Lawyers for the poor

MANCHESTER
1824

Manchester University Press

Lawyers for the poor

Legal advice, voluntary action and citizenship in England, 1890–1990

KATE BRADLEY

Manchester University Press

Published by Manchester University Press
Altrincham Street, Manchester M1 7JA
www.manchesteruniversitypress.co.uk

British Library Cataloguing-in-Publication Data
A catalogue record for this book is available from the British Library

ISBN 978 1 5261 3605 3 hardback

First published 2019

Typeset by Deanta Global Publishing Services

For Peter and Alexander

Contents

Preface

This book aims to uncover the ways in which activists sought to make access to the civil law easier and fairer for people of limited means in the period from 1890 to 1990. In this period, there was a rapid expansion in legislation, much of which aimed to protect the citizen from the risks of the modern world, from health and safety at work to standards in housing. The concept of who a citizen was also changed in this period, with the enfranchisement of all men and certain groups of women in 1918, and all women in 1928, and a series of nationality Acts. The experiences of total war, the Depression, the establishment of a welfare state and nationalised industries, and the challenges faced by oppressed and excluded groups also encouraged shifts in ideas about what it was to be a citizen – and how citizens might best have their voices heard. Access to the law was one mechanism for upholding the rights of citizens, by offering guidance on the best course of action in a difficult situation, as well as the possibility of legal action, in or out of court, to settle a matter. However, the legal profession in England and Wales was made up of private practitioners, whose fees could be far beyond the reach of those who needed them most. Lawyers who were concerned about this imbalance found various ways of making their services available to those who could not afford them at a commercial rate, working in conjunction with social workers, trade unionists, broadcasters and community activists, and making use of new technologies to reach out to people. Volunteering to offer one's services for free – known as pro bono work – was, on the face of it, the simplest solution, but it was difficult both to meet the demand for legal support and then to sustain it. This prompted campaigns for reforms to make the law more accessible through state funding, though, as this book will show, state involvement in legal aid and advice could be woefully inadequate or threaten the most innovative and inclusive work being done with vulnerable people.

These remain live issues at the start of the twenty-first century. This book looks at the period in which the Law Society – the professional body of solicitors – was responsible for legal aid and advice in its various forms. The Legal Aid Act 1988 shifted this responsibility from the Law Society to a new body, the Legal Aid Board, which meant that legal aid in both civil and criminal cases became the responsibility of central government. The Labour Government of 1997 brought in further change through the Access to Justice Act 1999, which created the Legal Services Commission, with the Community Legal Service responsible for civil matters. Both Acts brought legal aid and related services firmly into the purview of central government – a major concern of reformers. Yet, legal aid in both civil and criminal matters was one of the victims of austerity measures introduced from 2010, as the Legal Aid, Sentencing and Probation of Offenders Act 2012 drastically reduced both the funding for legal aid and the situations in which it could be used. For scholars and practitioners of the law, understanding the historical development of the legal aid system and the different strategies used to make the law as accessible as possible is a vital part of understanding the present and future of access to the law. For historians and scholars of social policy, this book offers critical new insights into the evolution of civil society and its institutions, and the ideas, individuals and groups who had varying degrees of agency within these processes.

Acknowledgements

The first people I would like to acknowledge are the volunteers, staff and users of the Free Legal Advice Centre at Toynbee Hall in East London. When I joined the settlement as a volunteer librarian in 1999, the only other people who were around in the evenings were the people running the Free Legal Advice Centre. I learned a tremendous amount from chatting to Brian Cunningham, then the organiser of the centre, about why this group of people were spending their evenings after work volunteering at a settlement. In a more observational way, I also began to appreciate why a queue of advice-seekers began to form outside the settlement from about 5.00 p.m. on legal advice evenings, regardless of how pleasant or inclement the weather, patiently waiting for the doors to open. I also began to appreciate the strengths and limitations of a service that relied on the work of volunteers to meet the needs of the advice-seekers – needs that could be considerable and highly complex.

I would also like to thank the librarians and archivists who have allowed me access to their collections: Jeremy McIlwaine at the Bodleian Library at the University of Oxford; the teams at the British Library; Cadbury Research Library at the University of Birmingham; the Keep at Brighton; Lambeth Palace Library; the London Metropolitan Archives; the London School of Economics Archives; the Modern Records Centre at the University of Warwick; the National Archives; and Nick Mays and Anne Jensen at the News UK Archive. I have had exceptional support from my colleagues in the Drill Hall Library at the University of Kent, particularly from Andy Major with interlibrary loans. I am very grateful to Eleanor Sier at Toynbee Hall for our conversations about Poor [Wo]man's Lawyers at the settlement and also to my colleagues at Kent, who have had all manner of conversations about legal aid, advice and social justice over the years. I have also deeply appreciated support from George Campbell Gosling, Daniel Grey, Kathleen McIlvenna, Sarah Roddy and Samantha Shave, with whom I have worked on various projects about the history of welfare and money. Likewise, I have a debt of gratitude to those who attended presentations on this work at the European Social Science History, Information and its Communication in Wartime,

Modern British Studies, Social History Society and Voluntary Action History Society conferences and the Lifecycles and Lifestages seminar at the Institute of Historical Research, who asked probing questions and offered valuable insights. I am also grateful to Martin Conway and Catherine Wright at the *English Historical Review* for their support and encouragement on my John Hilton Bureau article, which laid the foundation for this bigger project.

Last, but not least, thanks are due to my family for their moral and practical support over the last few years. Annette, Frank, Michael and Elaine have all helped with childcare at various points in this project, with Annette also proofreading and Michael helping me with the finer points of Old English. Peter and Alexander have lived with this project for the last few years – it started shortly before Alex was born – and they have offered endless love, support, motivation and distraction.

All errors are entirely my own.

Abbreviations

BARS	British Association of Residential Settlements
CA	Consumers' Association
CAB	Citizens' Advice Bureau
CABx	Citizens' Advice Bureaux
COPEC	Christian Conference on Politics, Economics and Citizenship
COS	Charity Organisation Society
CPAG	Child Poverty Action Group
CPGB	Communist Party of Great Britain
FWA	Family Welfare Association
GLC	Greater London Council
ICCUS	Inns of Court Conservative and Unionist Society
LCC	London County Council
LCSS	London Council of Social Service
NACAB	National Association of Citizens' Advice Bureaux
NCABC	National Citizens' Advice Bureaux Committee
NCCL	National Council for Civil Liberties
NCSS	National Council of Social Service
ODNB	*Oxford Dictionary of National Biography*
SLL	Society of Labour Lawyers
TGWU	Transport and General Workers' Union
TUC	Trades Union Congress

Introduction

Many everyday situations require some degree of engagement with the law. For example, the act of buying a loaf of bread in a shop is a simple one but, legally, is made possible through the legislation and regulations around hygiene, weights and measures, and customs and imports, as well as protections for both consumers and employees. Parking a car is not just about the technicalities of moving a car into a suitable spot but also about interpreting, often in a matter of seconds, a range of laws relating to public and private land, and the differences between the codification of best practice and the laws of the road. Some of this legal and related knowledge is provided through specific training and then tested, as in the case of learning to drive a car. Some paid jobs or forms of voluntary work have come to require knowledge of areas of the law, such as consumer law for retail workers or education law for school governors. Other parts of our everyday legal knowledge are passively acquired, perhaps through reading accounts of certain problems in a magazine or newspaper, or through following storylines in a soap opera. Aspects of the law may have been covered during citizenship classes in school. We may, through our absorption of the normative behaviour around us from early childhood, have a sense of what is 'right' and 'wrong' from observing others.

This everyday legal awareness is usually more than enough for a smooth passage through life. But what happens when things look like they might go wrong? Or when two opposing parties both think they are right? Or when dealing with a totally new situation? This is the point at which an individual might ask friends and family for advice, or search on the internet, perhaps posting on social media, or look up information in a book. Advice might also be sought in person, possibly by phoning a telephone service or consulting a website, or by going to a local branch of the Citizens Advice Bureau. Local community organisations may also offer advisory services, whilst community workers, religious leaders and social workers might also be able to help. A trade union representative might be able to give some advice in person, whilst the union is very likely to have its own advice and legal services. Advice can also be obtained from a lawyer. Home insurance policies often offer cover for legal expenses and costs, as well as an advice phone line. Anyone can also walk into a legal firm's offices and gain their advice or services for an agreed payment. In some circumstances, it is possible for the cost of legal advice, any mediation work or representation in court to be paid for through the state legal aid scheme.

The term 'anyone' here is at once accurate and misleading. Indeed, anyone can ask a friend for advice on a dispute with a neighbour, but not everyone has friends who have the knowledge or expertise to give them a useful, legally informed answer. Likewise, whilst anyone can walk into a legal firm, perceptions of the expense of consulting a lawyer may deter some people from going in because they fear that they would not have the money to pay for the service – and perhaps they don't have a suitable problem, so it could be a waste of money and time. Simply approaching a lawyer may be daunting.[1] 'Anyone' is anyone with the requisite social, cultural and financial capital, as well as the legal literacy and confidence to seek help with their problems. It is by no means a given that 'anyone' can access good, reliable and accurate support in terms of their legal affairs, despite the numerous ways in which legal advice or advice on legal matters can be obtained.

The ubiquity of sources of legal advice (advice as provided by a lawyer) and advice on legal matters (advice provided by someone with sufficient legal expertise but who is not a lawyer) is easy to take for granted. Citizens Advice Bureaux have been a feature of town and city centres since the Second World War, whilst community centres – often offering advice shops – were developed from the 1930s with the growth of suburban housing estates.[2] Legal advice centres, which rely on either the voluntary work of lawyers and law students or a combination of public contributions, state and philanthropic grants, and legal aid funding, have been around in different forms since the 1890s.[3] The idea of a little man against the big state or business drove the growth of the legal and consumer advice genres in newspapers, magazines, television, radio and online forums. New technologies have offered new ways of connecting advice-seekers with lawyers.[4] For those who need action – from the writing of a letter to representation in court – but who cannot afford to pay for it, legal aid was introduced in England, Wales and Scotland in 1949, and in Northern Ireland in 1965.[5]

The growth of these civil law forms of support was highly contentious. The criminal law had a very different trajectory, to avoid miscarriages of justice.[6] The civil law was a different matter, concerned as it was with such issues as divorce and family law, property and employment disputes. The established legal profession was loath to improve access to divorce in the interwar period and unwilling to promote litigiousness more generally amongst the working class. Yet members of the working classes still needed advice on civil law matters in terms of family or employment and increasingly needed guidance on welfare issues. This ran in tandem with the shift from discretionary practices in welfare to the more rules-based and 'scientific' approaches encouraged by the Charity Organisation Society (COS) from the late 1860s, and embedded in the Liberal governments' welfare schemes from 1906, as well as the growth of legislation that aimed to limit or prevent harm at work or in housing, for example.[7] As welfare claims became more about satisfying rules and less about personal petitioning, the need for expert advice and guidance became more important. A solution emerged through the work of charities, in the form of 'Poor Man's Lawyer' volunteering from the early 1890s. General William Booth of the Salvation Army called for a 'Poor Man's Tribune' in his 1891 book, *In Darkest London and the Way Out*, to allow working-class Londoners the chance to benefit from legal advice on their problems, as their middle-class counterparts might. As will be seen in Chapter 2, this idea was developed by Frank Tillyard, then a young barrister in residence at Mansfield House University Settlement, into a scheme of volunteering by lawyers. Tillyard's Poor Man's Lawyer involved solicitors and barristers regularly giving over an evening to providing advice for free to those who came to the Settlement House.[8] Tillyard took the concept to Sheffield and Birmingham, but his idea was also taken up by others at Settlement Houses, churches and community organisations like the Guild of Help in the 1890s and 1990s.

Whilst Poor Man's Lawyer evenings could be very useful to individuals, such services were not uniformly spread across the country. Even where they were provided, access was usually limited to one or two evenings a week. Whilst the Legal Aid and Advice Act 1949 and the Legal Aid and Advice (Scotland) Act 1949 made provision for legal advice and aid to be available on a sliding scale of affordability, successive waves of governmental parsimony from the 1950s onwards resulted, first, in the partial implementation of the Act and, second, in very strict qualifying criteria around income and capital.[9] Indeed, the Legal Aid, Sentencing and Punishment of Offenders Act 2012 (LASPO) dramatically restricted the types of civil cases for which legal aid could be sought.[10] In the 2010s, legal aid campaigners called for a more inclusive approach to legal aid and advice, very rightly pointing out the vital role that legal aid and advice play in ensuring that the most vulnerable members of society have their human rights upheld in the face of violence, corruption and discrimination.[11]

Buying a loaf of bread or parking a car may seem to be a long way in conceptual terms from the upholding of human rights, as they are, ultimately, mundane and everyday events. Yet it is these personal, everyday problems as experienced by individuals and the people around them that collectively fold into much bigger questions about human rights, social justice, trust in systems, and the use and abuse of power. The cost, availability and quality of bread and food as a whole have been a lightning rod for political imbalances for centuries.[12] Amongst the things that brought people to queue up to see a Poor Man's Lawyer were problems with landlords and employers: problems experienced by individuals, but which signalled the presence of major and persistent social inequalities.

In the context of Britain, having the ability to tackle these personal problems or the ability to find help with them matters because it is part of being able to exercise one's rights as a citizen and, on a wider level, of upholding social justice. Unlike many other modern nation states, the United Kingdom of Great Britain and Northern Ireland does not have a written constitution. There is no Bill of Rights that outlines what the rights and responsibilities of a citizen are. Since the mid-nineteenth century, the amount of legislation has grown considerably, and it has also become highly complex.[13] One of the drivers of this was the development of the welfare state. This process has created legislation and administrative structures that aim to protect citizens, at least in part, from the impact of unemployment or ill health, as much as trying to engineer a social good through the provision of education.

At the beginning of the period examined here, the state played little role in either regulating access to free or subsidised legal aid and advice or providing funds for this work. Access to welfare was shifting from a more discretionary to a rules-based system as legislation laying out restrictions or delineating rights increased. By the end, the state had rolled back some of the things that it would pay for but not the fundamental principle that it was the duty of the state to be responsible for upholding the rights of its citizens in this way. This marks a shift from seeing the responsibility for protecting rights as lying with private professional practitioners to the growing view that advice on legal and other aspects should be an element of the welfare state. This was, however, often in conflict with other views about the importance of maintaining a judiciary that was independent of the state. Great importance was also placed on the vitality of civil society organisations, such as trade unions, mutual aid associations and charities, as offering both services and associational life beyond or in place of anything offered by the state.[14]

A study of the historical development of legal aid and advice is necessarily a history of power, shifting imbalances and the desire for social justice. As Abel notes, the legal profession was dominated by middle-class men, and it was slow to diversify – if becoming a solicitor was somewhat more accessible. Women were excluded from both branches of the legal profession until the Sex Discrimination (Removal) Act 1919. People who were not British citizens were unable to qualify as solicitors until 1974, which excluded many black, Asian and minority ethnic people from joining the profession. The profession became younger and more diverse from the 1970s, partly through the lifting of restrictions on citizenship and the growth of university education as a precursor to a career in the law.[15] As will be seen, free legal advice and aid were largely given by white male lawyers from privileged backgrounds, and they also dominated strategic decision-making. Advice-seekers, on the other hand, were diverse: male or female, of any age, able-bodied or disabled, of any sexuality, of any religion and of any ethnic community. What united them was a need for assistance.

These imbalances were also embedded in the language of access to the law. From the twelfth century until the Legal Aid and Advice Act 1949, any form of support in legal matters, whether pro bono or through statutory provision, was couched in the language of paupers and of the 'poor', from the *in forma pauperis* to the Poor Man's Lawyer. The 'poor' was also a term that was used in a variety of formal and informal ways, and it was used by the legal profession and in legislation to refer to specific sections of the population. This usage continued into the mid-twentieth century, when in the aftermath of the Second World War, the language used to describe work on behalf of the 'poor' shifted dramatically. To this point, 'poor' had been both a broadly acceptable way of referring to those less well-off than oneself – the majority of the population – but it was also, most importantly, a term used in the law. Into the 1930s, it was perfectly acceptable to use such terms as 'Poor Persons' Rules', but the Legal Aid and Advice Act 1949 had pointedly dropped the term 'poor' in favour of 'persons of small or moderate means'.[16] This shift in language does not reflect fashion: it reflects a change in the perceived relationship between the law and working-class citizens.

In Modern English, the words 'poor' and 'poverty' have Latin roots, as terms introduced by the Normans, who conquered England and parts of Wales. Latin became the language of the Church and officialdom. Whilst Old and Middle English had many synonyms for 'poor', these did not become the lingua franca or operate in the same way as 'the poor'. From the early Tudor period, the use of 'poor' in legislative language reflected contemporary distinctions between 'vagabonds and beggars', on the one hand, and the 'impotent poor', on the other. Legislation passed between the Statute of Cambridge in 1338 and Gilbert's Act of 1782 was collectively known as the [Old] Poor Laws. The New Poor Law was itself termed the Poor Law Amendment Act 1834. The *in forma pauperis* procedure was introduced through a statute in 1495, enabling those who were paupers – not just 'poor' but at this point, in receipt of the then-nascent Poor Law relief – to have a lawyer acting on their behalf without charge and with no fear of being charged court fees.[17] As will be seen, the organised pro bono activities of the legal profession positioned the economic status of the recipient of the legal services first, as in the Poor Man's Lawyer. The reforms of the interwar period, around divorce and criminal law, used the same phrasing: namely, in the Poor Persons' Rules and the Poor Prisoners' Defence Acts of 1903 and 1930.

Why the emphasis on economic status? Funding for the courts came partly from the public purse, but the fees for solicitors and barristers were meant to be met by the plaintiff and the defendant. Various strategies were implemented for dealing with the costs of legal action involving those who could not afford to pay them. The introduction and expansion of free legal aid for criminal cases in the early twentieth century was uncontroversial, because there was little desire to allow miscarriages of justice to take place, and, whilst the first Finlay Report of 1926 recommended improvements to the system, it concluded that the system was fundamentally working satisfactorily.[18] The civil law was a different matter. Here, the legal profession had evolved to service the needs of those with property or looking to exchange it with others; it was also involved in enabling the business community to navigate its growing responsibilities in adhering to safety and financial regulation. The legal profession was not set up to include service to those without property or on the lowest incomes, because its raison d'être was to be a service to those with property. The potential for lawyers to provide legal advice in civil matters for the benefit of those who could not afford to pay for their services outright was contested and negotiated slowly both in England and Wales, as well as in the United States, Belgium and other Western nations.[19]

Not only did the civil law side of the profession have no reason to engage with the legal needs of the working classes in the nineteenth century, but also its social composition was resolutely middle-class.[20] Middle-class lawyers practising in an urban setting did not encounter the poor in the same ways that other professionals, such as doctors in voluntary hospitals, might have done. Whilst there were regular scares about the impact of unemployment and hunger on the working classes of London and other towns and cities, there is also evidence from the second half of the nineteenth century to the early twentieth that negative sentiments about the 'poor' were widespread. Unemployment was commonly understood as laziness or incompetence rather than as a result of cyclical downturns in the economy; poverty, likewise, was interpreted as being incapable of managing one's resources and being a slave to one's vices.[21] As McKibbin points out, there was also a view amongst the middle classes that the working classes were problematic, calling endless strikes and living on dole money at the expense of the middle-class taxpayer.[22] The legal profession had little reason to see the working classes as anything other than potential nuisances. The question is how the legal profession came to see the working classes as being one of the legitimate audiences for their work.

Researching the Poor Man's Lawyer

The earliest analyses of the development and impact of free legal advice work in Britain came from the practitioner-activist field. One of the earliest pieces of research into the provision of Poor Man's Lawyer work was undertaken by Gurney-Champion, a lawyer with strong connections to the settlement movement. He was given the task of mapping the provision of free legal advisory services on behalf of the Christian Conference on Politics, Economics and Citizenship (COPEC). In the early 1920s, COPEC was lobbying the government to further investigate the provision of legal aid to the working classes, alongside other social issues.[23] Gurney-Champion's findings – that the existing voluntary system was inadequate and a system of legal dispensaries would be much more appropriate – were driven by his empirical research but equally reflected the concerns of the organisations with which he associated.[24]

Two other works on voluntary-provided legal advice were published in the early 1940s. Again, these two came from the practitioner-activist field. J. Mervyn Jones's *Free Legal Advice in England and Wales* was prepared with funding from Trinity Hall at the University of Cambridge. Trinity Hall was one of the colleges that supported the Cambridge House University Settlement's Poor Man's Lawyer service. Jones offered a mapping of services across England and Wales rather than obvious polemic about the need for a national legal dispensary system. Yet the political dimensions were there: whilst Jones's tone may have been balanced, by delineating, mapping and describing, he was attempting to demonstrate the importance and scale of the movement by the late 1930s. The politics also extended to what was mentioned but then explicitly excluded from his study of Poor Man's Lawyer services. The first exclusion was the so-called 'ambulance-chasers', or legal firms who actively pursued accident victims to take out claims through them in order to profit from the costs, damages and compensation of a successful prosecution. The second and third exclusions were closely related. Jones excluded the trade unions because their member legal services were usually only for matters to do with employment, and he also excluded the political parties' legal advice clinics offered in London.

Egerton's *Legal Aid*, on the other hand, was concerned not just with mapping Poor Man's Lawyer-style provision but also with providing a synthesis of the historical development of legal aid up to the mid-1940s and the burgeoning demand for advice support. Egerton also called for major reform of the system. Egerton's book was published as the Rushcliffe Committee was considering reform of legal aid and advice, and offered a timely, strongly argued case for reform. Egerton was also active in the provision of free legal advice, working as a Poor Man's Lawyer at Cambridge House in the early 1940s before going on to be the Honorary Legal Advisor to the National Citizens' Advice Bureaux.[25]

It is unsurprising that the first studies to explore and delineate the provision of free legal advice were written by practitioner-activists. All three mentioned here were trying to identify and add importance to the work that they and their colleagues were doing, as part of a bigger project to increase the amount of state involvement in upholding rights. After the partial implementation of the Legal Aid and Advice Act 1949, academic commentary tended to critique the scheme and its partial implementation.[26] This situation changed in the later 1960s, when there was a period in which university academics, charities, political law groups and foundations had the ear of government. Abel-Smith undertook three major studies of the legal profession and access to justice, in conjunction with Stevens (1967 and 1968) and with Zander and Brooke in 1973.[27] Abel-Smith was one of the 'Titmice', academics who worked closely with Richard Titmuss at the London School of Economics in the 1950s and 1960s and who had close working relationships with the Labour Party.[28] The first, *Lawyers and the Courts*, was a groundbreaking sociological and historical study of the legal profession and the legal system in England, looking at the period from 1750 to 1965.[29] Stevens and Abel-Smith were highly critical of how less affluent Britons were neglected in this specific area of welfare, pointing to how

> By 1965 education and health services were available to all irrespective of income. The same could not be said of England's legal services and legal institutions – and yet many claimed that they represented the very fabric of the democratic state.[30]

Their position in *In Search of Justice* remained as critical, pointing to the ways in which the legal profession expected to cater only to the middle and upper classes, despite the provision of legal aid and years of pro bono voluntary work being undertaken.[31] As Sheard notes, the legal profession's response to both books' call for rapid social and legislative change was one of distaste.[32] These emphases on the role of the legal profession in being part of the welfare state and the intricate relationship between the public and the law of the country were part of a process of the radical thinking of what it meant to be a citizen in a country with a universal franchise, a welfare state, mass literacy and growing affluence.

Abel-Smith and Stevens opened a space for a critical understanding of law in everyday life. This was also a space that was deeply influenced by developments in policy, practice and academic research in the United States around the question of access to justice. Carlin, Howard and Messinger's *Civil Justice and the Poor* was highly influential on both sides of the Atlantic in highlighting the imbalances in access to justice and framing it as a civil rights issue, shaped by poverty, class and race.[33] Abel-Smith, Stevens and others spent time in the United States, studying the 'neighborhood law offices' that were created in the light of President Lyndon Johnson's 'War on Poverty'.[34] Whilst one result of this was the creation of Neighbourhood Law Centres, the other was academic interest in access to the law and its relationship to social inequalities. In terms of British research, Paterson's *Legal Aid as a Social Service* explored the tensions between the legal profession and the idea and practice of legal aid as a social good, and the profession's begrudging acceptance of the need to do something about widening access to the law.[35] Paterson has also contributed to our understanding of how the concept of 'access to justice' became an important principle for organising community legal work. He is highly critical of a profession that has had the privilege of defining what is or is not a public good whilst simultaneously excluding lay people from making any contribution to this. Further, he has also drawn attention to the ways in which politicians in the Attlee governments of 1945–51 enacted the Legal Aid and Advice Acts for England and Scotland, yet at the same time 'did not see law as a way of enforcing the new welfare rights – and neither [did] Beveridge, the architect of the welfare state'.[36] Spencer's work on the Attlee governments and the creation of the legal aid scheme points to how the scheme was an acknowledgement of the potential of the law to help people in need but was couched in a deeply conservative view of what the legal profession was, with little consideration of what it *could* be.[37]

This question of who the law is for, and how it should be used, also informs research by Goriely, who has examined the debates within the legal profession about creating and extending legal aid provision in response to growing demand for divorce during the First World War and up to the outbreak of the Second. Goriely emphasises the importance of voluntary legal services in establishing the ideals and priorities of the legal profession, and also of marking the status boundaries between solicitors and barristers, though her emphasis is largely on the legal profession.[38] She has also explored the development of legal aid since the 1950s, exploring the development of Neighbourhood Law Centres by groups on the left of the political spectrum in the 1970s and the Thatcher governments' embracing of consumer rights and reduction of the public sector in the 1980s.[39] The importance of divorce as a pressure on the legal profession to at least consider some sort of reform, and the ways in which such reform was piecemeal and often half-hearted, is also a finding of both Morgan and Abel.[40]

Although the legal academics mentioned earlier have considered the voluntary action undertaken by both branches of the legal profession and its relationship to the economics and business of law, as well as the evolving sense of the need for the legal profession to better serve society, their approach is ultimately (and appropriately) lawyerly. Their starting point, as lawyers and legal academics, was with the legal profession and its concerns, focusing on the relationships between the Law Society and the Bar Council with the legislature – mainly the Lord Chancellor's Office and the Treasury. Historians of Britain in the twentieth century have tended to approach legal advice and legal aid as instruments in a bigger political, social or cultural picture. For historians of family and romantic relationships, such as Cohen and Langhamer, the impact of access to divorce lawyers and growing legislation around sexuality, adoption and domestic violence is an important dimension of their work.[41] Questions of advice and advocacy, and who could provide this, have arisen in studies of the Co-operative Movement, campaigns against rationing, and the emerging 'consumer-citizen' of the 1950s and 1960s.[42] The new political history of the 1990s and 2000s, and its emphasis on the ways in which citizens engaged, or failed to engage, with political parties and social movements, has also considered the question of legal and other advice, albeit in passing. For example, Fielding et al. mentioned the work of Constituency Labour Parties in providing advice to their local communities, whilst Thorpe has examined the work of the Conservatives and the Labour Party in providing advice bureaux during the Second World War.[43] The advice and advocacy work of national organisations such as the National Council for Civil Liberties (NCCL), the Child Poverty Action Group (CPAG) and others has also been explored by historians such as Moores, and Thane and Davidson, whilst Jones has looked at community organisation at a local level.[44] In terms of voluntary action and welfare, however, historians have largely focused on the organisations that provided advisory services, such as the Citizens Advice Bureaux or as part of the activities of settlement houses.[45]

The history of legal aid and advice, and advisory services generally, was influenced by practitioner-activists, who were keen to delineate what legal advice was (and what it was not) as part of making a case for greater intervention. This has created a literature that, on the socio-legal side of things, is based largely on the responses of the legal profession to demands for change and their negotiations with the government. On the social, cultural and political side of the literature, access to affordable, reliable and accessible advice, legal or otherwise, was very important in many areas, from the reformation of the role of the MP to supporting the interests of needy families. It cut across different parts of the economy, from charitable and voluntary organisations through to the growing welfare state, and through a raft of different parts of the private or profit-making sector. Although work on the consumer-citizen has addressed the intersections between individual consumers, consumer groups, manufacturers, retailers and regulators, historians of voluntary action and welfare have tended to focus on charities, non-governmental organisations and the state, rather than straying into looking at the work of the private sector or those whose individual work was intended to make a profit. This is generally true of voluntary action and welfare history of the twentieth century, though historians working on the funding of voluntary hospitals and medical care are an important exception to this rule.[46]

In consequence, there is a considerable gap in our understanding of the role that legal aid and advice has played in the lives of working- and lower-middle-class Britons, especially those who did not regularly encounter lawyers. There are also parallels to be drawn between interactions between the public and professionals in different welfare arenas, with the most apparent contrast being between the medical and legal professions. There is, finally, the issue of the extent to which private or profit-making bodies are involved in providing social goods and how this has changed during the twentieth century. These gaps lead to a series of questions. In what ways was 'the law' harnessed as a means of developing citizenship? To what extent did the provision of legal aid and advice intersect with the development and growth of the welfare state? Or the interests of other professions, industries and interests, such as the media, the publishing industry and the major political parties? How did ideas about money, justice, and the independence of professions and civil society institutions from the state intersect?

This book seeks to address these questions through examining how legal and other types of advice were provided on an accessible basis to the public from the 1890s. This could be advice given for free, or free on the grounds of a means test, or with a contribution made to the costs of the advice and action. It could also be available in less affluent areas, at a time or place to suit residents, or accessed remotely. The public in this context usually meant members of the working classes and the less affluent parts of the middle classes, but class background was not always a reliable guide to whether an individual would be able to afford legal aid and advice on a commercial basis. Chapter 1 maps the policy developments in the funding of legal aid and advice by the government from the late nineteenth century to the 1980s. It establishes the landscape in terms of the legal profession and the government, and maps the overarching debates about class, morality, litigation and money that form the background to the situations and processes examined in the following chapters.

There were four broad constituencies with an interest in facilitating access to the law in the first half of the twentieth century: the proto-voluntary sector; the political parties and their affiliate groups within the legal profession; the trade unions; and the media. Chapter 2, therefore, looks at the efforts to create a Poor Man's Lawyer movement from the later nineteenth century, which intersected with efforts to better implement charitable services to needy individuals and communities. Advice was a critical element of the work of the institutions that were associated with the National Council of Social Service (NCSS), the British Association of Residential Settlements (BARS) and other groups with a keen eye on positioning themselves as the experts on 'welfare' and building up closer relationships with local and national government. Such Poor Man's Lawyer work was positioned as 'neutral' by interwar researchers like J. Mervyn Jones, but it sat in contrast to overtly political provision by political parties. Chapter 3 examines the ways in which the Labour Party and the Conservatives offered legal advisory services as a means of connecting with voters by solving their problems. It also explores the wider role of lawyers in the Labour Party and the involvement of radical lawyers' groups in encouraging the view that the workers were as much the business of lawyers as any other group in society. Chapter 4 explores the involvement of the trade unions in shaping policy around legal aid and in providing legal services to their members through their mutual aid provision. Chapter 5 also looks at the trade publishing of popular law guides and the use of this part of the publishing industry by consumer groups and campaigning bodies as a means of literally putting the law in the hands of their members. It also evaluates the provision of advice columns and features in newspapers, alongside the provision of free-to-access advice bureaux. Radio programming around rights and advice is also considered, as an evolution of the principle of 'public service broadcasting'. It also looks at the way in which new telephone technologies were harnessed to help support advice-seekers who could not attend a clinic in person for reasons of either distance or personal safety. Finally, Chapter 6 explores the ways voluntary providers of legal advice managed a volatile funding climate, and the impacts of shifts in city, local and central government funding on such precarious institutions.

Why look at the 1890s to the 1990s? As will be seen in Chapters 1 and 2, the idea of a Poor Man's Lawyer was by no means a new one in the nineteenth century. What was new was its harnessing by charities and voluntary associations whose aim was to try to first alleviate and ultimately eradicate poverty in the 1890s. Legal advice formed part of their understanding that the working classes needed to be given the tools – either through their personal education or through having access to people with expertise – to be effective citizens. This in turn formed part of the growing pressure to enfranchise all working men. It found resonance amongst members and supporters of the Liberal Party and then within the new Labour Party, especially during the interwar period. During the interwar period, the expansion of a network of Poor Man's Lawyer services as part of a proto-voluntary sector, along with an emerging left-wing network of lawyers, helped to create an environment in which access to the law could be part of the welfare state. Although the Rushcliffe and Cameron Reports of 1945 recommended the introduction of legal aid, and their proposals met with favour from Labour and the Conservatives, legal aid did not receive the same power and energy in being pushed through as other welfare initiatives of the Labour governments did. Legal aid also remained in the hands of the legal profession, as the Law Society managed the scheme until the Legal Aid Act 1988 shifted the responsibility to central government. Although there were other areas in which the provisions of 1948 were rolled back for reasons of cost, the legal aid budget was hit by successive waves of governmental parsimony throughout the post-war period. As will be seen, particularly in Chapter 6, this meant that the free legal advice centres were never able to plan to consolidate or expand their services or to know whether they would be put out of business by a new, enhanced legal aid scheme. They were joined in the 1970s by the Neighbourhood Law Centres and supported by new networks to share expertise and build capacity. All were affected to varying degrees by a volatile environment in terms of access to funding throughout the 1970s and 1980s. This study ends around the year 1990, because this period marks the point at which the Legal Aid Act 1988 created a new system for organising legal aid and transferred responsibility from the Law Society to the new Legal Aid Board. Although a mixed economy of legal advice and aid provision has continued into the twenty-first century, the Legal Aid Act 1988 effectively ended the environment created by the campaigns of the 1920s and 1930s and the Legal Aid and Advice Act 1949.

Methodological issues emerge with any study of advice that attempts to stray from an institutional perspective. Throughout the twentieth century and beyond, advice was provided verbally in many cases – largely because that was all that was needed. As researchers in the 1920s and 1930s found, very few Poor Man's Lawyer services had any form of clerking system. In some cases, letters from legal advice centres were kept for future reference, but these tend to appear occasionally in the archives of organisations.[47] Many more may survive in individuals' personal papers – an example of these being the letter my grandfather received from the *Daily Mirror*'s Philip Wright Readers Service, which was uncovered and then subsequently disappeared in the process of clearing his house after his death in 2008. The John Hilton Bureau of the *News of the World* retained some sample letters sent to members of the public and a selection of letters sent in by people who had benefited from its service, but these are a tiny fraction of the letters it sent out. Through the publications and broadcasts, we have a clear sense of what blanket advice was given. In gauging a sense of what problems people took to advisory services, we are reliant on the ways in which those services recorded the complaints that people brought. At the time of writing, only the papers of the Mary Ward Settlement and Brighton Legal Advice Centres are available to the public – and then, only the operational papers of the groups, not case papers. Any papers relating to cases are restricted by privacy laws for a minimum of fifty years, which means that the Toynbee Hall papers are closed until the 2050s.[48] However, the voluntary provision of legal advice was researched at the time by individuals associated with proto-voluntary sector organisations like COPEC and the NCSS; there is a reasonable degree of rigour in these research projects, even if some of the sources have a tendency towards impressionistic accounts of their subject.[49] Engagement with umbrella groups throughout the period also provides a means of assessing the extent of services, the diversity within the sector, and the kinds of issues and concerns that providers had through the papers, publications and correspondence. Aside from extant oral histories and radio or television programmes, this is largely a history that relies upon the written word of those who provided these services rather than the voices of those who used them.

Notes

1 See A. Paterson, *Legal Aid as a Social Service* (London: Cobden Trust, 1971), p. 16; *Justice for All* (London: Fabian Society, 1968), pp. 22–3.

2 O. Blaiklock, 'Advising the Citizen: Citizens Advice Bureaux, Voluntarism and the Welfare State in England, 1938–1964' (PhD dissertation, Kings College London, 2012); S. Kirwan, M. McDermont and J. Clarke, 'Imagining and

practising citizenship in austere times: The work of Citizens Advice', *Citizenship Studies*, 20:6–7 (2016), pp. 764–78; J. Citron, *Citizens Advice Bureaux: For the Community, by the Community* (London: Pluto, 1990); B. Jones, *The Working Class in Mid-twentieth Century England: Community, Identity and Social Memory* (Manchester: Manchester University Press, 2012).

3 See A. Byles and P. Morris, *Unmet Need: The Case of the Neighbourhood Law Centre* (London: Routledge & Kegan Paul, 1977); P. Kandler, 'North Kensington Law Centre', in H. Curtis and M. Sanderson (eds), *The Unsung Sixties: Memoirs of Social Innovation* (London: Whiting and Birch, 2004); Newham Rights Centre, *Newham Rights Centre: Two Years Work 1975–7* (London: Newham Rights Centre, 1977); T. Goriely, 'Rushcliffe fifty years on: The changing role of civil legal aid within the welfare state', *Journal of Law and Society*, 21:4 (1994), pp. 545–66.

4 K. Bradley, '"All human life is there": The John Hilton Bureau of the *News of the World* and access to free legal advice, c.1938–1973', *English Historical Review*, 129:539 (2014), pp. 888–911.

5 Legal Aid and Advice Act 1949, Legal Aid and Advice (Scotland) Act 1949, and Legal Aid and Advice (Northern Ireland) Act 1965.

6 See R.I. Morgan, 'The introduction of civil legal aid in England and Wales, 1914–1949', *Twentieth Century British History*, 5:1 (1994), pp. 38–76.

7 See P. Thane, 'The making of national insurance', *Journal of Poverty and Social Justice*, 19:3 (2011), pp. 211–19; G. Finlayson, 'A moving frontier: Voluntarism and the state in British Social Welfare, 1911–1949', *Twentieth Century British History*, 1:2 (1990), pp. 183–206.

8 W. Booth, *In Darkest England and the Way Out* (London: International Headquarters, 1890); A. Blott, *Legal Dispensaries: An Account of the Poor Man's Lawyer Movement* (London: Avenue Press, 1903 and 1911); 'Obituary: Sir Frank Tillyard', *The Times*, Tuesday, 11 July 1961, p. 12.

9 Paterson, *Legal Aid*, p. 22.

10 LASPO full text: www.legislation.gov.uk/ukpga/2012/10/contents, correct at 29 May 2017. See also Law Society, 'Legal Aid Changes: Key Information and Advice', 13 March 2013, www.lawsociety.org.uk/support-services/advice/articles/legal-aid-changes-key-information-and-advice/, correct at 29 May 2017; C. Baksi, 'Civil Legal Aid: Access Denied', *Law Society Gazette*, 7 April 2014, www.lawgazette.co.uk/law/civil-legal-aid-access-denied/5040722.article, correct at 29 May 2017.

11 See Amnesty International UK, *Cuts That Hurt: The Impact of Legal Aid Cuts in England on Access to Justice* (London: Amnesty International UK, 2016).

12 I. Zweiniger-Bargielowska, 'Bread rationing in Britain, July 1946–July 1948', *Twentieth Century British History*, 4:1 (1993), pp. 57–85; P. Pickering and A. Tyrell, *The People's Bread: A History of the Anti-Corn Law League* (London: Bloomsbury, 2000).

13 For example: H. Street, *Justice in the Welfare State* (London: Stevens and Sons, 1975), p. 1.

14 M. Spencer, 'Public subsidies without strings – Labour and lawyers at the birth of legal aid', *International Journal of the Legal Profession*, 9:3 (2002), pp. 251–82; J. Harris, *Private Lives, Public Spirit: Britain 1870–1914* (Penguin: Harmondsworth,

1993), pp. 116–41; *Civil Society in British History: Ideas, Identities, Institutions* (Oxford: Oxford University Press, 2005), pp. 167–9; 'Political thought and the welfare state 1870–1940: An intellectual framework for British social policy', *Past and Present*, 135 (1992), pp. 116–41; R. McKibbin, *The Ideologies of Class: Social Relations in Britain 1880–1950* (Oxford: Clarendon, 1990).

15 See R.L. Abel, *The Legal Profession in England and Wales* (Oxford: Blackwell, 1988), pp. 170–6.

16 Legal Aid and Advice Act 1949, 12 & 13 Geo.6, Chapter 51, 624.

17 T. Goriely, 'Gratuitous assistance to the "ill-dressed": Debating civil legal aid in England and Wales from 1914–1939', *International Journal of the Legal Profession*, 13:1 (2006), p. 42.

18 *First Report of the Committee on Legal Aid for the Poor*, Cmd. 2638 (London: HMSO, 1926), p. 5.

19 See, for example, F. Batlan, *Women and Justice for the Poor: A History of Legal Aid, 1863–1945* (Cambridge: Cambridge University Press, 2015); S. Gibens, 'Legal aid in Belgium: The absence of a tradition?' *International Journal of the Legal Profession*, 13:1 (2006), pp. 3–18; J.T. Johnsen, 'How has the complexity of the law and the market for legal expertise impacted on the development of legal aid in Norway?' *International Journal of the Legal Profession*, 13:1 (2006), pp. 19–39.

20 R.L. Abel, 'England and Wales: A Comparison of the Professional Projects of Barristers and Solicitors', in R. Abel and P.S.C. Lewis, *Lawyers in Society: The Common Law World* (Washington DC: Beard Books, 2005), pp. 24–6.

21 McKibbin, *The Ideologies of Class*, p. 167; E.P. Hennock, 'Poverty and social theory in England: The experience of the Eighteen-Eighties', *Social History*, 1:1 (1976), pp. 67–91.

22 McKibbin, *The Ideologies of Class*, p. 273.

23 'Legal justice and the poor: A movement for reform', *United Methodist*, 25 December 1924, p. 639.

24 F.C.G. Gurney-Champion, *Justice and the Poor in England* (London: George Routledge and Sons, 1926).

25 R.M.J., 'Legal aid', *Cambridge Law Review*, 9:2 (1946), p. 259; M. Seasongood, 'Legal aid', *Harvard Law Review*, 60:5 (1947), p. 854.

26 For example, L.C.B.G., 'Legal Aid and Advice Act 1949', *Modern Law Review*, 13:1 (1950), pp. 81–7.

27 P. Townsend, 'Professor Brian Abel-Smith', *Independent*, 8 April 1996, www.independent.co.uk/news/obituaries/obituary-professor-brian-abel-smith-1303950.html, correct at 22 April 2019; S. Sheard, *The Passionate Economist: How Brian Abel-Smith Shaped Global Health and Social Welfare* (Bristol: Policy Press, 2013). See also B. Abel-Smith, 'Richard Morris Titmuss', *Journal of Social Policy*, 2:3 (1973), i–ii.

28 Sheard, *The Passionate Economist*.

29 B. Abel-Smith and R. Stevens, *Lawyers and the Courts: A Sociological Study of the English Legal System 1750–1965* (London: Heinemann, 1967).

30 Ibid., p. 348.

31 B. Abel-Smith and R. Stevens, *In Search of Justice: Society and the Legal System* (London: Allen Lane, 1968), p. 161.

32 Sheard, *The Passionate Economist*, p. 213.
33 J. Carlin, J. Howard and S.L. Messinger, *Civil Justice and the Poor: Issues for Sociological Research* (New York: Russell Sage Foundation, 1966).
34 Sheard, *The Passionate Economist*, pp. 210–11; D. Sugarman, 'Beyond ignorance and complacency: Robert Stevens' journey through *Lawyers and the Courts*', *International Journal of the Legal Profession*, 16:1 (2009), pp. 11–15.
35 Paterson, *Legal Aid*, p. 15.
36 A. Paterson, *Lawyers and the Public Good: Democracy in Action?* (Cambridge: Cambridge University Press, 2012), p. 65.
37 Spencer, 'Public subsidies without strings'.
38 Goriely, 'Gratuitous assistance'.
39 Goriely, 'Rushcliffe fifty years on'.
40 Morgan, 'The introduction of civil legal aid'; R.L. Abel, 'Law without politics: Legal aid under advanced capitalism', *UCLA Law Review*, 32:474 (1985), pp. 474–642.
41 D. Cohen, *Family Secrets: The Things We Tried to Hide* (London: Penguin, 2014); C. Langhamer, *The English in Love: The Intimate Story of an Emotional Revolution* (Oxford: Oxford University Press, 2013).
42 L. Black and N. Robertson (eds), *Consumerism and the Co-operative Movement in Modern British History: Taking Stock* (Manchester: Manchester University Press, 2009); F. Trentmann (ed.), *The Making of the Consumer. Knowledge, Power and Identity in the Modern World* (Oxford: Berg, 2006); M. Hilton, *Consumerism in Twentieth-century Britain: The Search for a Historical Movement* (Cambridge: Cambridge University Press, 2003); L. Black, '*Which?* craft in post-war Britain: The Consumers' Association and the politics of affluence', *Albion*, 36:1 (2004), pp. 52–82; J. Benson, *The Rise of Consumer Society in Britain, 1880–1990* (London: Longman, 1994).
43 S. Fielding, P. Thompson and N. Tiratsoo, *'England Arise!' The Labour Party and Popular Politics in 1940s Britain* (Manchester: Manchester University Press, 1995); A. Thorpe, *Parties at War: Political Organisation in Second World War Britain* (Oxford: Oxford University Press, 2009).
44 C. Moores, *Civil Liberties and Human Rights in Twentieth-century Britain* (Cambridge: Cambridge University Press, 2017); P. Thane and R. Davidson, *The Child Poverty Action Group 1965 to 2015* (London: Child Poverty Action Group, 2016); B. Jones; 'The uses of nostalgia', *Cultural and Social History*, 7:3 (2010), pp. 355–74.
45 J. Richards, *Inform, Advise and Support: 50 Years of the Citizens Advice Bureau* (Cambridge: Lutterworth, 1989); Citron, *Citizens Advice Bureaux*; Blaiklock, 'Advising the Citizen'; K. Bradley, *Poverty, Philanthropy and the State: Charities and the Working Classes in London, 1918–1979* (Manchester: Manchester University Press, 2009).
46 See G. Campbell Gosling, *Payment and Philanthropy in British Healthcare, 1918–1948* (Manchester: Manchester University Press, 2017); B. Doyle, *The Politics of Hospital Provision in Early Twentieth Century Britain* (London: Pickering and Chatto, 2014).

47 See, for example, Wolverhampton Archives, D-SO-26/3/2/33 Correspondence: www.wolverhamptonart.org.uk/collections/getrecord/GB149_D-SO-26_3_2_33, correct at 22 April 2019.

48 London Metropolitan Archives, ACC/2486/230 'Papers Relating to Various Cases', https://search.lma.gov.uk/scripts/mwimain.dll/144/LMA_OPAC/web_detail/REFD+ACC~2F2486~2F230?SESSIONSEARCH, correct at 22 April 2019 – closed until 2052.

49 A particularly impressionistic account is given in Gurney-Champion, *Justice and the Poor.*

1

Making free legal aid and advice the business of state and profession

Until the beginning of the twentieth century, poorer Britons had access to the civil law in the High Court through the *in forma pauperis* procedure, a provision established in the thirteenth century that enabled those who declared themselves as paupers to be given legal support free of charge. The procedure was infrequently used, as it required the lawyers to act for free, with all incurred expenses to be met from their pockets. By the early twentieth century, the legal profession had contrived to put enough obstacles in place to make obtaining legal help through this avenue almost impossible.[1] However, whilst 'poor' people could and did find themselves in the High Court, it was by no means the main court that people on lower incomes used for civil matters. Rather, the 'everyday' courts for most people were the county courts in the case of civil matters and magistrates' courts for criminal cases – and there was no provision for those cases.

Before the end of the nineteenth century, seeking advice or support on legal and welfare matters could take various forms. Historians of the late eighteenth and early nineteenth centuries have written about the omnipresence of law in everyday life, from the spectacle of public executions, as examined by Thompson or Gatrell, to the implementation of law in everyday, personal relations, as in the work of Steedman.[2] Steedman has examined magistrates, the public and the writing of legal letters, with a focus on what has come to be known as the civil law. Magistrates were the individuals tasked with implementing and policing statutory law on the ground and thus with the governance of the nation.[3] As Gray and Davis have both noted in respect to different time periods, the London magistrates' or police courts were also highly accessible to ordinary people who needed additional help in righting wrongs.[4] The Old and New Poor Laws also brought people into contact with the law and officials. King and Jones note how the Poor Law of 1601 created a national welfare framework, delivered through each Anglican church parish and funded through local taxes on property.[5] Charlesworth further notes how the system before 1865 allowed local autonomy, reflecting the different realities faced by communities.[6] It was, further, a discretionary system, in which individuals could write in support of their case or ask a respected member of the community to serve as an advocate for them, writing a supportive letter, which often had the power to change the official decision made. Where such advocates did not get the response they wanted, they would help to escalate the issue to the local magistrates. People knew the law and were able to make their case as to how it applied to them. Scandals, as Shave notes, were also an important means of reforming and shaping the system.[7] Writing 'pauper letters' and making use of advocates – members of the local community in good standing, who were not usually lawyers – defined the ways in which people engaged with the Poor Law and were in turn part of the bigger picture of political participation before mass democracy in the twentieth century.[8] King and Carter's initial findings from their research on Poor Law correspondence in the National Archives demonstrate how the culture of writing a letter to make one's case for support continued throughout the New Poor Law, from c.1834 to 1900.[9] Hurren also draws our attention to the ways in which paupers pushed back against the New Poor Law in the later nineteenth century, despite attempts to make the system harsher.[10]

Whilst people could go to the magistrates for advice as well as practical help, they could also have a letter written by a 'low' lawyer on their behalf to be given to someone who had offended them or to someone who owed them money.[11] The term 'Poor Man's Lawyer' was in common use well before the nineteenth century, referring to solicitors or barristers who were willing to offer their services to those in need for free or for a reduced rate. Some made this available through cheap publications explaining the law, such as Pearce's 1755 book, *A Poor Man's Lawyer*.[12] However, such publications still required the reader to have a relatively high degree of literacy, and not all cases could be easily resolved in this way. Therefore, those who could provide advice verbally and in person remained important in this area of the legal economy. For example, William Unwin of Sheffield used his profitable conveyancing and estate law work to subsidise work for those who could not afford to pay him.[13] Others, like the prominent freethinker and MP Charles Bradlaugh, or Robert Thompson, a bankrupt grazier from Wellingborough, were not lawyers but provided advice on legal matters for free when approached.[14] Taking together the criminal and civil areas of law outlined earlier, what historians have shown is the considerable extent to which 'ordinary' people were aware of the law in the eighteenth and nineteenth centuries. It was something that could be accessed locally, through the magistrates' courts, and was also visible to the community, as people could sit in a magistrate's justicing room and see their work in action. Both the Old and New Poor Laws were malleable, with individuals able to challenge decisions about their entitlement and officials able to exercise discretion.

Over the course of the nineteenth century, the administration of law changed dramatically, with powers being progressively handed over from the Assizes and Quarter Sessions to the magistrates' courts. Magistrates became more important as the 'bloody code' ended and the 'administrative turn' in criminal law meant that more people would be dealt with summarily, which was faster and more cost-effective.[15] Likewise, police forces were set up from the late 1820s to provide a professional, dedicated response to the problems of policing in (particularly) urban environments and increasingly took over the responsibility of bringing prosecutions against offenders, reducing the need for victims to do this.[16] From the 1880s, 'prosecuting authorities' like the National Society for the Prevention of Cruelty to Children (NSPCC) emerged: charities and agencies that trod the line between voluntary activities and carrying out the work of the state.[17] At the same time, the reforms of the administration of the Poor Laws and the management of public health gradually increased the responsibility of both central and local government and necessarily introduced more legislation with which to comply.[18] As Hurren notes, the 1870s were marked by calls for New Poor Law administration to strictly abide by the 1834 Act, reducing the amount of the supposedly generous and wasteful 'out-relief' for the able-bodied poor in favour of stricter proofs of poverty before recourse to the workhouse.[19] The most vulnerable members of society were increasingly being moved out of the Poor Law into specialist provision through such measures as the Metropolitan Poor Act 1867, which attempted to better address the medical and psychological needs of poorer Londoners.[20] The mid-nineteenth-century boom in middle-class women's voluntary action with the needy created a 'maternalist' public sphere, in which women could be active beyond the confines of their homes, and opened up a space for professionalised social work. For example, the COS, founded in 1869, aimed to rationalise indiscriminate, duplicated and therefore potentially ineffective voluntary action and almsgiving through careful 'case work' with families and coordinating welfare; the National Union of Women Workers (NUWW) was founded in 1895 to support women's voluntary social work.[21] Collectively, these changes were part of a shift away from discretionary decision-making in welfare towards a rules-based system driven by 'experts' and professionals.

The legal worlds and economies presented by Steedman, Gray, Davis, King and others, in which members of the working classes were well-versed in the law, seem to be at odds with the relative paucity of affordable and reliable legal knowledge in the later nineteenth century, at least as seen by voluntary social workers and their circles. Davis points to a decline in the authority and reach of the police courts in the later nineteenth century, ostensibly due to a shift in attitudes to respectability amongst the capital's working classes and a desire to avoid the stigma of being 'criminal' and 'undeserving'.[22] The division between the 'deserving' and 'undeserving' poor was part of the operations of the Poor Law and, from the 1870s, also entered the language of welfare and voluntary action through the 'efficient' and 'scientific' approaches of the COS. Whilst the New Poor Law continued until its abolition in 1948, the Liberal Governments' introduction of National Insurance in 1911 created a rules-based system for unemployment and sickness and a means-tested old age pension, effectively sealing the shift away from discretion at local level to the enforcement of national rules. The culture of writing letters in support of one's case or finding an advocate to champion one's needs was out of step with the new culture, which prioritised rules, case work and expertise in the context of burgeoning legislation. The need to advocate did not go away: it shifted from a petitioning and letter-writing culture with advocates from the local community to one in which lawyers and other professionals were involved in advising on rules and legislation and crafting responses.

The Royal Commission on Divorce

A broad consensus exists amongst historians of legal aid that the primary driver behind the reform of access to financial help with legal cases was the Royal Commission on Divorce of 1909–12.[23] Obtaining a divorce was possible following the Matrimonial Causes Act 1857. However, divorce was only permitted in limited circumstances and could only be dealt with in the High Court. A High Court case was an extremely costly exercise, with deeply personal matters aired in the very public court.[24] As Cohen shows, divorce was very difficult to obtain because of the prevailing social view that marriages were for life and beyond. The idea that further sin in the form of adultery or bigamy could be unintentionally created by insisting on a couple remaining unhappily married emerged later in the nineteenth century; the concept of divorce to bring an end to unhappiness itself took longer to embed.[25] The proto-feminist movement that emerged around female suffrage from the 1860s also raised demands for women's property rights, legal guardianship of their children, and access to divorce on more equal terms for husbands and wives.[26] Likewise, other areas of family life were increasingly subject to public regulation. The Children's Charter of 1888 established a legal precedent for the punishment and prevention of cruelty to children, whilst the Children Act 1908 made it illegal for children to buy alcohol and cigarettes, and adoption was legally formalised in 1926.[27] What can be seen is the process of establishing adult women as full citizens and children as future citizens, with these claims being granted on a gradual and piecemeal basis. These claims to rights and protections were typically pushed through statutory provisions rather than the precedent-driven case law as practised in the courts: these were the fruits of campaigns and policy networks putting pressure on the legislature.

As Morgan notes, the Royal Commission on Divorce called for a reorganisation of the legal profession in order to make access to divorce more broadly available. The Royal Commission was intended to liberalise divorce law, but, largely, its recommendations were not acted upon. Rather, divorce remained relatively inaccessible, particularly as the legal profession was stretched throughout and after the First World War and to a considerable extent blocked access to what many practitioners saw as an undesirable social development.[28] The Royal Commission undoubtedly drew attention to the demands made on the legal profession and its ability (and willingness) to respond. This led to two further committees looking at the question of legal aid: Lawrence, which reported in 1919 and 1925, and Finlay, reporting in 1926 and 1928.[29] Access to divorce was part of the shift towards the acceptability of providing for the legal needs of the working classes. The First World War brought matters to a head, as the pressures of war created an increased demand for divorce, whilst the legal profession felt overstretched. Despite the concerns of the legal profession that enabling the poor to have support in pursuing divorce claims would lead to declining moral standards, the Royal Commission called for reform to ensure equality of access to the law for such groups. One consequence was the establishment of the Poor Persons' Department, operating under the Lord Chancellor's Department, which means-tested applicants for legal aid and assigned them to lawyers who would act voluntarily for them. This system came under intense pressure in the aftermath of the First World War due to a shortage of solicitors and a rise in divorce cases.[30] In light of this, there were further calls to reform the Poor Persons' Rules system for both criminal and civil cases.

The Lawrence Committees

The Lord Chancellor's Department set up two committees to look at the Poor Persons' Rules in divorce cases, both chaired by Sir Paul Ogden Lawrence. Lawrence was called to the Bar in 1882 and built up a Chancery practice from the 1890s. He acted for various private firms whose property was requisitioned by the Government during the First World War. As Rubin points out, whilst Lawrence's political views cannot be ascertained from his legal practice, his antipathy towards greater state involvement came through clearly in the findings of both committees.[31] The first Lawrence Committee was comprised solely of lawyers: Robert Frederic Bayford, a barrister who had recently been made a King's Counsel; Henry Maddocks, MP; A.H. (Alfred Henry) Coley, a Birmingham-based solicitor; and Charles Goddard, a London-based solicitor. Both Coley and Goddard were members of the Council of the Law Society, with Coley being active in the Birmingham Law Society over many years.[32] Maddocks was also a barrister whilst serving as the Conservative MP for Nuneaton between 1918 and 1923.[33] Bayford, Coley and Maddocks returned to join the second Lawrence Committee. The second Lawrence Committee was larger, and it had a slightly wider representation. Sir Roger Gregory was a solicitor as well as the treasurer of the Foundling Hospital.[34]

Sir Claud Schuster was on the committee due to his work as the permanent secretary to the Lord Chancellor's Department, though he was trained as a barrister.[35] Roderick Sinclair Meiklejohn was also a civil servant.[36] Lawrence Roger Lumley, later Governor of Bombay, was appointed to the committee whilst serving as Conservative MP for Hull East.[37] The final two members of the committee were not lawyers. William Leach was a Labour Bradford city councillor and MP for Central Bradford between 1922 and 1924.[38] Ethel Snowden was a suffragist, socialist and pacifist with a background in Labour politics in West Yorkshire; she was married to Phillip Snowden, Labour MP and Chancellor of the Exchequer from January 1924 in the first Labour Government.[39] Whilst neither Leach nor Snowden was from a working-class background, their appointments marked the growing influence of Labour in political life.

The first Lawrence Report focused on the major obstacle people on lower incomes encountered when trying to pursue cases: finding around £10 to cover the out-of-pocket expenses required before a case could begin. Potential cases collapsed through lack of funding.[40] Problems also arose with finding a solicitor willing to take on the work. The report claimed that few solicitors were willing to take on 'distasteful' cases and that many of the solicitors who would take on this work were based in London. There were also suspicions that many of the reports required by the courts were done shoddily and that people were billed for expenses before work began.[41] The first Lawrence Report focused on recommendations to improve the Poor Persons' Rules in this area. The committee called for an income test, for the reporting solicitor to be able to administer the necessary oaths required to progress the case, and for the reporting solicitor to be required to meet with the applicant. They also wanted the conducting solicitor to report on the progress of the case and to report instances where it was found that the Poor Person had understated his or her means. The committee also wanted to prevent both the reporting and the conducting solicitor from receiving any money directly from the Poor Person and wanted any expenses to be dealt with by the prescribing officer.[42] The aim of these rules was to discourage, if not prevent, solicitors from unnecessarily causing delays in the system or exploiting cases for profit.

The committee vehemently rejected the notion of the state intervening in legal aid. They did not believe that a government official was needed in most types of cases. In divorce cases, however, there would need to be two officials appointed, one for the petitioner and one for the respondent. The committee also felt that officials would not give due diligence to checking the means of those coming to the courts. Therefore, those who could afford to pursue their own divorce cases would pass this responsibility and cost on to the state. They also felt that a government department would also be more inclined to raise the limits on means and to start taking on cases that would normally be profitable. The committee felt that Poor Persons' work should be done by private practitioners, who 'would have the greatest interest in seeing that the privileges granted to Poor Persons were not abused' because of the direct financial loss to them.[43] Morgan points out that the Lord Chancellor's Department was equally loath to create additional governmental responsibility and keen to avoid a scandal about solicitors exploiting divorce clients. State takeover was used as a threat to those who would not uphold the moral boundaries of their profession.[44]

Yet this view of the state also assumed that governments had endless capacity to absorb the costs of divorce cases and that state officials could not be efficient arbiters of an individual's means because there was no direct cost to them in the form of lost earnings. This interpretation of what a state might do in moving into a private business arena spoke to Lawrence's experiences of working for those companies whose property was requisitioned in wartime. It was not an unreasonable view, as the peacetime governments of the late 1910s and early 1920s tried to offer welfarist provisions such as 'Homes fit for Heroes' – Lawrence and colleagues could not have known that the 'Geddes Axe' would shortly fall. It did, however, overlook the years of case assessment and means-testing in the welfare professions. This emerged first through the COS's development of case work to best identify the needs of families and individuals.[45] Hospital almoning was a development of this form of social work. Hospital almoners used social work skills to prevent those who could afford to pay for treatment from abusing the system, whilst referring those who could afford to pay into a hospital savings scheme to a suitable society and those who were destitute to the Poor Law.[46] There was an element, here, of overlooking and dismissing the claims to expertise of the emerging, female-dominated social work profession.

As Morgan argues, the first Lawrence Report's recommendations were implemented, making it harder for solicitors to exploit Poor Persons' divorce cases, but they failed to make any provision for the profession's capacity to do the work. The solution was to strongly encourage solicitors to volunteer to take the work on. When this did not succeed, the second committee was launched to review the scheme. However, the second committee maintained the principle of this work being done without a fee.[47] The second Lawrence Report again pointed to a shortage of solicitors willing to undertake divorce work, with most of the willing lawyers based in London.[48] This report recommended the further decentralisation of divorce cases, by enabling more courts around the country to hear them, and the abolition of the Poor Persons' Department in favour of the Law Society taking over the administration of this work through regional committees, which was put into effect the following year.[49] The committee felt that, whilst it was the responsibility of the state to ensure that everyone who needed it could take divorce proceedings to the High Court, it was not desirable for the state to deliver this. First, the committee argued that it would require either the formation of a new government department or the major expansion of the Poor Persons' Department, and that either method would be very expensive. Second, they felt that the state taking on the responsibility for this work would necessarily lead to the 'loss of much voluntary energy'. The committee further felt that a solicitor acting voluntarily for a client maintained a relationship of trust and honesty between the client and the solicitor. Handing the responsibility over to the Government would result in the loss of this type of relationship. The committee further felt that the return for the legal profession's considerable autonomy was the moral responsibility to offer free services to those who could not afford to pay for them. Finally, they felt that the state should only step in if the profession had failed to discharge its moral obligations to the wider community.[50] Money figured in two ways here: first, the desire to avoid the state directing taxpayers' money to Poor Persons' divorce cases; and, second, the desire to push solicitors to ensure that their divorce work was done in a timely and fair fashion and thereby to avoid accusations of profiting from misery. This plan rationalised where divorce cases could be heard and brought more responsibility for the system into the hands of the Law Society. It did not engage in any meaningful sense with widening access to the law.

The Finlay Committee

Whilst the two Lawrence Reports were concerned with the problem of people on lower incomes accessing divorce proceedings without being exploited in the process, the Finlay Committee and its reports were tasked with looking at access to the law more generally. The impetus for the Finlay Committee's appointment came from campaigning outside the profession. As Goriely notes, it came first from the National Conference of Labour Women, with a campaign led by three women – Gertrude Tuckwell, Clara Rackham and Marion Phillips – who were amongst the first women magistrates and were concerned about the problems faced by women in court. The campaign was also picked up by BARS and the Salvation Army and was then followed by a letter to *The Times* from a number of senior Anglicans, by which point Schuster could no longer ignore it.[51] Justice Finlay was a barrister who had first worked as junior counsel to the Board of the Inland Revenue before taking up various government support roles during the First World War and later returning to private practice.[52] The Finlay Committee produced two reports, the first on legal aid in criminal matters and the second looking at the provision of legal advice and legal aid in the county courts. They found that legal advice was provided by lawyers acting in a voluntary capacity on behalf of settlement houses, community associations or political parties. The greatest need was for advice, but some cases needed to be taken to the county courts, which dealt with such issues as debt and recovery or problems with landlords. Legal aid in the county courts mattered, because it would enable working-class people to effectively deal with the legal problems that beset them – and the solicitors and barristers who offered advice for free were often unable to take a case further without some sort of financial assistance.

The first Finlay Report, published in 1926, was uncontroversial. It made some relatively minor recommendations about expanding existing provision under the Poor Prisoner's Defence Act 1903.[53] However, the second report on civil legal advice revealed that the committee was split between a majority and a minority. As with the Lawrence Committees, the membership heavily favoured the legal profession, with – as Rubin notes – relatively few people having any experience of the needs of the working classes or administering welfare.[54] With such a bias on the committee, it was unsurprising that the majority were happy with the existing provision and the philanthropic efforts of the legal profession. Ideologically, the Finlay Committee had much in common with the Lawrence Committees. The signatories to the majority report were Finlay, Sir Ernley Blackwell, Sir Geoffrey Butler, Dennis Herbert and Rhys Hopkin Morris, and Coley, Maddocks, Meiklejohn and Schuster from the Lawrence Committees. Blackwell was born into a prominent St Andrews family and became a barrister in 1892. He entered the Civil Service as the Assistant Undersecretary of State for the Criminal Department of the Home Office in 1906 and remained there until his retirement in 1933.[55] Butler was then the Conservative MP for the University of Cambridge, having grown up in a very well-connected and influential family and worked as a historian at Cambridge.[56] Dennis Herbert had begun his career as a solicitor before being elected as the Conservative MP for Watford.[57] Rhys Hopkin Morris was a barrister turned Liberal MP for Cardiganshire.[58] H.D. Roome was a barrister, serving as Junior Crown Counsel at the Old Bailey from 1920 and also as Treasury Counsel. Roome had also stood as a Liberal MP in Reading in the 1922 General Election.[59] These men were extremely distinguished in terms of their legal expertise, or their capabilities in public administration or politics, but had little to no experience of working-class people.

This was reflected in the majority report's findings. The committee noted how impressed they were with the various voluntary groups, but they called only for more lawyers to volunteer for this work.[60] They were keen to avoid encouraging litigation by working-class people.[61] This was in stark contrast to the minority report and its signatories. The minority report, presenting the views of Dorothy Jewson and Rhys J. Davies, called for legal advice to be absorbed within local authorities, as the existing system was failing to meet people's need for advice on social legislation. This was compounded by the massively uneven distribution of Poor Man's Lawyer services across the country.[62] Jewson came from a prominent Norwich industrial family. She was heavily involved in activism, including working with Mary Macarthur for the National Federation of Women Workers and serving as the Labour MP for Norwich between 1923 and 1924.[63] Rhys J. Davies was a former coal miner and Labour MP for Withington in Manchester.[64] Jewson and Davies amplified the concerns of the voluntary organisations who had given evidence.

Goriely makes important observations about the majority report of the Finlay Committee. First, its adherence to voluntary principles was already out of step with the legal profession, and the profession proved largely resistant to further calls for volunteering.[65] Second, there was a question of professional identity. As Abel notes, barristers had a long-standing professional identity. In contrast, the definition of a solicitor only came into shape in the nineteenth century, with the profession developing a monopoly in conveyancing work, dealing with litigation in the lower courts and preparing cases for barristers to take into the higher courts.[66] With great effort, solicitors had acquired respectable status by the early twentieth century, and the social standing of the client reflected on the social standing of the solicitor. Voluntary service was also part of this wider staking of a claim as a profession, but by the 1920s, the need for solicitors to prove themselves had reduced.[67] The second Finlay Report failed to find a way of enthusing lawyers to volunteer to take on Poor Persons' work, and it also failed to satisfy growing demands for better access to the law.

The Rushcliffe Committee

The Second World War both replicated and exacerbated the problems of the First, since there was additional demand for divorce cases as lawyers and clerks were called up into the armed forces or war work.[68] Divorce was not the only area that caused concern. In a debate in the House of Lords, the Lord Chancellor, Viscount Simon, said:

> It must be very worrying to a serving soldier when at a distance from home not to know what to do about some civil difficulty such as the rent of his house or the claims of a building society or a hire purchase contract or the complaint of a neighbour reported to him by his wife.[69]

For those in the forces, the Services Divorce Department in 1942 was established to expedite divorce proceedings alongside other types of provision. As Cohn notes, the forces set up both Legal Advice Bureaux and Command Legal Aid (Civil Affairs) to support the whole range of civil legal needs of those serving.[70] Crang also notes that legal assistance was part of the broader provision of welfare to those in the forces. The Army set up civil legal advice bureaux to support those whose problems could not be dealt with through the CABx in Home Commands, drawing upon qualified lawyers in service or volunteer civilian lawyers. Beyond this, the command legal branches were run by full-time serving lawyers, who were able to help with more complicated cases and, where necessary, prepared cases to be passed over to the relevant

Poor Persons' Committee. This scheme was free and open to all soldiers up to the rank of sergeant, but it left out junior officers, who were often unable to afford legal expenses from their own pocket. The Royal Air Force joined the Army's scheme, whilst the Royal Navy made its own arrangements. As Crang states, their work was primarily matrimonial, with 140,000 of the 175,000 cases they dealt with between 1942 and 1945 being divorce cases.[71] Along with the establishment of the civilian CABx from 1939, different models of offering legal advice were available to the public – and they were working.

The Rushcliffe Committee was appointed in 1944 to examine the availability of legal advice and what could be done to improve it, as well as the possibilities for expanding access to legal aid. That the committee was appointed with this purpose reflected considerable shifts in the landscape of legal aid and advice provision. As Goriely notes, the interwar Poor Persons' Procedure had proved unworkable by the late 1930s, as Welsh solicitors refused to take on cases. With a rise in divorce cases in wartime, it was essential to rethink what a legal aid and advice scheme could look like – and how it could go far beyond divorce work.[72] The advice landscape had also shifted since the Finlay Committee had released its second report on civil legal aid. The Poor Man's Lawyer movement had continued to grow, as had the NCSS and its reach. The NCSS led the establishment of CABx on the outbreak of the Second World War. However, CABx could only provide legal advice if they were able to call upon the services of a volunteer lawyer. The CABx nonetheless offered a national network of advice that was open to anyone, and they could serve as a portal to legal advice. An informed and compliant public was critical to maintaining the home front during the war. CABx and other advisory services were not just a means of ensuring that citizens could get the best information and help but also a way for the Government to keep an eye on morale.[73]

The Rushcliffe Committee had more members than any of the interwar committees, and its membership was more diverse. Unlike the earlier two committees, it comprised people who were active in the field rather than just being asked to provide written evidence or be interviewed: George Haynes was the director of the NCSS, whilst Felix E. Crowder was the secretary of the Manchester Poor Man's Lawyer Association.[74] The trade unions, major providers of legal services, were represented through F.J. Burrows. Burrows was a railway porter by trade and very active in the trade union movement, becoming the President of the National Union of Railwaymen in 1943. Burrows left the Rushcliffe Committee in early 1945, when he was sent by Winston Churchill to (then) Ceylon to work on the Ceylon Constitutional Reform Committee; by November 1945, Clement Attlee had appointed him as the Governor of Bengal.[75] The Lord Southwood was the chair and managing director of Odhams Press, which published the *Daily Herald*, one of the bestselling British newspapers in the 1930s and 1940s and a paper explicitly linked to the

Labour Party.[76] Mabel Crout was a member of Woolwich Borough Council and one of the first women Justices of the Peace (JPs) in London.[77] The Hon. Mrs Bickford-Smith was the daughter of Lord Simon.[78]

There was also a considerable amount of legal expertise on the committee. Baron Rushcliffe began his career as a barrister, becoming the Conservative MP for Rushcliffe in Nottinghamshire in 1918, and was later chair of the Unemployment Assistance Board.[79] W.A. Gillett was a solicitor and a senior figure in the Law Society.[80] Moelwyn Hughes was a member of the Haldane Society and Labour MP for Carmarthen.[81] Sir James Aitken was a district registrar of the High Court and the group registrar of county courts and served on Lancashire County Council from the early 1920s.[82] Sir Frank Burnand was the master of the Queen's Bench Division between 1930 and 1960. Burnand worked on the Army and Royal Air Force Legal Schemes between 1941 and 1947, holding the rank of honorary lieutenant colonel at the War Office.[83] Justice Hodson began his career at the divorce bar, later becoming a divorce judge.[84] Justice Lewis was junior counsel to the Treasury and was appointed to the King's Bench Division of the High Court in 1935.[85] S.C.T. Littlewood was a solicitor with expertise in the magistrates' courts and town planning and was also a member of the Law Society's council.[86] Reginald Manningham-Buller was a barrister, then freshly elected as the Conservative MP for Daventry, and he would later serve as the Lord Chancellor.[87] Theobald Mathew was a solicitor who joined the Civil Service on the outbreak of war and by 1944 was head of the Home Office Criminal Division.[88] Sir Bertrand Watson was the Chief Metropolitan Magistrate in London.[89] The Lord Chancellor's Office (LCO) was represented on the committee by Schuster and Sir Albert Napier. Napier had been assistant secretary to the LCO and the deputy clerk of the Crown in Chancery from 1919 to 1944, when he replaced Schuster as permanent secretary and clerk. Napier was, therefore, the civil servant who would steer the Rushcliffe reforms into law.[90] In 1944, Schuster moved to become head of the legal branch of the Allied Control Commission (British zone) in Austria, thereby relinquishing the role to Napier.[91]

The Rushcliffe Committee found the existing system wanting and recommended the following: that legal aid should be granted in all criminal cases where it was seen to be in the 'interests of justice' and in civil matters, that it should be available to all with a net annual income of no more than £420. Single men and women who earned £3 or less per week and married men who earned £4 or less would receive legal assistance for free. Capital above £25 for the single and £50 for the married would be taken into account. Assistance would be available in all criminal courts, as well as the House of Lords, the Court of Appeal, the High Court, county courts, the Coroner's Court and the Courts of Special Jurisdiction, as well as special tribunals. The scheme would remain in the hands of the legal profession, overseen by the Law Society and in turn by the Lord Chancellor. It would be administered through area committees, which would follow the boundaries of the regional Law Societies. The area committees would in turn oversee local committees, which would be responsible for awarding legal aid certificates. Legal advice would also be provided at a local level with a charge of 2s 6d, unless it was clear that the applicant could afford to pay more. Area committees were to run offices with paid solicitors, whose job it would be to provide this advice, with branches and advice sessions run as necessary. The local and area committees would work as closely as possible with the CABx. Finally, the scheme would be underwritten by the Treasury.[92]

The scheme offered much. First, it was concerned with reducing economic barriers to the law. Second, it kept the legal profession in charge of the scheme, negating concerns about the impact of a state takeover of legal aid and advice. As Spencer notes, this was a long-standing orthodoxy in English constitutional history and law, and the Rushcliffe Committee did not challenge the assumptions that all litigation is private, and that the legal profession needed to remain independent of the state to work effectively.[93] Third, it retained the principle of voluntarism. Those who served on area committees could expect to receive payment for their expenses, whilst panel schemes would be set up to provide a ready supply of lawyers to take on cases.[94]

The Rushcliffe Report was published in 1945 and met with a favourable response in Parliament. Unlike other reports on the National Health Service (NHS), housing and education, it and the Cameron Report, which commented on the application of Rushcliffe's recommendations in Scotland, dropped down the agenda. Ground was regained in 1948 with broad support on both sides of the House. Unlike the other forms of social service or welfare, which were in the process of being brought under state control or nationalisation, access to the law remained in the hands of the profession. As Abel-Smith and Stevens argued, the eventual deal was favourable to lawyers: it kept legal services independent of the state for democratic reasons, and control of access to Poor Persons' relief remained with the Law Society. Rather than a new system being created, a system by which the state refunded lawyers for their work was implemented.[95] It worked on the assumption that such work did not need specialist knowledge and therefore could be fitted in alongside a solicitor's fee-incurring work. It was this question of paying lawyers back – along with the implicit sense that solicitors and barristers *could* make more money in other areas of their work – that undermined attempts to address the legal needs of some of the most vulnerable members of society.

The Legal Aid and Advice Act 1949 gained Royal Assent in July 1949, and it was followed by the establishment of the Advisory Committee on the Legal Aid and Advice Act, enabling the Trades Union Congress (TUC), the NCSS and others to have input into the management of the Act and its provisions.[96] The Act was not fully implemented, however. As Paterson notes, some of this related to differences between the Rushcliffe Committee and the Treasury.

The Rushcliffe Committee recommended a blanket payment of 2s 6d for legal advice with no means test, unless it was apparent that the advice-seeker could afford to pay the normal fee; the Treasury opposed this, blocking the development of a framework for paying for advice.[97] The devaluation of the pound in 1950 meant that only legal aid for High Court actions was made available through this scheme. Legal advice and aid in the county courts were not made available until 1955. The uncertainty and eventual outcome did not help the voluntary organisations providing advisory services – some closed down in the expectation of a new system, whilst others had to find funding in an uncertain climate, with potential donors always mindful of what the state might be providing around the corner.[98]

Legal aid in the welfare state

The partial implementation of the Legal Aid and Advice Act 1949 and the existence of the Advisory Committee created a space for the critical observation of developments. This was particularly the case for Labour, who were in opposition from 1951 to 1964. But the legislation that created the welfare state brought with it a panoply of tribunals to serve as a means of challenge or redress regarding decisions made by various local and central government departments or officials. As Spencer notes, barristers and solicitors were prevented from appearing in tribunals. This was partly due to various governments wanting to keep costs down and also to a desire to keep tribunals simple and accessible – and the view that lawyers would complicate matters.[99] Tribunals were supposed to offer a straightforward, common-sense approach to a problem. For example, under the provisions of the National Insurance (Industrial Injuries) Act 1946, an individual wishing to claim disablement benefit would need to be referred by their insurance officer to a Medical Board. The Medical Board, comprised of two or more medical practitioners, would come to a decision on the individual's condition and prognosis. If the individual was not happy with the Medical Board's decision, they had a right of appeal to the Medical Appeal Tribunal via the Minister of National Insurance. Appeals against ministerial decisions could be taken to the High Court.[100] In theory, setting up a benefit claim and dealing with dissatisfaction with a decision on that claim were straightforward and should not have needed a lawyer's support unless the case needed to be taken to the High Court, where legal aid was available. But not all people who needed to challenge a decision on their benefits were able to make their case effectively in a tribunal or to gather the reports and information needed in the time required by the tribunal and appeals process. Not everyone had ready access to the kinds of people who might be able to help them navigate the system, such as a trade union representative, a social worker, or even a family member or friend with the requisite literacy and organisational skills. Legal representation could make all the difference. For example, Alan Counsell, who had cerebral palsy, was excluded from mainstream school for eighteen months in the late 1940s because his head teacher thought he should have been in a special needs school. His grandmother paid for a lawyer, who obtained a medical expert, who went to the tribunal to speak on Counsell's behalf. The doctor found Counsell to be of above average intelligence and Counsell went straight back to his mainstream school, exactly as he and his family wished.[101] As Abel-Smith and Stevens pointed out, advice was often needed to work out which tribunal or court needed to be applied to before it would be clear whether the individual could represent themselves – and if the other party had professional support, it was usually a good idea for the individual in question also to consult a lawyer.[102] Solicitors and barristers were later given the right of appearance at tribunals in the light of the Franks Report and the subsequent Tribunals and Inquiries Act 1958, but there was no legal aid for this.[103]

Various pieces of legislation were passed in the mid-1950s that raised the issue of legal aid in the county courts, largely as the work of the county court was expanded in the light of the Evershed Report of 1953. In 1947, the Evershed Committee was tasked with looking at the operation of the Supreme Court, the final court of appeal for civil cases in all British jurisdictions, and for criminal cases for all but Scotland.[104] Reviewing Supreme Court processes necessarily meant looking at processes and procedures in all lower courts, and the Evershed Committee recommended in its first interim report that the county courts should have their jurisdiction widened.[105] The Jones Committee was tasked with looking at how the procedures in the county courts could be made swifter and less costly.[106] The Advisory Committee's annual report in November 1954 claimed that the need to make contributions was not having an impact on people claiming legal aid.[107] The results of Evershed, on the back of other committees, led to the introduction of the County Courts Bill in June 1955, which in turn would bring legal aid into the county courts.[108]

Two further adjustments were made to the Legal Aid and Advice Act 1949. First, in 1960, the Legal Aid Act 1960 changed the income and capital limits of the scheme to make more people eligible. Then, in 1964, a subsequent Legal Aid Act allowed those who were being pursued by a legally aided person also to be supported through the scheme. It also figured as an element of tackling other social policy issues. The Molony Committee on Consumer Protection reported in 1962. This committee had a wide remit, which included quality standards, clothes sizing and hire purchase. Consumer advice, with recourse to legal support if necessary, was an important part of better protecting the public.[109] The Finer Committee was established by Richard Crossman, the Secretary of State for Social Services in 1969, to investigate the difficulties faced by lone-parent families and to explore possible avenues of support. The report brought out the numerous points at which legal advice and aid were critical to lone-parent families, from guidance as a marriage or relationship broke down, to advice on the services and support available, to obtaining legal documents, such as affiliation orders against the father of a child, to taking out and enforcing a maintenance order against a liable parent.[110]

A change of government in 1964 and the controversy over Abel-Smith and Stevens's books prompted further rethinking of legal aid and advice. Two reports into the state of access to justice and possible solutions were published in December 1968: *Justice for All*, by the Society of Labour Lawyers, and *Rough Justice*, by the Society of Conservative Lawyers. Both agreed that access to solicitors was inadequate, but their proposals were very different. Whilst the Conservatives favoured subsidising legal firms to open in areas with a shortage of lawyers, the Labour lawyers called for the introduction of neighbourhood law centres. These followed a model that had been recently adopted in the United States, in which salaried lawyers provided legal advice to deprived communities and also offered education to communities on rights and the law. As will be seen in Chapter 4, this idea did not meet with favour from the Lord Chancellor's Advisory Committee. It did, however, prompt the Law Society to develop the £25 scheme, or 'green form' scheme, which allowed solicitors to means-test potential clients themselves. They also proposed the appointment of twelve liaison officers to work with the CABx and experimentation with legal centres. The Law Society's amended proposals met with Gardiner's approval, including the continued appointment of one liaison officer at the Law Society. When Labour lost the 1970 election, Gardiner was replaced by Lord Hailsham, who developed these proposals into the Legal Advice and Assistance Act 1972. This Act was divided into two parts. The first covered the £25 scheme and the second the establishment of an Advisory Liaison Service, along with providing for offices of salaried solicitors in communities where there was particular need. However, only Part I of the Act was implemented when the Act came into force on 2 April 1973. Despite consolidations and amendments made through the Legal Aid Acts 1974 and 1979 to the Legal Advice and Assistance Act 1972, state provision for legal advice failed to reach its full potential. This also meant that the neighbourhood law centres had to seek special permission from the Lord Chancellor to be able to undertake legal aid work, which was granted and offered the burgeoning movement a lifeline.[111]

The Royal Commission on Legal Services

In July 1976, the Home Secretary, Roy Jenkins, launched the Royal Commission on Legal Services, chaired by Sir Henry Benson. The Benson Commission was to examine the provision of legal services in England, Wales and Northern Ireland and to recommend any necessary changes to the legal profession. The commissioners were to look at how people became lawyers, how they were trained, paid and regulated, and the overall structure and organisation of the legal profession. These initiatives both raised the problems of access to legal advice and offered possible solutions to them. But the Benson Commission was also prompted by the perception that the legal profession was not fit for the twentieth century. This centred upon the concept that the members of the profession became wealthy by charging excessive fees for their work. As the report pointed out, when compared with such everyday expenses as having a car repaired or decorating the external walls of a house, lawyers' fees were not extortionate. The difference was that it was easier for a lay person to see what had been done and therefore to have a sense of where the expense came from. The work that a solicitor or barrister would do was less immediately obvious or tangible, and therefore, as the Commission argued, fees felt excessive.[112] In their evidence to the Commission, the TUC highlighted the importance of recognising that many people were put off by going into an unfamiliar office and their reluctance to become involved in what could be a very expensive process.[113] The potential cost of legal remedy clearly mattered, and it also mattered that there was a perception that too few lawyers had expertise in the areas where people needed advice or assistance: in navigating social security, divorce, childcare and housing.[114]

The Benson Commission had a very different composition from the previous investigations into legal aid and advice. First, the Commission was not dominated by lawyers. The chair of the Commission, Sir Henry Benson, was an accountant by training. Zander pointed out that whilst several Commission members were trained lawyers, only three practised: David Seligman was a solicitor in Cardiff; Sir Sydney Templeman was a High Court judge; and Max Williams was a member of the Law Society's Council and a partner in a City of London law firm. Other members had a legal background but did not practise, such as Susan Marsden-Smedley. Marsden-Smedley had originally trained as a barrister but joined the Consumer Council and later the Legal Action Group. Mark Littman was also a barrister by training, but he had ceased to practise. Tom Harper had been the editor of the *Law Society Gazette* before moving to the *New Law Journal*. The committee also included business representatives, in the shape of Sally Ramsden, recently the President of the UK Federation of Business and Professional Women, and William Marshall, a Northern Irish company director.[115] The TUC were given representation through Len Edmondson of the Amalgamated Engineering Union.[116] Joe Haines worked as Prime Minister Harold Wilson's press secretary, but after Wilson's resignation in March 1976, Haines joined the *Daily Mirror* as a journalist. Peter Goldman was director of the Consumer Association, having previously been director of the Conservative Political Centre. He also served on the Community Relations Commission between 1973 and 1975.[117] Unlike the earlier committees exploring access to the law, this committed included social scientists. Alwyn Roberts was a sociologist at Bangor University, whilst Peter Morris Oppenheimer was an economist at the University of Oxford.[118] Ralf

Dahrendorf was the director of the London School of Economics.[119] As providers of legal services and a major political force in their own right, the TUC lobbied to ensure that they had representation on the Advisory Committee, but they had begun to lose ground to bodies like the Nuffield Foundation and Rowntree Trust, and academic social scientists. The academic social scientists here, as on the Advisory Committee, brought to the table an understanding of structural inequality, social structures and economic operations. The commission included members who represented not only the more radical parts of the legal profession, in the shape of Marsden-Smedley and Harper, but also the emerging areas of advice provision, in the shape of the Consumer Association.

The Benson Commission reported in 1979. The resulting report ran to two volumes, with the substantive report over 800 pages. It was a comprehensive study of many aspects of the legal profession. In terms of legal aid and advice, it made a number of findings. First, although the commission considered the idea of a national legal service, they rejected it in favour of maintaining an independent judiciary – though they felt that the salaried elements of the profession could be extended.[120] They also wanted the Law Society to remain in charge of civil legal aid through the creation of regional committees, with ultimate oversight coming from the Lord Chancellor's Office (LCO). The Legal Aid Advisory Committee would be replaced by a Council for Legal Services, which would support the Lord Chancellor.[121] The commission were generally interested in the journeys people took to resolve issues and wanted to ensure that there were bias-free sources of advice in the community, which could provide advice in a majority of circumstances and sift out cases that needed legal intervention. Whilst the commission recognised the work of other advice providers, they agreed with the National Consumer Council that the CABx should be the 'basic general practitioner or first tier service' for advice. CABx workers would be able to identify a case that needed to be taken down a legal route and to help the advice-seeker find a suitable solicitor.[122] The National Association of Citizens' Advice Bureaux (NACAB) and the Government would need to work together to develop a programme for setting up CABx in areas that were not currently served by branches, whilst the CABx would need to provide training in paralegal and tribunal representation services.[123]

Whilst the commission valued the work of voluntary-run law centres, they felt that the expansion and enhancement of the CABx in terms of their legal support and the development of a national network of community law centres (CLCs) would mean that the need for the free legal advice centres would be phased out, with the volunteers and funding moving over to the CABx and CLCs.[124] Citizens' law centres were a possible solution to those problems that were not covered by legal aid and to the shortage of lawyers. Whilst the commission thought that they had proposals that would solve these problems in time, they believed that law centres were a valuable interim service. The CLCs would specialise in welfare law and take referrals from CABx. The term 'citizens' law centre' marked the difference between this type of service and the service that had been developed by the neighbourhood law centres in the 1970s, which had placed the greatest emphasis on trying to tackle social inequality rather than necessarily dealing with individual legal cases.[125] The Law Centres Working Group presented evidence arguing that it was usually better to focus meagre resources on tackling the root of a problem rather than putting energies into dealing with a series of individual cases.[126] However, the Benson Commission felt that, ultimately, the neighbourhood law centres were campaigning organisations supporting particular sections of the community rather than being open for legal advice for all. They were not, therefore, an impartial legal service, and their community development work should be funded through the urban aid scheme for urban regeneration rather than through the legal aid system.[127] The CLCs would effectively be a hybrid of the existing free legal advice centres and the neighbourhood law centres, insofar as they would be staffed by salaried solicitors who offered advice to individuals, and would be embedded within a particular neighbourhood. The CLCs would be overseen by a quango, which would oversee standards and impartiality.[128]

The Benson Commission had to wait four years before the Conservative Government responded to them, and their proposals were not acted upon in any substantive way. What followed the Benson Commission was a period of crisis in advisory services, as the local authority budgets that funded neighbourhood law centres and their free legal advice colleagues were constrained during the 1980s. The abolition of the Greater London Council in 1986 disrupted the funding of many law centres; prior to this, many had been presented by Conservative councillors as being part of a 'loony left' in London and therefore less worthy of public funds. However, the Legal Aid Act 1988 took up some of the recommendations of the Benson Commission. It introduced the Legal Aid Board, whose members were appointed by the Lord Chancellor and would comprise representatives of the Law Society, the Bar Council, and others with experience of the courts and management. This would eventually replace the Lord Chancellor's Advisory Committee in the early 1990s, although the Act did not abolish it.

Conclusion

The provision of legal aid and advice in the twentieth century is book-ended by two Royal Commissions that addressed it as part of a bigger concern. In 1909, the Royal Commission on Divorce was tasked with finding a means of making divorce law fairer and easier, but it took the impact of the First World War on the legal profession to prompt the creation of the Poor Persons'

Department. The Lawrence and Finlay Committees were dominated by lawyers who were conservative in their vision of the legal profession and its relationship to the needs of the working classes. The Finlay Committee heard evidence from those involved in Poor Man's Lawyers associations, but the findings revealed that the lawyers on the committee remained wedded to the idea of voluntary work with no state funding. Voluntarism centred on the idea of lawyers doing their work without charge to advice-seekers. This work was 'free' in the sense that no fees or expenses were billed, but it ignored the commitment required by the lawyers and their host organisations and placed a disproportionate burden on junior members of the profession. Calls to do more of this 'free' work for the good of the profession and society had little impact, and little thought was given to how volunteering could be arranged in a sustainable manner in terms of either divorce work or more general legal advice. The idea of legal advice as offering the means for working-class people to assert their agency – replacing, perhaps, the older letter-writing and petitioning cultures of the nineteenth century – was overlooked in discussions about avoiding state involvement in proceedings. A shift in the terms of the debate by the later 1920s was marked by Jewson and Davies's argument for legal advice being harnessed as part of ensuring working-class citizens' rights, even though they were overruled.

The Rushcliffe Committee and the Benson Commission differed in drawing upon a wider range of experience and engaging more deeply with the initiatives to widen access to justice that were taking place. Critically, both engaged with the more radical innovators as well as the more mainstream. Whilst the Lawrence and Finlay Committees were trying to prevent scandals, Rushcliffe and Benson were more concerned with trying to make it easier for people to assert their rights. The Rushcliffe Committee's findings came alongside the abolition of the Poor Law in 1948 and the completion of the shift to rules-based national schemes for welfare and health. If the Legal Aid and Advice Act 1949 had been fully enacted, it would have offered better redress for working-class people; it took considerable effort to extend provision into the county courts and tribunals and for legal advice to be more widely available.

Both Rushcliffe and Benson, however, kept to the same ideological concepts that the state and judiciary should be separate and that a state-funded national legal service with salaried solicitors and barristers was intolerable. The Benson Commission, on the other hand, was willing to consider the radical idea of a national network of citizens' legal centres, which would have, if enacted, provided a legal corollary to the CABx. It was concerned with rationalising voluntary legal activity into the CABx and these centres for reasons of efficiency and efficacy. Although, as Spencer and Sommerlad note, all committees and commissions were consistent in thinking about maintaining the independence of civil society and the state, the vision of a feckless working-class person desperate to take out vexatious litigation dissolved.[129] This was a result of greater diversity on the committees and commissions as well as – in the case of Benson – a shift towards undertaking research into the needs and wants of working-class advice-seekers. Legal advice as a tool of making the welfare state work in the interests of citizens emerged most strongly in the period after 1945, in the wake of a rules-based welfare and health system based on taxation and contribution, but it was difficult to make the case for greater state involvement.

Notes

1 T. Goriely, 'Gratuitous assistance to the "ill-dressed": Debating civil legal aid in England and Wales from 1918–1939', *International Journal of the Legal Profession*, 13:1 (2006), p. 42.
2 See E.P. Thompson, *The Poverty of Theory and Other Essays* (London: Merlin, 1978); V.A.C. Gatrell, *The Hanging Tree: Execution and the English People, 1770–1868* (Oxford: Oxford University Press, 1996); C. Steedman, 'At every bloody level: A magistrate, a framework-knitter, and the law', *Law and History Review*, 30:2 (2012), pp. 387–422; 'A lawyer's letter: Everyday uses of the law in early nineteenth-century England', *History Workshop Journal*, 81, Spring (2016), pp. 62–83.
3 Steedman, 'At every bloody level', p. 393.
4 D.D. Gray, 'The People's Courts? Summary justice and social relations in the City of London, c.1760–1800', *Family and Community History*, 11:1 (2008), pp. 7–15; J. Davis, 'A poor man's system of justice: The London police courts in the second half of the nineteenth century', *Historical Journal*, 27:2 (1984), pp. 309–35.
5 S.A. King and P. Jones, 'Testifying for the poor: Epistolary advocates and the negotiation of parochial relief in England, 1800–1834', *Journal of Social History*, 49:4 (2016), pp. 784–807.
6 L. Charlesworth, 'Big Society, legal structures, Poor Law and the myth of a voluntary society', in A. Ishkanian and S. Szreter (eds), *The Big Society Debate: A New Agenda for Social Welfare?* (Cheltenham: Edward Elgar, 2012).
7 King and Jones, 'Testifying for the poor', p. 801; S.A. Shave, '"Great inhumanity": Scandal, child punishment and policymaking in the early years of the New Poor Law workhouse system', *Continuity and Change*, 33 (2018), pp. 354–5.
8 See P. Jones and S. King (eds), *Obligation, Entitlement and Dispute under the English Poor Laws* (Newcastle: Cambridge Scholars, 2015); C. Tilly, *Popular Contention in Great Britain 1758–1834* (London: Routledge, 2005).
9 See 'In Their Own Right: Contesting the New Poor Law 1834–1900', AHRC Project AH/R002770/1, January 2018 to December 2020, and project website www2.le.ac.uk/projects/own-write, correct at 7 January 2019.
10 E.T. Hurren, *Protesting about Pauperism: Poverty, Politics and Poor Relief in Late-Victorian England, 1870–1900* (Woodbridge: Boydell and Brewer, 2015).
11 Steedman, 'A lawyer's letter', p. 64.
12 T. Pearce, *The Poor Man's Lawyer* (London: Homer's Head, 1755).

13 'Mr William Unwin', *Sheffield Daily Telegraph*, Monday, 2 March 1896, p. 2.
14 'The Day's Gossip', *Nottingham Evening Post*, Thursday, 7 December 1893, p. 2; 'Northampton Bankruptcy Court', *Northampton Mercury*, Friday, 21 October 1892, p. 6.
15 L. Radzinowicz and R. Hood, *The Emergence of Penal Policy in Victorian and Edwardian England*, vol. 5 (Oxford: Clarendon Press, 1990); J. Briggs et al., *Crime and Punishment in England: An Introductory History* (London: UCL Press, 2001), p. 221.
16 See C. Emsley, *The English Police: A Political and Social History* (London: Longman, 1996).
17 M. Flegel, 'Changing faces: The NSPCC and the use of photography in the construction of cruelty to children', *Victorian Periodicals Review*, 39:1 (2006), pp. 1–20.
18 See G. Finlayson, *Citizen, State and Social Welfare in Britain 1830–1990* (Oxford: Clarendon, 1994), pp. 2–6; J. Garrard, *Democratisation in Britain: Elites, Civil Society and Reform since 1800* (Basingstoke: Palgrave, 2002).
19 Hurren, *Protesting*, p. 1.
20 D.R. Green, *Pauper Capital: London and the Poor Law, 1790–1870* (Farnham: Ashgate, 2010), pp. 237–8.
21 See J. Lewis, *The Voluntary Sector, the State and Social Work in Britain: The Charity Organisation Society/Family Welfare Association since 1869* (London: Edward Elgar, 1995); D. Glick, *The National Council of Women of Great Britain: The First One Hundred Years* (London: NCW, 1995).
22 Davis, 'A poor man's system of justice', p. 334.
23 See A. Paterson, *Legal Aid as a Social Service* (London: Cobden Trust, 1971); R.I. Morgan, 'The introduction of civil legal aid in England and Wales, 1914–1949', *Twentieth Century British History*, 5:1 (1994), pp. 38–76; F. Regan et al., *The Transformation of Legal Aid* (Oxford: Oxford University Press, 1999); Goriely, 'Gratuitous assistance'.
24 Morgan, 'The introduction of civil legal aid', pp. 53–5.
25 D. Cohen, *Family Secrets: The Things We Tried to Hide* (London: Penguin, 2014).
26 See M.L. Shanley, *Feminism, Marriage, and the Law in Victorian England* (Princeton: Princeton University Press, 1993).
27 K. Bradley, A. Logan and S. Shaw, 'Editorial: Youth and crime: Centennial reflections on the Children Act 1908', *Crimes and Misdemeanours*, 3:2 (2009), pp. 1–17.
28 Morgan, 'The introduction of civil legal aid', p. 48.
29 *Committee to Enquire into the Poor Persons Rules*, Cmd. 430 (London: HMSO, 1919); *Poor Persons' Rules Committee*, Cmd. 2358 (London: HMSO, 1925); *Committee on Legal Aid for the Poor – First Report*, Cmd. 2638 (London: HMSO, 1926); *Committee on Legal Aid for the Poor – Final Report*, Cmd. 2016 (London: HMSO, 1928).
30 Morgan, 'The introduction of civil legal aid', pp. 46–8.
31 G.R. Rubin, 'Lawrence, Sir Paul Ogden', *ODNB*.
32 'Bayford, Robert Frederic', *Who Was Who*. Coley's firm was Coley and Tilley; 'Mr Charles Goddard', *The Times*, 29 May 1922, p. 18; 'Noted Lawyer Dead', *Birmingham Daily Gazette*, 30 June 1933, p. 5.

33 'Well-known KC', *Gloucester Citizen*, 11 June 1931, p. 8; 'Sir Henry Maddocks', *The Times*, 11 June 1931, p. 18.
34 'Gregory, Sir (John) Roger (Burrow) (2 April 1861–27 February 1938)', *Who Was Who.*
35 A. Napier and M. Pottle, 'Schuster, Claud, Baron Schuster (1869–1956)', *ODNB.*
36 'Sir Roderick Meiklejohn', *The Times*, 20 January 1962, p. 10.
37 K. Prior, 'Lumley, Lawrence Roger, Eleventh Earl of Scarbrough (1896–1969)', *ODNB.*
38 'Poor Persons' Legal Assistance', *Scotsman*, 26 July 1923, p. 10; 'Leach, William', *Who Was Who.*
39 J. Hannam, 'Snowden [Nèe Annakin], Ethel (1881–1951)', *ODNB.*
40 *Committee to Enquire into the Poor Persons Rules*, Cmd. 430, paras 8–10, p. 3.
41 Ibid., pp. 3–4.
42 Ibid., pp. 9–10.
43 Ibid., p. 9.
44 Morgan, 'The introduction of civil legal aid', p. 47.
45 See Lewis, *The Voluntary Sector.*
46 G. Campbell Gosling, 'Gender, money and professional identity: Medical social work and the coming of the British National Health Service', *Women's History Review*, 27:2 (2017), pp. 310–28; L. Cullen, 'The first Lady Almoner: The appointment, position, and findings of Miss Mary Stewart at the Royal Free Hospital, 1895–99', *Journal of the History of Medicine and Allied Sciences*, 68:4 (2013), pp. 551–82.
47 Morgan, 'The introduction of civil legal aid', pp. 48–9.
48 *Poor Persons' Rules Committee*, Cmd. 2358, pp. 3–4.
49 Ibid., pp. 9–13.
50 Ibid., pp. 6–7.
51 Goriely, 'Gratuitous assistance', p. 54.
52 G.R. Rubin, 'Finlay, William, Second Viscount Finlay (1875–1945)', *ODNB.*
53 *Committee on Legal Aid for the Poor – First Report*, Cmd. 2638, pp. 10–11.
54 Rubin, 'Finlay'.
55 'Obituary', *The Times*, 23 September 1941, p. 7.
56 'Obituary', *The Times*, 8 April 1929, p. 16; also S. Parkinson, 'Sir Geoffrey Butler and the Tory tradition', *Conservative History Journal*, 2:2 (2014), pp. 18–26.
57 Herbert, 'Obituary', *The Times*, 11 December 1947, p. 6.
58 'Morris, Sir Rhys Hopkin (1888–1956)', *Who Was Who.*
59 'Obituary', *The Times*, 10 June 1930, p. 14.
60 *Committee on Legal Aid for the Poor – Final Report*, Cmd. 2016, para. 8, p. 5; Morgan, 'The introduction of civil legal aid', p. 51.
61 *Committee on Legal Aid*, p. 7.
62 Ibid., pp. 2, 12.
63 J. Hannam, 'Jewson, Dorothea [Dorothy] (1884–1964)', *ODNB.*
64 'Mr R. J. Davies', *The Times*, 2 November 1952, p. 2; 'Davies, Rhys John (1877–1954)', *Who Was Who.*
65 Goriely, 'Gratuitous assistance', p. 60.
66 R.L. Abel, *The Legal Profession in England and Wales* (Oxford: Blackwell, 1988), p. 139.

67 Goriely, 'Gratuitous assistance', pp. 60–2.
68 *Report of the Committee on Legal Aid and Legal Advice in England and Wales*, Cmd. 6641 (London: HMSO, 1945), pp. 4–5.
69 *Hansard*, HL Debate, 14 July 1942, vol. 123, cols 808–30.
70 E.J. Cohn, 'Legal aid to soldiers in the British Army', *University of Pennsylvania Law Review*, 92:2 (1943), pp. 171–2.
71 J.A. Crang, *The British Army and the People's War, 1939–1945* (Manchester: Manchester University Press, 2000), pp. 102–5.
72 T. Goriely, 'Law for the poor: The relationship between advice agencies and solicitors in the development of poverty law', *International Journal of the Legal Profession*, 3:1–2 (1996), pp. 222–3.
73 R. Mackay, *Half the Battle: Civilian Morale in Britain during the Second World War* (Manchester: Manchester University Press, 2003), pp. 9–10.
74 A.P. Baker, 'Haynes, Sir George Ernest (1902–1983)', *ODNB*; 'Best Legal Skill to Aid Poor', *Newcastle Journal*, 30 May 1944, p. 1.
75 'Sir Frederick Burrows', *The Times*, 24 April 1973, p. 14; D. Howell, 'Burrows, Sir Frederick John (1887–1973)', *ODNB*.
76 H. Richards, 'Elias, Julius Salter, Viscount Southwood (1873–1946)', *ODNB*.
77 'Crout, Dame Mabel (1890–1984)', *Who Was Who*.
78 D.J. Dutton, 'Simon, John Allsebrook, First Viscount Simon', *ODNB*.
79 R.C. Davison and M. Brodie, 'Betterton, Henry Bucknall, Baron Rushcliffe (1872–1949)', *ODNB*.
80 'Gillett, Col Sir (William) Alan (1879–1959)', *Who Was Who*.
81 G.R. Rubin, 'Hughes, Goronwy [Ronw] Moelwyn (1897–1955)', *ODNB*.
82 'Aitken, Sir James (1880–1948)', *Who Was Who*.
83 'Sir Frank Burnand', *The Times*, 26 April 1969, p. 10; 'Burnand, Sir (Richard) Frank (1887–1969)', *Who Was Who*.
84 Devlin and M.C. Curthoys, 'Hodson, Francis Lord Charlton [Charles], Baron Hodson (1895–1984)', *ODNB*.
85 'Obituary: Mr Justice Lewis', *Manchester Guardian*, 16 March 1950, p. 4; W.N. Stable and M.C. Curthoys, 'Lewis, Sir Wilfrid Hubert Poyer (1881–1950)', *ODNB*.
86 E. Sachs and S. Doyle, 'Littlewood, Sir Sydney Charles Thomas (1895–1967)', *ODNB*.
87 R.F.V. Heuston, *Lives of the Lord Chancellors, 1940–1970* (Oxford: Clarendon, 1987); D.J. Dutton, 'Buller, Reginald Edward Manningham-, First Viscount Dilhorne', *ODNB*.
88 M. Evelyn and M. Pottle, 'Mathew, Sir Theobald (1898–964)', *ODNB*.
89 'Sir Bertrand Watson', *The Times*, 17 February 1948, p. 7.
90 R. Stevens, 'Napier, Sir Albert Edward Alexander (1881–1973)', *ODNB*.
91 A. Napier and M. Pottle, 'Schuster, Claud, Baron Schuster (1869–1956)', *ODNB*.
92 *Report of the Committee on Legal Aid and Legal Advice in England and Wales*, Cmd. 6641, pp. 40–3.
93 See M. Spencer, 'Public subsidies without strings: Labour and the lawyers at the birth of legal aid', *International Journal of the Legal Profession*, 9:3 (2002), p. 261.
94 *Report of the Committee on Legal Aid and Legal Advice in England and Wales*, Cmd. 6641, p. 42; p. 34.

95 B. Abel-Smith and R. Stevens, *Lawyers and the Courts: A Sociological Study of the English Legal System 1750–1965* (London: Heinemann, 1967), p. 327.
96 *Report of the Committee on Legal Aid and Legal Advice in England and Wales*, Cmd. 6641, pp. 39–40.
97 Paterson, *Legal Aid*, pp. 13–14.
98 Abel-Smith and Stevens, *Lawyers and the Courts*, p. 328.
99 Spencer, 'Public subsidies', pp. 257–8.
100 National Insurance (Industrial Injuries) Act 1946, s37–40.
101 British Library, Sounds collection. Alan Counsell interviewed by Dean Thomas, Speaking for ourselves: an oral history of people with cerebral palsy. Interviewed 26 January 2005, shelf mark C1134/08/01–08. Transcript and recording available at: https://sounds.bl.uk/Oral-history/Disability-Voices/021M-C1134X0008XX-0100V0, correct at 22 April 2019.
102 B. Abel-Smith and R. Stevens, *In Search of Justice: Society and the Legal System* (London: Allen Lane, 1968), p. 10.
103 Conservative Party Archive (hereafter CPA) CPA PUB 173/34 *Rough Justice* (London: Conservative Political Centre, 1968), pp. 12–13.
104 *Final Report of the Committee on Supreme Court Practice and Procedure*, Cmd. 8878 (London: HMSO, 1953).
105 *Interim Report of the Committee on Supreme Court Practice and Procedure*, Cmd. 7764 (London: HMSO, 1949), pp. 17–18.
106 *First Interim Report of the Committee on County Court Procedure*, Cmd. 7468 (London: HMSO, 1948), pp. 12–13.
107 LSE, SLL/6/17, SLL Questionnaire on Legal Aid.
108 *Hansard*, HC Debate, 24 June 1955, vol. 543, col. 1650.
109 *Final Report of the Committee on Consumer Protection*, Cmnd. 1781 (London: HMSO, 1962), pp. 128–9.
110 *Report of the Committee on One-Parent Families*, Vol. 1, Cmnd. 5629 (London: HMSO, 1974), pp. 139, 141, 376, 441.
111 S. Pollock, *Legal Aid: The First Twenty-Five Years* (London: Oyez, 1975), pp. 96–8.
112 *Royal Commission on Legal Services – Final Report*, Vol. 1, Cmnd. 7648 (London: HMSO, 1979), p. 34.
113 Ibid., p. 35.
114 Ibid.
115 M. Zander, 'Commission with Legal Minority', *Guardian*, 30 June 1976, p. 6.
116 'Len Edmondson', *Journal*, 5 December 2006, www.thejournal.co.uk/news/north-east-news/the-death-of-len-edmondson-4543890, correct at 22 April 2019.
117 'Goldman, Peter (1925–1987)', *Who Was Who*.
118 'Oppenheimer, Peter Morris', *Who's Who 2018*; 'Roberts, Alwyn', *Who's Who 2018*.
119 'Dahrendorf, Ralf (1929–2009)', *Who Was Who*.
120 *Royal Commission on Legal Services – Final Report*, Vol. 1, Cmnd. 7648, pp. 51–2.
121 Ibid., p. 68.
122 Ibid., pp. 69–71.

123 Ibid., p. 74.
124 Ibid., p. 77.
125 Ibid., p. 83.
126 Ibid., p. 80.
127 Ibid., pp. 83–4.
128 Ibid., p. 65.
129 Spencer, 'Public subsidies'; H. Sommerlad, 'Some reflections on the relationship between citizenship, access to justice, and the reform of legal aid', *Journal of Law and Society*, 31:3 (2004), pp. 345–68.

2

The Poor Man's Lawyer

Before the 1890s, a 'Poor Man's Lawyer' was an individual solicitor or barrister who made his services available as an act of good will or a working-class autodidact who was happy to share knowledge with others. By the end of the century, it was a common term for regular volunteering by members of the legal profession, primarily giving advice and occasionally representing a pro bono client in court. It spread not only through the settlement movement but also with the development of umbrella groups concerned with improving the efficiency of voluntary action and campaigning for the extension of state welfare. It was also successful in providing the basic model for legal aid and advice that informed the Legal Aid and Advice Act 1949 – and, at the same time, deeply unsuccessful in terms of opening up the more radical approach to access to the law that its supporters wanted.

The origins of the Poor Man's Lawyer

The first articulation of a plan for a 'Poor Man's Lawyer' as a recognisable form of organised *service* was made by William Booth, the founder of the Salvation Army, in his book *In Darkest England and the Way Out* in 1890.[1] Booth wrote this tract with the help of W.T. Stead, the campaigning journalist and erstwhile editor of the *Pall Mall Gazette*.[2] The book garnered considerable attention, selling over 100,000 copies by the end of 1890.[3] Booth's idea for a 'Poor Man's Lawyer' emerged from his belief that, for many people, their difficulties were 'not material, but moral'.[4] 'Moral' was in the sense of having the kind of advice, sympathy and support that could come from the voluntary action of a concerned community. Booth believed that there were no means by which those on lower incomes could find legal advice in the city at that time and that they had little in the way of contacts to help them find support:

> While the 'well-to-do' classes can fall back upon skilful friends for direction, or avail themselves of the learning and experience of the legal profession, the poor man has literally no one qualified to counsel him on such matters. In cases of sickness he can apply to the parish doctor or the great hospital, and receive an

> odd word or two of advice. But if his circumstances are sick, out of order, in danger of carrying him to utter destitution, or to prison, or to the Union, he has no one to appeal to who has the willingness or the ability to help him.[5]

Booth's analysis essentially pointed to the differences in social capital between classes. A middle-class family might well include a lawyer or two, or family members might be friends with or employ one, or have the connections to ask for a recommendation; a working-class family was unlikely to have such connections, formal or otherwise. Booth saw the utility of offering legal advice to help people to unpick an array of personal problems through a number of cases in which the Salvation Army's solicitors intervened.[6] The Salvation Army started its own 'Poor Man's Lawyer' in 1906; in the 1920s, it paid for a firm of solicitors to provide legal advice for free.[7]

Frank Tillyard, then a twenty-five-year-old barrister in residence at Mansfield House University Settlement in Canning Town, was inspired by Booth's book.[8] Historians of the settlement movement and its legal advice work have credited Tillyard and the London settlement movement, rather than Booth or any other potential influences, with initiating the Poor Man's Lawyer movement.[9] Mansfield House was a settlement house, and it drew on the model of Toynbee Hall in Whitechapel by bringing young male graduates to a deprived urban area to live, volunteer and learn something of what it was to be poor.[10] Tillyard and the founding warden of Mansfield House, Percy Alden, studied together at Oxford, and Tillyard followed his friend to the settlement. Tillyard was then studying for the Bar and volunteered to serve as the Poor Man's Lawyer at the settlement, spending his free time offering advice to the working classes of Canning Town.[11] The first sessions were offered in March 1891, with thirty visitors on average coming to a session in the early years of the project, rising to sixty visitors by 1903 and seventy by 1911.[12] Whilst Tillyard provided the legal advice on his own to begin with, the first annual report for the settlement mentioned that he was supported by a committee, who 'investigate the various cases, and give practical help to their satisfactory settlement' as part of a 'Poor Man's Friend and Lawyer, or Mutual Aid Society'. The report did not provide any detail on the composition of the committee, but – given that a sister settlement, Canning Town Women's Settlement, opened in 1892 – it was possible that this work was picked up by female volunteers. This is supported by the highlighted work of the committee, which focused on dealing with abused women and children and helping them to find work outside the area, along with emigration support and pressurising for better sanitation in the area.[13] Certainly, there was a division of labour between the legal advice given by Tillyard and what was effectively case work offered by the committee. Tillyard was joined in 1891 by Arthur Blott, a local solicitor, who volunteered at the Poor Man's Lawyer for the next twenty years.[14]

The Poor Man's Lawyer was featured in the weekend regional papers in 1893. A reporter apparently observed Tillyard and Blott at work one evening, sitting in on the confidential cases to create pen portraits of the work for the readers of the *Leeds Times*. It was noted that the pair saw around thirty people each Tuesday evening. A considerable amount of their work revolved around helping with problems between landlords and tenants, followed by domestic violence and marriages that had broken down, and then by accidents and workers' compensation cases. Other cases included those who believed that they had a claim to a pension from the military through either their own service or that of their husbands. As there were no state old age pensions before 1909, and the Employers' Liability Act 1880 and the Workmen's Compensation Act 1897 did not cover military personnel, success in these cases could make an enormous difference to the fortunes of the individuals involved. In these cases, the advice of the Poor Man's Lawyer could either help an individual focus their efforts on getting the pension due to them or disabuse them of any notion of having a case. However, the article also very clearly demonstrated that the transaction between a Poor Man's Lawyer and a working-class client was in the mould not of business but, rather, of social work. Further, the Poor Man's Lawyer was not in sympathetic thrall to the client, and the power and social imbalances between them were made explicit. One client asked whether a landlord could evict them for being a week in arrears, whilst another tried to pretend that she had not been drinking alcohol. The clients were presented as requiring skill to understand, with the lawyers investigating the client as much as they were attempting to ascertain the case that had brought them there.[15]

Tillyard left Mansfield House following his marriage in 1891 but continued to undertake Poor Man's Lawyer work until 1898, when the family moved to Sheffield.[16] Tillyard became involved with Sheffield's Neighbourhood Guild, founded the previous year.[17] The Guild's purpose was to enable the very poorest members of the community to develop the skills needed to help themselves.[18] Tillyard served both as the Neighbourhood Guild's Poor Man's Lawyer and as its honorary secretary.[19] Tillyard and family remained in Sheffield for nearly a decade until Tillyard took up a lectureship in law at the University of Birmingham. On arrival in Birmingham, Tillyard set up a Poor Man's Lawyer Association in the city in 1908.[20] Tillyard combined his work as a lecturer in commercial law with working for the COS and on the University's diploma in social studies. Tillyard was the director of practical work on the diploma, arranging for students to gain experience of social work at the Women's University Settlement in Birmingham.[21] The settlement and the university were closely linked.[22] The diploma was one of the first offered to would-be professional social workers and laid the foundations for the development of the social work profession in Britain.[23] The creation of such programmes was a significant step in the creation of social work as a profession, as much as it was in terms of the higher education and professional work of women.

Tillyard also published *Legal Hints for Social Workers*, an accessible, pocket-sized booklet, which ran to four editions. The various editions were published in conjunction with the NUWW (later the National Council of Women).[24] *Legal Hints for Social Workers* was a triage manual for female social workers. The first section gave 'hints of general interest' before moving on in the second to providing information on where clients could be sent for help. The third outlined the courts where legal redress could be obtained by those with limited means, whilst the fourth gave advice on 'Friendly Intervention, Compromise and Arbitration' – essentially forms of mediation and dispute resolution. The final and most extensive section provided brief notes on a number of common legal points but referred readers who wanted more 'plain language' information on the law to *Law for the Million*, published by the *News of the World* newspaper. The introduction also directed social workers to the COS's library at their London headquarters as well as to a similar collection at the Royal Colonial Institute for cases with an imperial angle.[25] The book also outlined the specific legal jurisdictions of factory and sanitary inspectors, NSPCC inspectors, Poor Law relieving officers and medical officers of health in addition to the police.[26]

The foreword to the 1916 edition was prepared by Louise Creighton, the first President of the NUWW, who stated:

> In proportion as a social worker fulfils her vocation of being a real friend to those amongst whom she works, she will find herself consulted about all kinds of difficult and puzzling questions.
>
> Women are too often content to be ignorant of the legal aspect of their own personal affairs, and having little experience in managing these are not likely to be of much use in helping those who in the course of their work turn to them for advice and help.[27]

Creighton came to voluntary social work in the earliest years of her marriage to Mandell Creighton, Bishop of London between 1897 and 1901, when he was a parish priest in Northumberland. Like many other clergy wives of the nineteenth century, she played an active role in visiting parishioners and engaging with groups such as the Girls' Friendly Society.[28] Her assumptions about the legal knowledge and experience of middle-class women reflected the broader social and legal position of women in that class, whose rights in terms of owning property and having custody of their children had grown in a fairly piecemeal fashion in the later nineteenth century.[29] Those women whose male relatives and spouses did not have a stable income or capital to call upon would find themselves in need of support more urgently than those women who did. In this way, the middle-class female social worker who was somewhat oblivious to legal matters was at a real disadvantage in helping a working-class family navigate the pitfalls of renting, hire purchase, employment law and community disputes.

As much as this booklet was attempting to address a perceived deficit on the part of female social workers, it also illuminated the expansion of regulatory bodies within and without the state. All these agencies were established (or reformed in the case of the Poor Law) in the nineteenth century, reflecting the development of bodies of knowledge about health, safety and sanitation, awareness of child psychology and well-being, or the perceived need to rationalise and professionalise public order. They were also the fruits of successful campaigns either to create roles under a local or national state remit or, in the case of the NSPCC, to be a charitable organisation vested with state-sanctioned powers.[30] Voluntary social workers were themselves part of this world, in which the role and remit of the state were expanding along with rapidly developing professions. These legal responsibilities *needed* to be mapped out because they were recent and complex developments. They were also arenas in which middle-class women were increasingly exerting power and carving out a role for themselves, particularly as these were areas that were less desirable to middle-class men.[31]

Tillyard's career consistently welded the 'male' discipline of legal learning with the 'female' discipline of social work. He was unusually prepared as a lawyer to involve himself within the female-dominated field of social work.[32] Whilst women could study law at university – Mary Sykes, one of the first four women solicitors, studied for an LLB degree before she was able to train – they could not qualify and work as solicitors or barristers before the Sex Discrimination (Removal) Act 1919, despite vigorous campaigns.[33] On the other hand, men were not excluded from doing social work, but it was not deemed to be 'their' sort of work. Members of the clergy had always performed an element of 'social work' as part of their pastoral role in their parish, but a considerable amount of parish voluntary work was done by women. Those who wanted to dedicate themselves to full-time voluntary social work often had a struggle to persuade family that it was a suitable career for them – as was the case for William Beveridge when he applied to work at Toynbee Hall as its sub-warden.[34] It was more acceptable for those who were not planning to enter the ministry to do something on top of their paid work, which ideally drew upon their professional skills. In that sense, Poor Man's Lawyer work was a way in which the socially minded late Victorian and Edwardian man could do social service without losing face. The guidance and training on the law that Tillyard and others provided for social workers in one way acknowledged the extent to which social workers – broadly defined – were applying new legislation in the course of their jobs. It also outlined the educational and advocacy role that those in front-line contact with the needy – such as social workers – could play in their communities and the potential place for legal advice and aid in an expanding welfare state.

A Poor Man's Lawyer *movement*?

The vignette of Frank Tillyard presented here throws a series of other issues into relief. The first question is the extent to which there was a Poor Man's Lawyer *movement*. This is a term that has been somewhat heuristically applied by researchers looking at the later nineteenth and early twentieth centuries, rather than a term used by its contemporaries. For example, Goriely uses the term to refer to the spread and scale of this specific kind of activity between the 1880s and the 1920s, as such activities caught the attention of the Lawrence and Finlay Committees.[35] By 1940, when Jones surveyed the field, there were distinct signs of a 'movement' insofar as he was able to count recognisable Poor Man's Lawyer services across the United Kingdom.[36] However, Gurney-Champion was keen to point out the lack of coordination between the different groups.[37] A spreading of activity does not, however, make a social movement in the sense in which it is understood by social scientists.

In addition to Tillyard taking his model of the Poor Man's Lawyer to Sheffield and Birmingham, it was also transplanted to other settlement houses by his friends from Mansfield House. Following Mansfield House's lead, Cambridge House in Camberwell set up a Poor Man's Lawyer in 1894, and Toynbee Hall did so in Whitechapel in 1898.[38] At Toynbee Hall, the explicit motivation for setting up such a project was because residents 'felt that the means of administering the law in the just interests of the poor, have been inadequate' – though their aim was to 'advise, not prosecute'.[39] The Poor Man's Lawyer here operated in the context of considerable activism around housing rights and conditions, with a Tenants' Protection Committee being formed around the same time. The Tenants' Protection Committee had the services of a solicitor and would try to take cases to court.[40] The two merged in 1905.[41] As Pimlott notes, the Toynbee Hall Poor Man's Lawyer was first run by Gustaf Oscar Roos and William Coldstream.[42] Roos was a solicitor who volunteered at Toynbee in his spare time until he left to fight in the South African Wars.[43] The service was revived when Dr A.E. Western, a solicitor, moved from Mansfield House to Toynbee Hall. Pimlott wrote in 1935 that Western's service with the settlement was 'long and invaluable and he was primarily responsible for the establishment of the work on a permanent basis'.[44] Western and Tillyard overlapped by a few months at Mansfield House. Coldstream was one of a handful of former colonial judges and administrators who gave over some of their retirement in London to Poor Man's Lawyer work. F.H. Hamnett, who revised the fourth edition of Tillyard's *Legal Hints*, also volunteered at the Toynbee Hall service and the Hampstead Council of Social Welfare after a career as a district and sessions judge in India.[45]

Consideration of who was undertaking Poor Man's Lawyer work at settlement houses demonstrates that it was largely done by men who had graduated from Oxford and Cambridge Universities, a good proportion of whom were embarking on careers in the law – particularly the Bar – and by those moving back to England after careers in the empire. Settlement houses provided a congenial and affordable living environment that was in reasonable travelling distance of the Inns of Court in Central London and the big legal and financial firms in the City: this mattered, because income for junior barristers in particular was often highly precarious.[46] In the case of Toynbee Hall, associate status was available for those men who were active in voluntary work at the settlement but who did not want to reside there.[47] Associates could use the settlement as something like a gentleman's club, being able to dine and stay overnight there as they wished. For those Poor Man's Lawyer volunteers who lived at a distance from the settlement, this could prevent the need to take a late-night train home whilst also providing an opportunity for sociability.[48] Despite several women's settlements being established from the 1880s in London, Poor Man's Lawyer evenings were the province of men's settlements or those women's settlements that had links with men's settlements, as was the case with Canning Town Women's Settlement and Mansfield House. Given women's exclusion from the legal profession, this was unsurprising.[49] Yet this changed once the legal profession was opened to women, as some of the first women lawyers began to offer their services to the Poor Man's Lawyer. Carrie Morrison, the first woman to be admitted as a solicitor in England, volunteered at Toynbee Hall's Poor Man's Lawyer as she worked to establish her practice.[50] Mary Elizabeth Pickup, a friend of Morrison, combined motherhood, paid work and voluntary work with the Soroptimists and the Birmingham Poor Man's Lawyer.[51]

The spread of settlements outside London also brought the Poor Man's Lawyer with it. The Manchester University Settlement was founded in 1895 with separate settlements for men and women.[52] It established a Poor Man's Lawyer evening in 1898, and in 1909 it set up a Poor Man's Lawyer Association to coordinate work in the city.[53] The men's Liverpool University Settlement and the women's Liverpool Victoria Settlement each offered a Poor Man's Lawyer service, but in 1919 the Liverpool Personal Service Society took over the responsibility of coordinating advice in the city. Other Liverpool community associations, such as the Norris Green Community Centre, cooperated with the society – itself part of the trend to professionalise and better coordinate voluntary activities, as will be seen later in this chapter.[54] When the short-lived Croydon settlement opened in 1905, the offer of a Poor Man's Lawyer was the first service to be listed, followed by a Poor Man's Doctor, educational classes, employment support, savings clubs and a soup kitchen.[55]

The settlements were not the only voluntary organisations interested in legal advice and aid work, as the London and National Councils of Social Service (LCSS and NCSS) were also keenly concerned about the legal rights of the working classes. However, as will be seen, whilst the LCSS, NCSS and COPEC were all separate entities, individuals and interest groups linked all of them in different ways and at different times. Sometimes, the links came through settlement houses; at other times, through religious affiliation and alliance.

The origins of both the NCSS and the LCSS lay in the 'new philanthropy' of late Victorian and Edwardian England in the Guild of Help and Social Welfare Movement. These were, as Moore states, responses to the COS and its philosophy, which had a better reception in London than it did across the country.[56] As Lewis argues, the COS and these new organisations had very different understandings of the relationship between the voluntary personal service organisation or charity and the state.[57] The first Guild of Help was set up in Bradford in 1904. As Cahill and Jowitt note, the COS failed to gain much traction in Bradford because, as elsewhere, it did not approve of the use of volunteers to undertake social work. The publication of Julie Sutter's *Britain's Next Scheme* in 1903 presented the middle classes of Bradford with an alternative script for organising social work. Sutter's book presented the case of Elberfeld in Germany, which operated a neighbourhood district visiting scheme, and challenged her English readers to volunteer to help their neighbours rather than allowing them to go to the Poor Law.[58] The Bradford Guild was set up in 1904 and was swiftly followed by a further six in northern towns in 1905, with a total of eighty-three in operation by 1917.[59] The Social Welfare Movement took a different philosophical starting point from both the Guilds and the COS by rejecting any home visiting in favour of setting up a body that would be responsible for coordinating welfare activities in each locality as well as acting as a clearing house for funds raised. The first of these was founded by former Toynbee Hall resident Thomas Hancock Nunn as the Hampstead Council of Social Welfare in 1907.[60] In 1910, Nunn established the Social Welfare Association for London, a citywide iteration of his Hampstead work.[61] Around the same time, Frederick G. D'Aeth was developing the Liverpool Council of Voluntary Aid (1909), which was affiliated with the Guilds movement, and sought to promote community organisation in the same way as Nunn was doing in the capital.[62] In the years shortly before the First World War, the three groups began to collaborate with each other, but the outbreak of the war and the demands made of charities and the state brought the groups closer still. In consequence, the NCSS was founded in 1919.[63] The Social Welfare Association for London changed its name to LCSS at the same time.[64]

Further to this again was what might be broadly termed religious philanthropy. COPEC was one element of various Christian churches' desire to engage with the impact of industrialisation, urbanisation and consumerism.[65] Frederick Gurney-Champion was a lawyer connected with the Bermondsey Settlement in south-east London, founded as a Methodist settlement in 1892 by the Reverend John Scott Lidgett. Gurney-Champion was tasked with researching free legal advice and aid to the poor for COPEC and other groups – including the settlements and the Councils of Social Service – to try to challenge the Government to make provision for the least affluent members of society.[66] His findings were published as *Justice and the Poor in England* in 1926. Gurney-Champion claimed that religious groups provided the majority of free legal advisory services, albeit with no substantiation of this claim.[67] He made impressionistic reference to individual parishes and missions arranging for Poor Man's Lawyer meetings, often for short periods of time, and mentioned the work of the Salvation Army and an unnamed Roman Catholic legal charity.[68] This was probably the Society of Our Lady of Good Counsel, formed in April 1926 to support and provide advice to those in need, as well as aid with cases in the police and county courts.[69] Gurney-Champion's lack of precision about the extent of religious legal advice provision partly reflects how Poor Man's Lawyer evenings were enthusiastically set up but ran out of steam as other calls were made on the lawyer's time.[70] It also, however, frustrates attempts to map this dimension of advice provision, and particularly the points of overlap with other groups of providers – such as the settlement houses, which could be very closely connected with a particular religious denomination. As will be seen in the next section of this chapter, there were many points of cooperation and coordination between the various associations.

Building networks

As Egerton noted, there was an abortive attempt by the Law Society to create some form of network between the different Poor Man's Lawyer groups in 1913. However, Poor Man's Lawyer groups preferred to follow rules and patterns that made sense in their locale.[71] The creation of a network of settlement Poor Man's Lawyer activities came in 1924 after BARS was approached by the LCO for evidence for the Finlay Committee. BARS established a subcommittee that was tasked with reviewing legal work.[72] The League of Nations was also investigating legal aid and assistance in different nations as a means of trying to ascertain the degree to which human legal needs and rights were being met, particularly in the case of migrants or people in transit.[73] BARS saw this as a timely opportunity, with legal aid being on both national and international policy agendas, to make their case. The BARS initiative was a post hoc creation of a network that was convened by the centre in response to these external prompts. That BARS took on this role also reflected the group's growing sense of itself as one of the leading bodies in the proto-voluntary sector of the interwar period. However, they were unsuccessful in pushing their agenda at this point.

The BARS network still enabled a key project to be taken to fruition. Former Toynbee Hall resident and Poor Man's Lawyer R.H. Turton was elected as the Conservative MP for Thirsk and Malton in 1929 and used his new position in parliament as an opportunity to try to improve the situation for those in need of criminal legal aid. There were various unsuccessful pushes to revisit the legislation in criminal cases in the later 1920s, with cross-party support; but Turton managed to find a window in the policy process, and it was successful on that occasion. The result of this was the Poor Prisoners' Defence Act 1930.[74] Although Turton was not working as part of a coherent settlement campaign, his success was nonetheless lauded by his settlement friends and colleagues, who saw it as part of the broader success of their work.[75] Certainly, it appears to have given E.S. Watkins confidence regarding his own project.

Ernest Shilston Watkins was in residence at Toynbee Hall at the same time as Turton, and both volunteered at the Poor Man's Lawyer service. Watkins left Toynbee Hall in 1926, returning in 1931.[76] Watkins graduated with a law degree from the University of Liverpool in 1922 and practised law in London from 1926 until the outbreak of the Second World War.[77] During his second residency, BARS passed a resolution at its 1932 Annual Conference to try to tackle the problems of hire purchase.[78] Settlements with Poor Man's Lawyer and similar services had noted rises in cases relating to problems with various forms of credit buying.[79] According to Tebbutt, hire purchase grew twentyfold between 1918 and 1938 and accounted for two-thirds of major item purchases.[80] Hire purchase, whilst not new, was an increasingly popular way for working-class families to fund purchases, and problems with hire purchase rose in line with its growth.[81] Ellen Wilkinson, MP for Jarrow, was alerted to the problems hire purchase was causing her constituents by a local solicitor. Watkins, Wilkinson and J.J. Mallon, the warden of Toynbee Hall, joined forces. Mallon and Wilkinson had worked together on campaigns against sweated labour before the First World War, remaining good friends.[82] Watkins set to drafting the Hire Purchase Bill, which was tested by Watkins, Wilkinson and others at a meeting of the Haldane Society of Socialist Lawyers on 15 November 1937 before it passed through Parliament the following year.[83] This was a major victory in terms of taking action to help the communities in which settlements worked. It also demonstrated the potential convening power that the settlement houses and their supporters could wield and their ability to influence the policy process. As will be further explored in Chapter 3, it also demonstrated the growing interest amongst lawyers in using the law for political ends.

The Poor Man's Lawyers that operated through the LCSS's councils and the settlement movement had done so without much cooperation with each other until the reform of the Poor Persons' Rules for High Court cases. This gave the responsibility for organising legal aid to the local Law Societies. The

LCSS had already given advice to the Finlay Committee for its second report, but they

> regarded the appointment of the second Committee as giving to social workers in this department an opportunity, long desired, for closer co-operation amongst Poor Man's Lawyers in London, and for an expression of their views as to some of the difficulties that surround their work.

Even allowing for a very loose understanding of 'social workers', this remark demonstrates both the LCSS's view that legal advice was part of their remit and their interest in those engaged in an array of voluntary and statutory social work activities being able to access legal support more easily. To this end, the LCSS invited colleagues at all the Poor Man's Lawyer teams in the city to join its Legal Aid Committee and to work together on a submission to the Finlay Committee. Settlement lawyers were largely found through the network of London settlement houses, but finding 'unattached' Poor Man's Lawyers outside this network was harder. The LCSS presented a conservative estimate of 14,000 annual applications to their Poor Man's Lawyer services for advice. The financial cost of the service was minimal, as most settlements provided rooms for free, and the vast majority of cases only required advice: there was some cost, however, in the form of out-of-pocket expenses for the relatively few cases that went to court.[84] The research also found that local CSS branches, the COS and other agencies tended to be happy to help find funds for needy cases and also that Poor Man's Lawyer evenings also attracted donations from people who had used them.[85] Such a service sounded remarkable in terms of both its performance and its cost. Yet this cost was dependent upon the goodwill of solicitors and barristers with the requisite expertise to give up their leisure time to provide their professional services for free, and it was further dependent on charities with suitable real estate they could make available. That so much could be offered for 'free' was laudable, as, indeed, the Finlay Committee noted; but this was a fragile 'freeness'.[86]

The LCSS had a legal and business advice standing committee: the committee was staffed by barristers and 'laymen (assisted by a rota of solicitors)' and could provide advice.[87] All London Poor Man's Lawyer services were invited to join this committee, and it continued to look for things to provide in the light of the Finlay Report's recommendations. A particular focus of its work was on ensuring that assistance could be provided for county court cases.[88] The impetus for this came from Patrick Harrington Edwards, who founded the Catholic Prisoners' Aid Society in 1898.[89] The LCSS network and the London Poor Man's Lawyer Council set up the Bentham Committee in 1929 to act as a clearing house for legal aid cases in the capital. The Bentham Committee offered financial support to enable cases with sufficient legal merit to be represented in court and, through having standard benchmarks for this, also created some consistency of practice across its fifty-five member organisations.[90]

In addition to taking cases from its members, it also received referrals from the Law Society's Poor Persons Committee.[91] Despite the scale of its work, the papers of the Bentham Committee appear to have been lost due to the personal papers of its chair, D.N. Pritt, being destroyed in an air raid in 1941.[92] The committee was shut down in 1949 in the light of the passing of the Legal Aid and Advice Act.[93] In order to be able to take cases to court, the Bentham Committee was reliant on and supported in part through solicitors recovering costs and returning these to the committee.[94] But it also undertook regular fundraising activities. For example, the Bentham Committee and the Society of our Lady of Good Counsel were the beneficiaries of a charity garden party held in Lincoln's Inn.[95] Other events garnered international attention. Another garden party, this time in the Temple Gardens and thrown by Jean Stewart, wife of Lord Chief Justice Hewart, was covered in *Life* magazine in 1938. At the same time, the Bentham Committee and its supporters continued to put pressure on the Law Society and the Lord Chancellor's secretary to create statutory provision for those working people who needed to go to the county courts.[96]

Providing advice in the interwar period

Attempts to map Poor Man's Lawyer work across London and the nation demonstrate the extent to which such voluntary action gained ground in the interwar period. The information on Poor Man's Lawyer and similar work undertaken by members of the NCSS and LCSS was reproduced in the appendices to the second Finlay Report. The NCSS reported the existence of ten services explicitly described as Poor Man's Lawyer services outside London: namely, those in Sheffield, Birmingham, Leicester, Manchester, Halifax, Liverpool (including Birkenhead and Wallasey), Chesterfield, Bristol, Leeds and Brighton. The Sheffield and Birmingham services were those originally founded by Frank Tillyard, as seen earlier in this chapter. In the cases of Halifax and Chesterfield, local government provided the steer through the Poor Law Union and a special committee of the Chesterfield Corporation, respectively.[97] Local law societies led on work in Brighton and Leicester, being involved to varying lesser extents in Birmingham, Liverpool and Bristol. In Sheffield and Liverpool, the predominant lead came from the local CSS. In Leeds and Bristol, settlement houses led activities. The Manchester and Salford Poor Man's Lawyer Association was effectively a broad group led by the settlement houses in the cities but also involving work with the local CSS. Outside the capital, there was no one dominant group leading on Poor Man's Lawyer work but rather, a reflection of the immense variations between different towns and cities in terms of their traditions of voluntary and civic action, and their industrial and economic development. With the exception of Brighton and Bristol in southern England, these Poor Man's Lawyers were to be found in the major industrial towns and cities of the

Midlands, the north-west and Yorkshire, where a considerable amount of the population was concentrated, along with a number of major red-brick universities. Bristol shared all these characteristics apart from the geographical location; Brighton was unusual in being a tourist resort on the south coast.

The LCSS information revealed a highly active Poor Man's Lawyer scene in London. It reported thirty-eight societies, of which all but four worked with the LCSS. It also noted the existence of eight services run by the Conservative Party, six by the Liberal Party and thirteen by the Labour Party, which will be explored further in Chapter 3.[98] Of those thirty-eight Poor Man's Lawyer groups, twenty-two were run under the auspices of settlement houses or missions, five by local councils of social welfare or service, two by Toc H (a Christian social service centre), others by two schools, an adult education centre and a public library, and two by housing charities, along with services provided by the Society of Our Lady of Good Counsel, the Salvation Army and the British Legion Headquarters. Whilst London had a plurality of providers, it was a plurality heavily dominated by the settlement movement, as the housing charities, the councils of social welfare and Toc H were part of the broader settlement networks. The London settlements were used to a degree of cooperation, having almost formed their own Association of Residential Settlements a couple of years earlier, and they were also very well networked into both the LCSS through Thomas Hancock Nunn and the NCSS through its general secretary, Lionel Ellis, both of whom had been residents at Toynbee Hall.[99] Manchester had a similar network of settlements and other providers forming an association. Whilst the legal profession provided the expertise in its spare time, the administration of the Poor Man's Lawyer was firmly in the hands of charities and churches.

Poor Man's Lawyer-style work continued to expand in the course of the 1930s. In 1940, J. Mervyn Jones, a legal scholar at Trinity Hall, Cambridge, published a report on free legal advice in England and Wales. This research was undertaken on behalf of the Executive Committee of Cambridge House, then the largest Poor Man's Lawyer service in the country.[100] Jones's aim was to assess all the main non-political free legal advisory services in operation. He did not include the services run by the political parties or the legal services offered by approved societies and trade unions. He noted, but did not include, those 'ambulance-chasing agencies' that sought out people on lower incomes to try to persuade them to take out claims for accidents and injury in order to profit from any damages awarded. 'Non-political' was only a partially appropriate term: it also included those who sought to directly profit from any legal action taken or where legal advice was available as a benefit from a subscription.[101]

Jones's report identified around 125 free legal advice centres, of which fifty-five were in London. Roughly sixty Poor Man's Lawyer or other free legal advice centres had been set up in a ten-year period, with the majority outside London. In the time between the Finlay Report and Jones's analysis, there had been numerous important developments, the first of which was the growth of the NCSS itself. Although the NCSS was founded in 1919, it took almost ten years for its work to be fully established. During the later 1920s and 1930s, it was presented with various challenges through the impact of the economic downturn, rural deprivation and the movement of inner-city dwellers to new suburban estates.[102] Of the seventy Poor Man's Lawyer services outside London, forty-seven were run by Councils of Social Service or equivalent organisations, reflecting the NCSS's work in building up community organisation and coordination of services nationally. A further ten were run by community associations on the new estates, such as the Watling Association in Edgware and the Norris Green Community Association in Liverpool, again demonstrating the important role of the NCSS in developing access to legal advice and its concern about the uprooting of working-class families to these new communities. This predated and pre-empted its more widely recognised role in the establishment of the CABx in anticipation of the outbreak of the Second World War.[103] Equally, the networks afforded by the settlement movement provided a forum for legal advice concerns to be aired and action taken.

Yet, for all these networks and their attempts to coordinate and improve access to free legal advice, the spread of these offerings was uneven. Within England, provision was far from universal, insofar as there were many major towns that did not have any form of Poor Man's Lawyer service. Blackburn, Exeter, Hereford, Huddersfield, King's Lynn, Norwich, Wigan and Wolverhampton were amongst the towns and cities that had a Poor Persons Procedures committee for dealing with divorce cases but no access to any form of help with other civil matters, such as through a Poor Man's Lawyer or any ad hoc arrangements.[104] Provision followed population clusters, with a profusion of services around Liverpool and Manchester in the north-west as well as Leeds and surrounding towns in the West Riding. Bristol, Newcastle and the Tees area were also relatively well served. The clusters evident in the 1920s had witnessed growth in neighbouring areas, some of which was the result of expansion within county boundaries of Law Society, settlement or CSS networks. However, for many across England, Wales and Scotland, a substantial trip to a nearby town, possibly in the next county, would be necessary.

Beyond geographical location, the next important factor was the capacity of the Poor Man's Lawyer to see clients. As Jones's survey revealed, most Poor Man's Lawyer services were open for one evening a week, with some operating twice per month; only one, the Wimbledon Guild of Social Welfare branch, was open daily between 10.00 a.m. and 12.00 p.m.[105] The volume of advice-seekers at these sessions were high. Toynbee Hall had 1,600 clients in 1938, with typically four or five lawyers on hand to deal with them. Assuming that the branch was open for every week that year, this meant an average of thirty unique clients each week – Jones's figures did not provide a picture of how many people returned throughout the year, as would be expected in complex cases. Cambridge House had an average of 3,000 clients each year from 1936, seen on Thursday evenings between 6.30 and 9.00 p.m. – an average of fifty-seven clients.[106] What evades measurement is the degree to which lawyers were consistent in their attendance and their enthusiasm for the work. The lawyers had considerable demand for their services but usually without any supporting infrastructure, be that a rota to share out the work between lawyers, a clerking system or a dedicated, appropriate space for their work at the hosting institution. Writing in 1926, Gurney-Champion provided a vivid description of what could happen at smaller Poor Man's Lawyer evenings:

> How at first the lawyer came down punctually and regularly every week, full of enthusiasm, for six months; how then he came unpunctually, because of business duties; how, after, he became irregular, not turning up at all at some meetings, because his wife or children were ill or lonely; and how, finally, he gave up, and sent his clerk to do his duty; who also arrived on the scene with great enthusiasm, and gradually went through the same process of disillusionment as his employer had already gone through; and when that stage was reached the [Poor Man's Lawyer session] was given up altogether.[107]

He also pointed to the case of a settlement lawyer whose room changed six times in a year, disrupting his work as well as the clients trying to find him.[108] These could be very trying circumstances, even for the most dedicated. The service may have been free to those who sought advice, but it came very much with costs to the lawyers and their charitable hosts.

Conclusion

The Poor Man's Lawyer – as something approaching a coherent, organised service – had its origins in the sensational writing of William Booth and W.T. Stead, who tried to jolt the consciences of Victorian England. By the end of the nineteenth century, the idea was taken up by Frank Tillyard and operationalised, to a degree, within the settlement movement and other reformist volunteer networks. It initially found resonance within the settlement movement because it offered those lawyers connected with it an effective way of volunteering and giving service that used their skills. This would also create a space that the first women lawyers could access to practise their profession. The Poor Man's Lawyer was also taken up by the NCSS and LCSS, who saw it as part of the armoury of the voluntary social work field, as a resource for social workers – and later, as part of the offer of a community centre.

The main transition in the period between Tillyard's first Poor Man's Lawyer evening and the outbreak of the Second World War was legal advice coming to be seen as something that should be available to all. Although the majority of the Finlay Committee, for example, were not convinced of the need for change, interest in the rights of citizens in terms of access to justice was growing both within England and on the international stage, as the League of Nations explored the issue in the 1920s. In theory, the individual citizen could harness their rights and secure their entitlement to fair treatment with the expert guidance of a lawyer or social worker; but this access to justice was dependent on the willingness of solicitors and barristers to give over their time to working without charge, and there were major inconsistencies in voluntary provision across the country. The 'freeness' avoided lawyers being paid from the public pocket, but it also meant that services were limited to what lawyers were willing to commit to doing in the time outside their main, fee-incurring work, in spaces that could accommodate them, rather than being driven by local need. It kept the legal profession free from the state but at the cost of the citizen.

The Poor Man's Lawyer was not a social movement in its own right but was co-opted by other social movements and institutions, from settlement houses to religious groups to law societies and Councils of Social Service, as an activity they thought important to provide. It provided a convenient outlet for those who had legal training to do social service through the institution of their personal choice. It also combined well with the work of these groups in presenting themselves as the representatives of a proto-voluntary sector that was increasingly lobbying government for additional welfare support and presenting itself as the source of expertise on need. The commitment of the NCSS, the LCSS, BARS, COPEC and others demonstrated that there was an understanding in the social reformist and religious circles that the law *should be* the business of the working classes and that it could have a powerful impact on the problems people faced. It was an aspect of voluntary social action to be coordinated at the local level as much as any other activity. As the next chapter will show, legal advice as a form of social justice was also becoming an important way of engaging with the newly enfranchised masses and thinking about the role of the law and the state within a modern nation.

Notes

1 W. Booth, *In Darkest England and the Way Out* (London: International Headquarters, 1890).
2 F.K. Prochaska, 'Booth, William (1829–1912)', *ODNB*; A. Woodall, *What Price the Poor? William Booth, Karl Marx and the London Residuum* (Aldershot: Ashgate, 2005), p. 197.
3 V. Bailey, 'In Darkest England and the way out: The Salvation Army, social reform and the Labour movement, 1885–1910', *International Review of Social History*, 29:2 (1984), p. 154.
4 Booth, *In Darkest England*, p. 255.

5 Ibid., p. 259.
6 Ibid., pp. 259–62.
7 Woodall, *What Price the Poor?* p. 199; F.C.G. Gurney-Champion, *Justice and the Poor in England* (London: Routledge, 1926), p. 21.
8 'The Poor Man's Lawyer', *Northampton Mercury*, 6 September 1912, p. 6.
9 J.A.R. Pimlott, *Toynbee Hall: Fifty Years of Social Reform* (London: Dent, 1935), pp. 116–17; D. Leat, 'The rise and role of the Poor Man's Lawyer', *British Journal of Law and Society*, 2:2 (1975), pp. 166–81; J. Glasby, *Poverty and Opportunity: One Hundred Years of the Birmingham Settlement* (Studley: Brewin, 1999), p. 46; T. Goriely, 'Gratuitous assistance to the "ill-dressed": Debating civil legal aid in England and Wales from 1914–1939', *International Journal of the Legal Profession*,13:1 (2006), pp. 41–67.
10 A. Briggs and A. Macartney, *Toynbee Hall: The First Hundred Years* (London: Routledge, 1984).
11 'Obituary: Sir Frank Tillyard', *The Times*, Tuesday, 11 July 1961, p. 12.
12 A. Blott, *Legal Dispensaries: An Account of the Poor Man's Lawyer Movement* (London: The Avenue Press, 1903), p. 3 and reprinted 1911, p. 2.
13 Mansfield House University Settlement in East London (Canning Town), *Report for the Year Ending September 1891*, pp. 4–5.
14 'The Poor Man's Lawyer'.
15 'A Poor Man's Lawyer', *Leeds Times*, 25 November 1893, p. 2.
16 'Obituary: Sir Frank Tillyard'.
17 'Mr Tillyard's Candidacy', *Sheffield Daily Telegraph*, Tuesday, 27 October 1903, p. 8; S. Pollard, *A History of Labour in Sheffield* (Liverpool: Liverpool University Press, 1959), p. 195.
18 Pollard, *A History of Labour*; 'Social Work in Sheffield Slums', *Sheffield and Rotherham Independent*, Tuesday, 2 May 1899, p. 3; 'History and Development', Croft House Settlement, www.crofthouse.org.uk/history.php, correct at 31 March 2017.
19 'Sheffield Neighbour Guilds', *Sheffield and Rotherham Independent*, Monday, 28 May 1900, p. 2.
20 Glasby, *Poverty and Opportunity*, pp. 46–7.
21 Cadbury Research Library, University of Birmingham, UB/COU/1/8 Birmingham University Council Minutes, 31 January 1912; J. Rimmer, *Troubles Shared: The Story of a Settlement 1899–1979* (Birmingham: Phlogiston, 1980).
22 Glasby, *Poverty and Opportunity*, p. 109.
23 Ibid., pp. 109–11.
24 J.T. Covert, 'Creighton, Louise Hume (1850–1936)', *ODNB*.
25 F. Tillyard and F.H. Hamnett, *Legal Hints for Social Workers*, 4th edn (London: National Union of Women Workers, 1916), p. 4; *Law for the Million: A Legal Handbook by a Practical Lawyer* (London: Simpkin, Marshall, 1904).
26 Tillyard and Hamnett, *Legal Hints*, pp. 8–9.
27 Ibid., p. 3.
28 Covert, 'Creighton'.
29 See M.L. Shanley, *Feminism, Marriage, and the Law in Victorian England* (Princeton: Princeton University Press, 1989); M. Berg, 'Women's property

and the Industrial Revolution', *Journal of Interdisciplinary History*, 24:2 (1993), pp. 233–50; B. Griffin, *The Politics of Gender in Victorian Britain: Masculinity, Political Culture and the Struggle for Women's Rights* (Cambridge: Cambridge University Press, 2012).

30 See, for example, V. Berridge, 'Health and Medicine', in F.M.L. Thompson (ed.), *The Cambridge Social History of Britain 1750–1950: Volume 3, Social Agencies and Institutions* (Cambridge: Cambridge University Press, 1990); R. Cooter, *In the Name of the Child: Health and Welfare 1880–1940* (London: Routledge, 1992); P. Thane, 'Women and Political Participation in England, 1918–1970', in E. Breitenbach and P. Thane (eds), *Women and Citizenship in Britain and Ireland in the Twentieth Century: What Difference Did the Vote Make?* (London: Continuum, 2010); H. Hendrick, *Child Welfare: England 1872 - 1989* (London: Routledge, 1994).

31 S. Koven, 'Borderlands: Women, Voluntary Action, and Child Welfare in Britain, 1840–1914', in S. Koven and S. Michel (eds), *Mothers of a New World: Maternalist Politics and the Origins of Welfare States* (New York: Routledge, 1993).

32 This should be compared with the tensions noted in the United States at the same time by F. Batlan, *Women and Justice for the Poor: A History of Legal Aid, 1863–1945* (Cambridge: Cambridge University Press, 2015).

33 See E. Cruikshank, 'Mary Elaine Sykes: The Wise Little Owl', *First Hundred Years*, Spark21, http://first100years.org.uk/mary-elaine-sykes-the-wise-little-owl/, correct at 15 August 2017; J. Bourne, *Helena Normanton and the Opening of the Bar to Women* (Hook: Waterside, 2016).

34 See J. Harris, 'Beveridge, William Henry, Baron Beveridge (1879–1963)', *ODNB*.

35 Goriely, 'Gratuitous assistance', pp. 52–3.

36 J. Mervyn Jones, *Free Legal Advice in England and Wales* (Oxford: Slatter and Rose, 1940).

37 Gurney-Champion, *Justice and the Poor*, pp. 15–21.

38 Jones, 14. Cambridge House, 'Our Story', http://ch1889.org/about-us/our-story/ (2017), correct at 25 April 2017.

39 'Occasional Notes', *Toynbee Record* (November 1898), p. 31.

40 'Tenants' Protection Committee', *Toynbee Record* (March 1899), p. 91.

41 Pimlott, *Toynbee Hall*, p. 119.

42 Ibid., p. 117.

43 'Gustaf Oscar Roos', in Westminster School and the First World War, http://firstworldwar.westminster.org.uk/?p=905 (2017), correct at 28 July 2017; 'Roos, Gustaf Oscar', in Herts at War, www.hertsatwar.co.uk/fluidcms/files/files/Haileybury%20College%20R%20to%20Se/ROOS%20Gustaf%20Oscar%20Captain.pdf (2017), correct at 28 July 2017.

44 Pimlott, *Toynbee Hall*, p. 118.

45 I. Elliott (ed.), *The Balliol College Register 1833–1933*, 2nd edn (Oxford: John Johnson at the University Press, 1934); Hampstead Council of Social Welfare, *Annual Report of the Executive Committee* (London: Hampstead Council of Social Welfare, 1916).

46 See description of housing in D.N. Pritt, *From Right to Left: The Autobiography of D.N. Pritt* (London: Lawrence and Wishart, 1965), p. 17.

47 Pimlott, *Toynbee Hall*, p. 48; Briggs and Macartney, *Toynbee Hall*, p. 34.
48 See particularly A. Milne-Smith, 'A flight to domesticity? Making a home in the gentleman's clubs of London, 1880–1914', *Journal of British Studies*, 45:4 (2006), pp. 796–818; L. Matthews-Jones, 'Centres of Brightness: The Spiritual Imagination of Toynbee Hall and Oxford House, 1880–1914' (PhD dissertation, University of Manchester, 2009).
49 See, for example, Bourne, *Helena Normanton*.
50 See E. Cruickshank, 'Carrie Morrison', in Spark 21 (eds), *First Hundred Years*, http://first100years.org.uk/carrie-morrison-2/, correct at 31 March 2017.
51 See E. Cruickshank, 'Mary Elizabeth Pickup', in Spark 21 (eds), *First Hundred Years*, http://first100years.org.uk/mary-elizabeth-pickup/, correct at 31 March 2017.
52 S. Eagles, 'Thomas Coglan Horsfall and Manchester Art Museum and University Settlement', Infed, www.infed.org/settlements/manchester_art_museum_and_university_settlement.htm, correct at 24 August 2018.
53 M.D. Stocks and B. Rogers, *Fifty Years in Every Street: The Story of the Manchester University Settlement*, 2nd edn (Manchester: Manchester University Press, 1956), p. 27; R. Douglas Waller (ed.), *Harold Pilkington Turner: Memories of His Work and Personality* (Manchester: Manchester University Press, 1953), pp. 12–13.
54 British Association of Residential Settlements, *Report 1935–38*, p. 15; Jones, *Free Legal Advice*, p. 33.
55 'Social Settlement', *Nottingham Evening Post*, 12 January 1905, p. 3.
56 M.J. Moore, 'Social work and social welfare: The organization of philanthropic resources in Britain, 1900–1914', *Journal of British Studies*, 16:2 (1977), p. 86. See also C.R. Attlee, *The Social Worker* (London: Bell, 1920), p. 68.
57 J. Lewis, 'The boundary between voluntary and statutory social service in the late nineteenth and early twentieth centuries', *Historical Journal*, 39:1 (1996), p. 158.
58 M. Cahill and T. Jowitt, 'The new philanthropy: The emergence of the Bradford City Guild of Help', *Journal of Social Policy*, 9:3 (1980), pp. 368–70.
59 K. Laybourn, 'The Guild of Help and the changing face of Edwardian philanthropy', *Urban History*, 20:1 (1993), p. 45.
60 Moore, 'Social work', pp. 98–100.
61 *Thomas Hancock Nunn: The Life and Work of a Social Reformer* (London: Baines and Scarsbrook, 1942).
62 Ibid., p. 101.
63 Cahill and Jowitt, 'The new philanthropy', pp. 381–2.
64 *Thomas Hancock Nunn*, p. 158.
65 COPEC, *The Social Function of the Church: Being the Report Presented to the Conference on Christian Politics, Economics and Citizenship at Birmingham, April 5–12, 1924* (London: Longman, Green, 1924), p. v.
66 'Legal Justice and the Poor: A Movement for Reform', *United Methodist*, 25 December 1924, p. 639.
67 Gurney-Champion, *Justice and the Poor*, p. 22.
68 Ibid., p. 19.

69 'The Society of Our Lady of Good Counsel', *The Tablet*, 25 March 1961, p. 20.
70 Gurney-Champion, *Justice and the Poor*, p. 19.
71 R. Egerton, *Legal Aid* (London: Kegan Paul, Trench, Trubner, 1945), pp. 27–8.
72 K.B. Beauman, *Women and the Settlement Movement* (London: Radcliffe, 1996), p. 196.
73 A.K. Kuhn, 'International regulation of legal assistance for the poor', *American Journal of International Law*, 19:2 (1924); League of Nations, *Legal Aid for the Poor* (Geneva: League of Nations, 1927).
74 P. Cosgrave, 'Obituary: Lord Tranmire', in the *Independent*, 21 January 1994, www.independent.co.uk/news/people/obituary-lord-tranmire-1408252.html, correct at 24 August 2018; Pimlott, *Toynbee Hall*, p. 247.
75 Jones, *Free Legal Advice*, p. 4; Pimlott, *Toynbee Hall*, p. 246.
76 Pimlott, *Toynbee Hall*, p. 295.
77 A.A. Mardon and E.G. Mardon, *Alberta Anglican Politicians, 1883–1999* (Edmonton: Golden Meteorite, 2013), p. 169.
78 British Association of Residential Settlements, *British Association of Residential Settlements, Report 1935–8* (London: BARS, 1938).
79 London Metropolitan Archives, ACC/2486, Toynbee Hall *Annual Report 1935–38*.
80 M. Tebbutt, *Making Ends Meet: Pawnbroking and Working-Class Credit* (Leicester: Leicester University Press, 1983), p. 193.
81 P. Johnson, *Saving and Spending: The Working-Class Economy in Britain 1870–1939* (Oxford: Clarendon, 1985), p. 157.
82 B.D. Vernon, *Ellen Wilkinson: A Biography* (London: Croom Helm, 1982), p. 149.
83 Haldane Society, *Annual Report for the Year 1937–38* (London: Haldane Society, 1938).
84 London Council of Social Service (hereafter LCSS), *Annual Report 1925–1926* (London: LCSS, 1926), pp. 23–4.
85 Ibid., p. 24.
86 *Committee on Legal Aid for the Poor – Final Report*, Cmd. 3016, pp. 5–6.
87 LCSS, *Intermediate Report for the year 1919* (London, LCSS, 1919); *First Annual Report 1919–1920* (London: LCSS, 1920), p. 23.
88 LCSS, *Unity and Co-operation: Year's Social Service in London. Annual Report 1927–1928* (London: LCSS, 1928), pp. 30–1.
89 'Law Society', *The Times*, 20 November 1897, p. 16.
90 Jones, *Free Legal Advice*, p. 13; *Report of the Committee on Legal Aid and Advice in England and Wales*, Cmd. 6641 (London: HMSO, 1945), p. 15.
91 'Legal Aid for the Poor', *The Times*, 21 June 1934, p. 9.
92 LSE Archives, Pritt, D.N. Fonds description, www.aim25.ac.uk/cgi-bin/vcdf/detail?coll_id=5916&inst_id=1 (2002), correct at 16 August 2017.
93 R.C.H. Briggs, 'Legal Aid', Letters to the Editor, *Guardian*, 3 July 1955, p. 13.
94 *Report of the Committee on Legal Aid and Advice in England and Wales*, Cmd. 6641, p. 15.
95 'Mr MacDonald at a Dance', *The Bystander*, 17 July 1929, pp. 120–1.
96 'Poor Man's Lawyers', *The Times*, 26 June 1929, p. 13.

97 Jones, *Free Legal Advice*, pp. 29–30.
98 *Committee on Legal Aid for the Poor*, Cmd. 3016, pp. 14–19.
99 Beauman, *Women and the Settlement Movement.*
100 Jones, *Free Legal Advice.*
101 Ibid., pp. 7–8.
102 M. Brasnett, *Voluntary Social Action: A History of the National Council of Social Service, 1919–1969* (London: National Council of Social Service, 1969), pp. 59–67.
103 See O. Blaiklock, 'Advising the Citizen: Citizens Advice Bureaux, Voluntarism and the Welfare State in England, 1938–1964' (PhD dissertation, Kings College London, 2012); J. Richards, *Inform, Advise and Support: 50 Years of the Citizens Advice Bureau* (Cambridge: Lutterworth, 1989).
104 Jones, *Free Legal Advice*, pp. 79–80.
105 Ibid., pp. 73–4.
106 Ibid., p. 18.
107 Gurney-Champion, *Justice and the Poor*, p. 19.
108 Ibid.

3

The political law

'Do you get paid for doing this?' said one applicant to a Poor Man's Lawyer.

'No.'

'Do you do it because you're standing for Parliament?'

'No.'

'Then what *do* you do it for?'[1]

The three main political parties also offered Poor Man's Lawyer clinics. Such contemporaries – the authors of the Finlay Report and J. Mervyn Jones – saw this 'political' work as being qualitatively different from what was being offered by the settlements and others. It was a provision that they acknowledged without paying it much attention, though it had more *positive* attention than was granted to legal insurance schemes and 'ambulance-chasers'.[2] There was a view that information and advice, as provided by the proto-voluntary sector and, later, by the CABx, were 'neutral'. In the early years of the Second World War, *The Times* praised CABx for being 'by the people for the people'.[3] Yet whilst advice could be given dispassionately, it did not follow that it was neutral. The proto-voluntary sector may not have been overtly political in their approaches, but they certainly had a clear agenda about the relationship of the state to the individual and the impact of the excesses of capitalism on housing and debt. As the epigraph to this chapter suggests, the motives of those making advice on the law and other matters freely available were not always clear to those who sought this support. As much as such offerings could come with the taint of 'charity', they could also come with the taint of the individual lawyer or advisor doing the work for personal gain in the form of being elected to Parliament or to convert people to a political cause. Yet electoral success and influence were just two of the reasons why political parties and political professional associations invested time and resources in such offerings. There were also strong similarities and connections between this work and the supposedly 'neutral' work of the proto-voluntary sector. Indeed, the engagement of political parties with the question of advice and rights was vital in the development of attitudes towards reform.

Politics and the law

The relationship between the 'law' and 'politics' is necessarily a very close one, as seen in the first chapter. As the British constitution has evolved over the last couple of centuries, laws are ultimately drafted, reviewed and approved by politicians, between those elected in the House of Commons and those appointed to the House of Lords. Two of the three strands of power in the United Kingdom – the executive and the legislature – are closely linked through the various levels of government and administration. The judiciary is, at least in principle, independent of the executive and legislature in order to ensure that 'justice' is upheld and not interfered with by political or administrative interests.[4] Although this principle of an independent judiciary is shared across the main political parties, the notion that the law needs to be harnessed to work in the interests of all citizens has been politicised, particularly from the interwar period onwards. The Reform Acts of the nineteenth century, along with the processes and campaigns behind them, started and then maintained debates about *who* was a citizen, *who* had the vote, *what* the rights and responsibilities of a citizen should be, and *what* the state owed the individual, their community and the country as a whole.[5] This also then caused shifts first in the relationship between political parties and the electorate, and then between government agents such as Members of Parliament and their constituents. It also led to the creation and growth of the Labour Party, which aimed to represent the needs of the working class in Parliament.[6] Alongside the campaign for the franchise to be extended to all working-class men was the campaign to extend it to women.[7] These shifts also had repercussions for those who worked to service the needs and rights of citizens, in terms both of what they did and of who did it. Indeed, the focus in this chapter is on the 'what they did', the ways in which the law and political life overlapped and merged.

Until the 1980s, political scientists and political historians tended to look either at the 'big picture' in politics, with a focus on the behaviour of parties as agents in themselves, or at 'high' political and diplomatic machinations. The 'new' political studies of the 1980s onwards sought to reappraise the MP as an actor in (mostly) his or (later) her own right, rather than as a puppet working on behalf of the political parties and their constituencies.[8] This branch of political science has looked not only at the social backgrounds of MPs but also at their behaviours and motivations in Parliament and their *everyday doings*. It enables us, first, to establish that solicitors and barristers have made up a considerable proportion of the membership of the House of Commons since the later nineteenth century and, second, the varying extents to which MPs with legal backgrounds populated the political parties. As Cairney demonstrates, by the end of the nineteenth century, barristers had grown to make up the second largest occupational background from which Conservative MPs came. By the mid-twentieth century, both the Labour and Conservative Parties had considerable numbers of MPs from both branches of the legal profession, though the proportion of Labour lawyers had declined by the end of the twentieth century.[9] Howarth further notes that the Labour landslide of 1945 brought with it the tendency for lawyer MPs to outnumber those MPs who came from skilled or unskilled manual labour backgrounds.[10] Arguably, this was itself part and parcel of the bigger Labour project to become the party of the Left in the later 1930s and 1940s and its reaching out to the professional middle classes in order to achieve this.[11] There was also a need to be able to call upon legal expertise as part of the construction of a mass political party. The significance of this greater presence of lawyers in the party will be returned to later in this chapter.

This field also allows us to interrogate the ways in which the role of the MP changed, particularly in terms of what they did in terms of meeting the needs and expectations of their constituents. Searing reminds us that, in the case of Britain, the original role of an MP was to seek redress for wronged constituents, and that this had declined in importance until it was largely revived by Labour in the interwar period, gaining further ground with the creation of the welfare state.[12] Searing and colleagues further found that there were no significant differences in the likelihood of Labour or Conservative MPs adopting this role but that Labour MPs were far more likely to see themselves as 'welfare officers', whilst their Conservative counterparts saw their role as being 'local promoters' of businesses and industries.[13] However, the provision of *advice* as part of this service of being an ombudsman emerged out of the increasingly close relationships between MPs and their (especially) working-class constituents. These relationships began to shift in the first half of the twentieth century, partly as the backgrounds of MPs themselves began to diversify. Before the First World War, MPs tended to be wealthy men who were called upon to serve as patrons of activities within their constituency and also as benefactors, giving donations to the local (Conservative) association as well as troubled members of the community – though the degree to which MPs of any party engaged with their constituency also varied greatly at this point.[14] As Norton noted in 1994, MPs did not have *official* job descriptions, but there were a general set of duties that had evolved over time.[15] At constituency level, Norton argues that the typical MP adopts some or all of the following typological roles when working with their constituents: a 'safety valve' for constituents to vent their frustrations; an 'information provider'; a 'local dignitary'; an 'advocate'; a 'benefactor'; a 'powerful friend'; and, finally, 'a promoter of constituency interests'.[16] Norton further argues that the constituency surgery – an opportunity for members of the public to discuss matters with their MP in person – and dealing with letters from constituents or other parliamentarians grew during the 1950s, increasing dramatically from the 1960s.[17] Norton identifies four causes for the increase: a growing electorate; the growth of the welfare state, resulting in greater opportunities for citizens to run into problems with the state; improvements in secondary education; and the general success of MPs in dealing with problems and issues raised by their constituents.[18]

The purpose here is not to look at the changing role of the MP with regard to the welfare state and beyond, though it informs the broader exploration of a political party or its elected representative as being a means for information, advice and advocacy at the grass-roots level and its crossover with Poor Man's Lawyer and other advice provision. More specifically, we need to ask *why* the political parties put energy, time and money into providing legal advice clinics from the interwar period. This was a period of intense competition for new working-class men's and an increasing pool of adult women's votes, and the Conservative and Labour Parties were rapidly innovating and refining their approach. This was by no means a service that MPs or constituency-level parties were mandated to do, so why did they do it? Although contemporary sources such as the Finlay Committee noted the provision of legal advice clinics by the major political parties in the interwar period, historians have overlooked the 1920s and 1930s in favour of focusing on the development of party political advisory services during the Second World War.[19] As Thorpe notes, the sheer impact of the Second World War in disrupting people's lives dramatically increased the amount of work MPs were doing on individual cases.[20] This was work that was undoubtedly important to the people whose lives had often been turned upside down, and it could also be an area of an MP's work that was 'above' party politics through its dedication. In one sense, if the political parties could use their knowledge of government and the law, and their powers of leverage, then this was an appropriate service to offer during a period of total war. However, the work of MPs and their local party organisations did not simply come out of nowhere at the outbreak of the war. Rather, the work during the Second World War was a development of strategies first explored in interwar London.

The Political Man's Lawyer?

According to the Finlay Committee, the three main political parties each offered 'Poor Man's Lawyer'-style clinics in London in the mid-1920s. The Liberals offered six, in Bethnal Green, Hackney, Lambeth, Shoreditch and Stoke Newington; the Conservatives eight, in Finsbury, Islington, Southwark, Camberwell, Bermondsey and North St Pancras. The Labour Party ran eleven, in Deptford, Fulham, Hackney (two branches), Hammersmith, Islington,

Paddington, Poplar, Southwark, Mile End and Stoke Newington, along with a further two that were run under the umbrella of the Kensington Trades Council (though this was effectively a branch of the Labour Party) and the Fabian Women's Group.[21] A letter sent by Enid A. Berthen, one of the Toynbee Hall Poor Man's Lawyers, to Sir Claud Schuster, the permanent secretary to the Lord Chancellor, provides insight into what these 'political' centres were doing in East London. Berthen noted that providing legal advice was one of the tactics used by those candidates who had legal training, such as Major Harry Nathan and Colonel Robert Bernard Solomon, who were running for the Liberal Party in Whitechapel and Mile End, respectively. She also referred to a barrister, John Duncan, who offered a service at Poplar Town Hall for the Labour Party, as well as to Lieutenant Colonel Meyer, formerly the Liberal MP for Blackpool, who offered legal advice for Labour in Pimlico.[22]

All these centres were in the densely populated central areas of London, which had been dominated by a working- or lower-middle-class population. By the interwar period, such areas were increasingly given over to industrial space, with London City Council (LCC) tenants being relocated out of these areas.[23] Hackney, Stoke Newington and Fulham were somewhat more suburban in character, but, as Steel notes, the major population growth in London in the interwar period was in newer suburbs beyond these areas, though the growth was strongest for private builds (and therefore largely middle-class homes) rather than council houses, which tended to be occupied by working-class families.[24] Although some were in the same or neighbouring districts as Poor Man's Lawyer centres, the political ones were relatively well spread out. The political legal advice centres were not formally part of the same networks as the other Poor Man's Lawyer groups, but there were informal links. For example, Frank Briant, the Liberal MP for Lambeth North, told the Finlay Committee that he had an office at Alford House, where he gave advice to his constituents, which included legal advice.[25] Founded in 1884 by Briant, Alford House was not a settlement, but as a youth club and adult men's institute, it had a similar social work and educational offering. Briant effectively served as a clearing house for those of his constituents with a legal problem, with his advice centring upon establishing the facts and then advising the constituent as to his or her rights; there was the option for Briant to call upon a small number of solicitors for further help.[26] Briant was not trained as a solicitor or barrister but had acquired legal knowledge through his decades of public service, including working as a civil servant before joining the LCC and then standing for Parliament.[27] It was not clear where Briant's social work ended and his political work began.

All the parties were competing for a winning share of the votes of all adult men and eligible women before all women gained the vote at twenty-one in 1928. During the 1920s, Labour made major gains across the nation and also in London at borough and LCC elections. Prior to 1918, the LCC was dominated by two factions. The Progressives broadly mapped to the Liberal Party and some Labourites, whilst the Municipal Reform bloc mapped to the Conservatives.[28] The gains that Labour made in the 1920s were generally at the expense of the Progressives and would be tempered by the turbulence that enveloped the party in the 1930s.[29] The Conservatives, on the other hand, were most perturbed about the new housing estates that were rapidly growing on the outskirts of London.[30] As Savage notes, the key to this shift in fortunes for the Labour Party, including in places where they had not had a foothold before 1914, was in neighbourhood organisation. In places like Deptford and Poplar South, the growth of the 1920s was also associated with this type of work.[31] By the 1930s, the London Labour Party and its constituency parties were extremely well organised.[32] The Mile End Labour Party in East London was deemed to be one of the best organised groups due to the efforts of its organiser, Israel Shafran, who was also the election agent for first, John Scurr and later, Dan Frankel.[33] The Mile End Party had over 2,000 members in 1930, along with a vibrant Labour Club, regular publications, social events and a free legal advice centre.[34] The Mile End Labour Party served a local community that was predominantly Jewish and faced strong and increasing competition from the Communist Party for their allegiance. The Communist Party favoured a far more proactive and combative response than Frankel and Labour to the problem of the British Union of Fascists, who were attacking and harassing members of the Jewish community, and the communists also put great efforts into organising rent strikes.[35] Housing had been a bone of contention in the East End for decades, as much of the accommodation was poorly maintained, insanitary, expensive and run by unscrupulous landlords. One solution to this was the building of model housing by philanthropists, housing societies and the LCC, but this was far from accessible to all working-class East Londoners.[36] The other solution was holding unscrupulous landlords to account and helping tenants to uphold their rights. In the case of the two Bethnal Green constituencies, the provision of a Liberal-run Poor Man's Lawyer and the (largely) Liberal domination of the seat was somewhat explained by the increasingly anomalous position of Bethnal Green as a redoubt of Liberalism as the party went into decline both nationally and in terms of London-wide and borough-level politics.[37] However, Linehan shows that, whilst the Liberals dominated in terms of returning MPs to Westminster throughout the 1920s and 1930s, they faced growing competition from the British Union of Fascists for the anti-socialist vote at a local level.[38]

This policy – especially, but by no means exclusively, on Labour's part – of being useful through offering advice was part of a much bigger project to work on Labour's offering to the electorate. As Wring demonstrates, the Conservatives were the first major political party in the United Kingdom to use proto-professional marketing, which they did in the wake of their landslide defeat by the Liberals in 1906. This marketing work included training candidates for election and adopting different techniques for marketing, such as cinema vans, particularly in the interwar period. Labour, on the other hand, did not have access to the same financial support as the Conservatives, but it did benefit from the contributions of Sidney Webb, who encouraged the party to use 'stratified electioneering' or finely targeting its message to the desired part of the electorate.[39] In the course of the 1920s and 1930s, party officials were increasingly aware of the need to try to attract different kinds of voters – women as well as young people – and that reaching different kinds of voters required different kinds of approaches.[40]

The Poor Woman's Lawyer

One of the legal advisory services under the Labour umbrella in the 1920s was run by the Fabian Women's Group. In March 1927, the annual meeting of the Fabian Women's Group voted unanimously to employ a 'Poor Woman's Lawyer' who would offer advice out of the Fabian offices for 'women in need of a legal opinion'. Jeanette Tawney was the chair of the Women's Group, and it fell to her to take the lead on the project. At their June 1927 meeting, Tawney introduced to the meeting Gwendolen Petersen, 'a fully qualified woman lawyer', who was willing to offer them a Poor Woman's Lawyer service. Petersen had previously offered advice to the Canning Town Women's Settlement in East London, and she was happy to give over Wednesday evenings on behalf of the Fabians.[41] It was not clear how Petersen was found, but Tawney was very well connected to the settlement movement through both her husband, R.H. Tawney, and her brother, William Beveridge. Jeanette Tawney undertook voluntary and paid social work in the earlier years of the Tawneys' marriage, and she was also linked into the networks of women's suffrage and equal citizenship campaigning.[42]

The Poor Woman's Lawyer project was off the ground quickly, with Wednesday evening sessions held in the Fabian Society offices. There was a small charge for the service, which was 1 d for advice and 3 d for a letter. These were very affordable amounts but nowhere near reimbursing Petersen for her work. A subcommittee comprising Jeanette Tawney, Gwendolen Petersen and Barbara Drake set to work on devising a leaflet to advertise the service and sending it to local Labour Parties, churches, hospitals and church missions, as well as placing an advertisement in the *Daily Herald*, the *London News* and the *Labour Woman*.[43] Frank Wallis Galton, Fabian Society secretary, gave his approval for the scheme and for the use of the society's offices over the summer of 1927.[44] By October 1927, attendance at the Wednesday evening sessions was strong and growing. With Tawney's consent, Petersen took a case to court, incurring expenses of over 30s. Tawney and the Group's Secretary resolved to set up an appeal to try to raise money for emergency cases.[45] By February 1928, however, donations of 30s had come from friends of the group, so that Petersen's court fees could be reimbursed, and plans for an appeal were shelved.[46] However, in late 1927, Elizabeth Haldane questioned the need to continue offering free legal advice, given that the Finlay Committee were due to report in a matter of months.[47] Haldane's view carried weight, as she was the sister of Viscount Haldane. Her brother, originally a Liberal, had been Labour's first Lord Chancellor in its 1924 Government. By 1927, Viscount Haldane's health was fading, but he was still an active Labour law lord.[48] However, Elizabeth Haldane was incorrect regarding the recommendations of the second Finlay Report, putting too much confidence in the power of the case made by the various representatives of Poor Man's Lawyer associations. The Poor Woman's Lawyer was not put out of business by the state taking on more responsibility for the working-class advice-seeker. After what had been a promising start, the Poor Woman's Lawyer fell victim to being displaced from its usual location when the Fabian Society offices were redecorated. The disruption caused by the move was compounded by the Labour Party opening a rival bureau on nearby Horseferry Road.[49] These were the issues of sustainability that Gurney-Champion had raised only a couple of years earlier. Although Elizabeth Haldane had hoped that the Finlay Report would put the Poor Woman's Lawyer out of business, the experiences of the Fabian Women's Group ironically demonstrated why the types of voluntary provision that the majority report so favoured were problematic. Yet the episode also shows how the idea of legal protection in a wide array of areas of law – not just divorce or custody matters – was an increasingly important part of campaigning work. It also demonstrated awareness of the complexity of working-class lives and the problems people faced, and that women might need dedicated support.

Agents and legal advice

The setting up of advisory services that were in addition to and different from the clinics offered by MPs as a matter of course began to spread beyond London in the 1930s. A considerable amount of this related to the shifts in what party agents did. Herbert Drinkwater founded the *Labour Organiser* in 1919, as part of the Labour Party's drive to build its movement during the interwar years, and edited it for twenty-five years.[50] The *Labour Organiser* was sent to agents across the country, providing tailored guidance on the activities that agents should be doing in order to build up the party at grass-roots level. In 1941, it had a monthly circulation of 1,800 copies.[51] The approaches to party-building laid out in the *Labour Organiser* shifted over time, reflecting the growing sophistication of the party in communicating with a wider electorate and the technological innovations of the mass media. For example, Beers outlines how the *Labour Organiser* had evolved from dismissing the need for agents to engage with the press in 1928 to calling for agents to devote an hour a week to working with the media in 1935.[52] Advice followed a similar pattern a couple of years later. In April 1938, its letters page responded to questions from organisers who had written in asking for guidance and support on setting up branch advice sessions. The *Labour Organiser* was cautious about encouraging such work. In ideological terms, they felt that it was not the party's mission, as a socialist party, to 'wipe up the mess of Capitalism' and essentially help to shore up the system. In more instrumental terms, they felt that advising members of the public was the duty of others, specifically the trade unions and MPs.[53]

In the space of a year, however, their advice had changed dramatically. During this time, war was declared against Germany, and the demand for information and advice was intense. One of the solutions to this had been the establishment of a national network of CABx. Much like their Poor Man's Lawyer counterparts, many of the CABx were run by volunteers on a part-time basis.[54] The demand for advice and the overall voluntary basis of CABx and similar initiatives provided an opportunity for the Labour Party to position itself as the place in the local community where the public could come for advice on a wide range of matters. Head Office provided bulletins with the latest information, which was circulated to members and branches. By March 1940, the *Labour Organiser* reported that fifty-one Borough and Divisional Labour Parties were responsible for running 117 advice centres, drawing upon the work of councillors, party officials and JPs.[55] Coverage of and advertisements for such bureaux in both the local press and the national Labour paper, the *Daily Herald*, give us a sense of the kinds of activity undertaken and its scale. The South Division Labour Party in Edinburgh offered an 'information and advice bureau' every Thursday evening from 6.30 to 9.00 p.m. with a councillor in attendance.[56] In London, both the West Lewisham and Leyton local parties set up information bureaux very early on in the war. The Leyton bureau was very specifically interested in tackling the issues of the home front, from paying the rent to being called up, being paid pensions and allowances, and the supply of food.[57] The Heston and Isleworth Borough Party in West London ran its own CAB, with Labour councillors serving as advisors. In 1941, the demand for advice and the limitations of containing it within their set evenings forced a change of arrangements, with the home addresses of councillors and other advisors provided so that people could go directly to them for guidance.[58]

Other insights into the impact of advice bureaux come from a short article in the *Labour Organiser* by Andrew Fleming, an organiser in Dumbarton Burghs. Fleming and colleagues started their advice bureau in the 1930s but found that its real value to the community came during the war. Fleming also felt that the act of running the bureau had kept the local party branch in contact with official channels, charities and everyone else at a point when 'everything else had stopped overnight'. Fleming also felt that the bureau had allowed the local Labour Party to be a friend to those who were not as able to assert their rights:

> Far better [critics of advice work] say, to leave such persons to some well-meaning social worker who knows better how to handle them. My experience of the well-meaning persons must be different from others. In times like the present we are polluted with them. Some have even reached the high rank of billeting officers. To do justice even some of them try to make a job of it but soon find out that if they would hope to success they must tread on somebody's toes. And they are not prepared to tread.[59]

As Fleming saw it, the Labour Party were the people who trod on toes to serve the interests of the people. Treading on toes was a means of challenging a bureaucracy that was overly interested in correct procedures being followed or incapable of dealing with complex cases or mistakes. It was a response to the lived experience of capitalism, of how the individual worker came up against those with far greater resources, including the ability to pay for legal services. None of this was necessarily innovative. As the *Labour Organiser* had itself pointed out, giving advice was part of the remit of being a councillor. What was new, for the Labour Party at least, was the use of the party machinery to drive this area of work as a means of building its political movement.

As Thorpe shows in his work on party political agents, the Conservatives were also extremely active in providing advice at the grass-roots level, particularly during the Second World War.[60] The Conservatives, however, had different motivations for undertaking this work. Sir Robert Topping, the general director of the Conservative Party, encouraged associations to consider setting up information bureaux to help those 'who are seeking advice on problems affecting their private lives'.[61] In the case of the Conservative Party, advisory work was a means of keeping local associations going and making them useful in the eyes of the constituency. In some cases, this was a service that the association itself provided: in Clitheroe, Lancashire, the local agent gave over a day a week to be available to any local person who needed help, with 2,000 cases being dealt with in 1941.[62] On the other hand, Major H.H. Little, a party agent in the West Midlands, called for his colleagues to support existing work being undertaken by the CABx or similar groups.[63] The contribution of the Conservative Associations to providing advice on the ground should not be underestimated. The associations helped thousands of people, either directly through their own advice bureaux or by providing volunteers to the CABx. However, in terms of understandings of the 'new' wartime citizen, the Conservatives had very different motivations for providing advice in comparison with the Labour Party and groups to the left of it, as will be seen. Advice was a means of supporting members of the community in their private lives and keeping useful connections going.

Politics, law and research

As the war progressed, so too did the commitment of the Labour Party and its associates to providing a breadth and depth of information to its agents for work at the grass roots. In the first couple of years of the war, the *Labour Organiser* promoted the use of Labour Research Department (LRD) publications, such as G. Grant McKenzie's *Rent Acts Guide*, to its organisers as sources of key information.[64] The *Labour Organiser* also began to highlight articles in other labour movement publications, such as *Plebs* and the *Trade and General Workers' Record*, which were written by lawyers such as R.S.W. Pollard in accessible language.[65] Whilst leaflets could help the individual worker or tenant to settle a dispute or prevent one, there was also a need to access other people who had a combination of expertise, the ability to interpret that expertise to the situation in an effective way, and the confidence to articulate the position in person or in writing. For members of the labour movement, this ability to marshal the same knowledge resources as 'capital' was important.

The LRD had progressively moved to the left of the labour movement and into the ambit of the Communist Party of Great Britain (CPGB) during the interwar period. It had been founded in 1912 by the Fabian Society as its Committee of Enquiry into the Control of Industry with a remit to develop theories about industrial development and the potential for socialism. It counted George Bernard Shaw, the Webbs and Maud Pember Reeves amongst its earliest Fabian researchers and directors.[66] In this way, it was firmly linked into the emerging body of social research and feminist activism of the Edwardian period.[67] In 1918, it was rebranded as the LRD to reflect its high standing within the Labour Party and wider labour movement. It was a mechanism through which the findings of these researchers could be disseminated and the labour movement could marshal knowledge and expertise to match that levelled against it by employers.[68] Whilst it remained dominated by the Fabians shortly after the First World War, staff who were members of the CPGB joined, namely Rajani Palme Dutt and Robin Page Arnot.[69] Such connections would prove troublesome for the LRD in 1942 when they were proscribed by the TUC and the Labour Party for being communists.[70] In the course of the 1920s, however, LRD publications were focused on providing useful reference to statistics around labour in Britain and beyond, as well as providing insight into the operations of capitalism and social structures.[71] Given the philosophy of arming the labour movement with the same depth of knowledge that the employers had, it was not unexpected that the LRD would move into publishing guides that would help individuals within the grass-roots movement. For example, the LRD issued *The Tenant's Guide to His Legal Rights* in 1938. This work expanded during the war. They provided leaflets such as *Health and the Blitz* and *Better Shelters* and set up a weekly bulletin, *Fact Sheet*. Their simple guide to the Beveridge Report sold 80,000 copies.[72] The advantage of McKenzie's booklet was that it contained 'no lawyers' language' and thus was very clear and accessible for advice centre volunteers.

Politics within profession

The LRD was not the only group seeking to build up the capacity of the Labour Party. According to the testimony of some of its earliest members, the Haldane Society was founded in 1929 and named after Viscount Haldane, who had died in 1928.[73] By the later 1920s and early 1930s, it was clear that the Labour Party needed professional and technical support in key areas. There were already groups involved with undertaking research on behalf of the party and trade unionists, but the XYZ Club for economists and financial journalists and the British Society for Responsibility in Science were founded in 1932 and 1930 to provide forums for Labour supporters to share their expertise.[74] An Inns of Court Conservative Society had been in operation for some time, according to Gardiner, and left-leaning barristers felt that the balance needed to be redressed.[75] As Pritt noted, Lord Sankey, then the Labour Lord Chancellor, addressed the society at a luncheon and hinted that the Labour Party would look to Haldane members for law officers and other legal assistance.[76] Sankey's papers for the earlier 1930s do not contain a copy of any address to the Haldane Club or Society, but there is some later corroboration of this idea of the relationship between the party and the society. In 1948, the Labour Party commissioned a report from the Haldane Society on 'such suggestions for Law Reform as it considers necessary and practicable at this present time'.[77]

The Haldane Society offered Labour-leaning lawyers an opportunity to network with like-minded people and to put their legal skills in the service of the Labour Party and the working classes. The club expanded its membership criteria during the course of the 1930s, admitting solicitors, law students and clerks; it also became affiliated to the Labour Party in 1937 and in doing so, changed its name to the Haldane Society.[78] Many of its members were also members of the Labour Party – 65 per cent of members in 1938 were also members of local Labour Party branches – but the Haldane Society welcomed a broad spectrum of left-wing opinion.[79]

According to Blake and Rajak, the Haldane Society went into a slump in the early 1930s, possibly due to the split within the Labour Party between those who followed Ramsay MacDonald into the national Governments and those who went into opposition under the leadership of Arthur Henderson. This was also compounded by the Independent Labour Party (ILP) disaffiliating from the Labour Party in 1932.[80] Around 1936, however, there was a cluster of barristers who joined.[81] One of the more established was Gerald Gardiner, later Harold Wilson's Lord Chancellor in 1964. Gardiner wrote of how he developed an interest in politics whilst an undergraduate at Oxford, but he was driven to join the Labour Party after witnessing the growth in unemployment in the 1930s. Ellen Wilkinson's work with the Jarrow marchers particularly piqued his conscience.[82] Gardiner was, however, not enamoured by the presence of communists in the society after the Second World War, and he went on to be chair of the Society of Labour Lawyers after they split from the Haldane Society over the question of needing to be a member of the Labour Party (and therefore not the CPGB) in order to be a member of Haldane.[83] One of the first solicitors to join the society was Jack Gaster.[84] During the disaffiliation of the ILP, Gaster was the leader of the Revolutionary Policy Committee, which was strongly linked at the time to the Communist Party, which he later joined in 1935, bringing his supporters with him.[85] Gaster was later a communist councillor in Stepney and remained a member of the CPGB up until its dissolution in the 1980s.[86]

A major push factor for many of these lawyers in joining the Haldane Society was the lack of legal protection for the working classes, not only in terms of such matters as dealing with rogue landlords but also with respect to their civil rights. The NCCL was founded in 1934, and there were close synergies between the two groups. Ronald Kidd, the founder of the NCCL, was outraged by police surveillance of hunger marchers and the use of agents provocateurs, and worked with the Haldane Society to make major amendments to the Incitement to Disaffection Act 1934.[87] As the NCCL grew, it welcomed members from across the spectrum of left-wing political positions and experienced the same sort of tensions in ensuring that more centrist or Liberal members were not discouraged by any association with the CPGB.[88] There was considerable crossover between the two groups – Clement Attlee, for example, was a member of both. Attlee was a barrister, but his working life was spent instead in politics.[89] The similar make-up of the two bodies was not always an advantage. Platts-Mills recalled being stopped from holding meetings of the Haldane Society immediately before NCCL meetings, as this was off-putting for Liberal members of the NCCL.[90] The other point at which the NCCL and the Haldane Society converged was on the question of defending anti-fascists involved in street fights with the British Union of Fascists. The communist tendencies of the anti-fascists did not encourage members of the English Bar to take their cases up. The NCCL worked with the Haldane Society to try to ensure that such individuals had a suitable and sympathetic defence brief.[91]

This broad church would cause controversy and conflict on various occasions, not least in terms of the society's relationship with the Labour Party. Most notoriously, two major figures in the society, Stafford Cripps and D.N. Pritt, were expelled from the Labour Party for their supposed communist sympathies. The presence of the hard left amongst the leaders of the society led to accusations that the society's policies and positions were dictated by this group to the exclusion of other points of view in the society.[92] This question of the relationship of the society to the Labour Party is an important one. Whilst the Haldane Society was a home for communists and 'fellow-travellers' such as Cripps, Pritt and John Platts-Mills, it also contained more orthodox and senior Labour figures, such as Clement Attlee. It was through its connections with these senior Labour figures that the Haldane Society was able to develop a role in shaping Labour policy and drafting legislation. This work was organised through subcommittees of the society's members, who either volunteered to take on or responded to calls for action. An example of this was the passing of the Hire Purchase Act 1938, as Ernest Watkins was a Haldane Society member as well as a Poor Man's Lawyer volunteer at Toynbee Hall. This was an example of the identification of a problem, here by organisations with links to the Haldane Society, demonstrating its varying courses through the grass roots and the use of networks within the Labour Party to enable it to be taken forward.

The Haldane Society was also keen to provide help to working-class people more directly. It published a series of books aimed at helping the working classes to navigate wartime legislation, *The Airman's Guide*, *The Soldier's Guide* and *The Sailor's Guide*, which were all published by Frederick Muller Ltd, whilst Sir Isaac Pitman published *The Industrial Worker's Guide*. These books were light and pocket-sized, easily carried around at work or in a kit bag, and sold at an affordable 1 s. In the preface to *The Industrial Worker's Guide*, Charles Dukes of the General and Municipal Workers Union wrote:

> Don't think that a book of this size is enough to teach you the law, or even to be a text-book. But it may be useful as a signpost to the general line of law affecting you. The industrial worker has as a rule only a vague idea of his general position in law in relation to his employer and his employment [...] No amount of legal knowledge can be as strong as a whole body of workers joined together to promote each other's common interests as in a trade union.[93]

In this understanding, 'the law' was not necessarily complicated or opaque, but it was unexplained. Not knowing about rights and responsibilities left both the individual and the collective vulnerable to an array of difficulties and punishments as a result through the basic legal principle of *ignorantia juris non excusat* (ignorance of the law is no excuse). The problem for conscripts during the Second World War was that they were first, by definition, thrown into situations that were new to them and, second, not necessarily welcomed as raw recruits to an industry. Trade unions could provide legal advice to their members, whilst knowledge of the law could be acquired through training and experience of different everyday situations by shop stewards and active union members – none of which was necessarily accessible to a conscript. Being conscripted into any of the armed forces also brought with it the reality of military law. As John L. Williams, the author of *The Airman's Guide*, pointed out, conscripts needed to collect all of their Royal Air Force-issued goods and uniform at the point of issue, as there would not necessarily be the opportunity to correct things later. Likewise, checking one's pay and dealing with any mistakes had to be done there and then at the issuing table at pay parade.[94] Uniform and kit were just the starting point of navigating an array of laws and regulations in the services. These books could explain the key points that an individual needed to know before service, the things that raw recruits were expected to know – but no-one told them. That these books were for the individual sparked another tension: where was the point at which a private trouble became a public one?

The society also became more concerned with grass-roots legal aid and advice, representing a move away from the concerns of a political party to dealing with the concerns of ordinary people. Whilst many of its individual members were also keen volunteers with a Poor Man's Lawyer evening, the society itself began to help groups and individuals in need, including advising on the legal constitution of a home factory for women doing part-time war work, and helping refugee organisations and the NCCL.[95] By 1943, the Haldane Society was pressing for the establishment of a national legal service as a counterpart to a national medical service, the latter having been mooted in the Beveridge Report.[96] This was fleshed out in a pamphlet, *The Law and Reconstruction*, which had a simple premise:

> It is undesirable, if workers in industry are to put forward their best efforts, that they should labour under a sense of injustice in any dispute they may have, civil or criminal, by feeling that the law is biassed [*sic*] against them, or that they cannot enforce their rights because legal advice and representation are not attainable except at exorbitant expense. So, too, is it undesirable that men in the Forces should be worried by doubts as to whether their wives at home are able to be properly protected against predatory landlords and other agents of oppression.[97]

Here was a clear statement that legal aid and advice was a *right* of the working classes, and linked it as such to the impact of personal worries on performance in war duties on all fronts.

The Law and Reconstruction recommended a radical overhauling of the legal system, including one suggestion of creating a Public Legal Service Department, which would create and oversee legal advice bureaux in every local authority. Other proposals included reforms to the payment of workers' compensation, the recruitment of magistrates, criminal law, divorce and the cost of appeals. Such a Public Legal Service Department would be overseen by a committee of eleven, comprising three barristers, three solicitors and five lay members from other public bodies. The local bureaux would decide whether cases should be taken forward to court, and if so, there would be a sliding scale of charges that would be levied. If the claimant was successful, these charges would be refunded. This Public Legal Service Department would be funded from a range of sources – from fees charged for advice at the local centres, from applicant contributions, from costs awarded and from the Treasury.[98] Where this scheme was radical lay in its aim of insisting that the legal profession use a set sliding scale for its services that matched the client's ability to pay; where it was less radical was in its insistence that legal assistance should still be paid for by the individual and not the state. The sense of legal expertise as something commanding a premium that had to be paid for was retained, as was the ability of lawyers to have no upper limits on their income. This was not at odds with the fundamental thinking of the Haldane Society: several of their most prominent and most left-leaning figureheads had made fortunes from their cases despite professing an affinity with socialism. Whilst the Haldane Society wanted to extend legal aid and advice to all, their thinking was still enmeshed within the orthodoxy of ideas about the shape of the legal profession.

Legal law groups and the post-Rushcliffe world

The Society of Labour Lawyers (SLL) was formed out of a split in the Haldane Society over the question of membership of the Labour Party. Following Labour's election victory in 1945, Haldane members either entered the Commons for the first time or found themselves in major positions: Stafford Cripps; Viscount Jowitt; Hartley Shawcross; Frank Soskice; Lewis Silkin; Arthur Henderson; and Clement Attlee as Prime Minister. Gardiner called for membership of the Haldane's executive committee to be restricted to members of the Labour Party, thereby excluding members of the CPGB – who were, as communists, unable to join Labour. This call was then extended to be a condition of membership. The ensuing discord resulted in those in favour of the Labour Party membership clause moving to the new SLL whilst the others remained in the Haldane Society. The Haldane Society remained active, but, as Blake and Rajak note, they were excluded from discussions about legal aid and its development just as changes were beginning to be made.[99]

The SLL were concerned about the continued failure of governments in the 1950s to fully implement the Legal Aid and Advice Act 1949, in terms of legal aid being available in courts other than the High Court, and for legal advice to be included in the scheme. Peter Benenson, a barrister and later founder of Amnesty International, was heavily involved in this work. In the 1950s, the SLL had a standing subcommittee on the Legal Aid and Advice Act 1949, of which Benenson was a member. The subcommittee had a number of concerns. First, with the scheme as it operated, they believed that the costs and contributions to be paid by people who earned £7–10 per week were disproportionately harsh, and that there was often too long a gap between applying for and being granted a legal aid certificate. Second, the subcommittee was particularly keen to see legal advice being brought into the scheme along with legal aid in the county courts. The obstacles to this were both financial and political. In a 1952 letter, Benenson pointed out that the Attorney-General, Lionel Heald, felt that it would be 'senseless' to introduce funding for legal advice without also having legal aid in the county courts, as it would be frustrating for qualifying members of the public to have funding for advice but not for the case itself. The subcommittee, on the other hand, pointed to how legal advice under the scheme would cost £120,000 a year in comparison with the estimated £3 million for legal aid in the county courts. In their eyes, it made no sense to hold up the advice element that the Government could afford for the sake of waiting for the Government to be able to also afford £3 million, particularly when Poor Man's Lawyers centres were struggling to stay open for want of advice funding.[100]

Calls for the introduction of legal aid in the county courts gained speed in 1954 and 1955. Arthur Skeffington, Labour MP for Hayes and Harlington and a recently qualified barrister, raised the question of extending the legal aid scheme in the Commons in October 1954. Skeffington pointed to the number of questions that had been previously raised in the House, as well as the NCSS's conference on legal advice in 1954 and the Labour Party's adoption of a resolution to bring the remaining parts of the 1949 Act into force at its autumn 1954 conference. He spoke of how 'the county courts are really the great social courts for masses of people. There it is that the problems of their wills, their homes, their inheritances, their nuisances and many other matters are dealt with.'[101] One focus, particularly for the TUC and others in the labour movement, was the Housing Repairs and Rent Act 1954, which would have meant many working-class people facing the prospect of county court cases with no financial support. The issue energised both the Labour and Conservative Parties ahead of the 1955 General Election.

In preparation, the SLL tried to interest independent and philanthropic research organisations in exploring the impact of the Act. They first approached Michael Young at the Institute of Community Studies, who advised them to contact the Acton Society Trust and the Fabian Society.[102] The Acton Society Trust had been founded by the Joseph Rowntree Social Service Trust (later the Joseph Rowntree Reform Trust) in 1948 to act as the Liberal Party's equivalent of the Fabian Society.[103] The Acton Trust were happy to put the proposal to their board, but the proposal went nowhere.[104] The SLL changed tactics and convened meetings with key individuals to help build up their evidence and case-making. They were more fortunate with their approach to George Corbyn Barrow. Barrow was part of the Quaker Barrow and Cadbury families that were integral to Birmingham's political and civic world by the late nineteenth century. Barrow qualified as a solicitor in 1928 and then joined a Birmingham law firm, where he remained for the rest of his career. Barrow was involved with the Poor Man's Lawyer in the city and was active in both the Birmingham Law Society and the Council of the Law Society from the 1940s until the 1970s. Barrow was also involved in the establishment of the legal aid scheme on the Law Society's side.[105] He was also on the Jones Committee.[106] He agreed to speak at a meeting of the SLL's executive committee in April 1955, drawing upon his views on how legal aid in the county courts could work from his experience of practising in those courts and serving on the Midlands Area Committee for legal aid applications.[107] Around the same time, the SLL sent a survey to members of the society who were solicitors, asking them about their experiences of financial contributions with legal aid cases in the High Court. Their sample was small – only twenty solicitors replied – but offered some powerful insights. One solicitor reported that an applicant had been granted a certificate but was unable to take it up because he could not afford the payments towards his contribution, whilst another solicitor took an unsatisfactory settlement to save his client paying contributions he could ill afford. As wages were rising, so too were rejections of cases for those who were just over the upper limit of £10 with an income of £12 per week, and for whom the full cost of a case was too much for their budgets to bear.[108]

In the summer of 1955, the SLL sent two papers to the LCO, the first on the extension of legal aid to the county courts and the second on the scale of financial contributions in the legal aid scheme.[109] Shortly afterwards, the SLL wrote to Labour MPs who were lawyers to draw their attention to the forthcoming County Courts Bill, which was due to have its second reading in June 1955. The Bill did not mention legal aid, but the Government had announced that the enactment of this Bill would trigger the introduction of legal aid in the county courts. Although this was desirable, there were two main issues that they wished members to refer to, if they were able to speak during the debate. First, without reform of the financial contributions, there would be no advantage for a person with a legal aid certificate taking a case to the county court. The letter gave the example of how a man on the national average earnings was liable to pay in full all legal costs up to £112 – but a county court case was assumed to cost no more than £50. The financial limits had been set using valuations from 1939, which were woefully out of date.[110] The other issue was the speed at which legal aid certificates were granted for High Court cases. It typically took two months for a legal aid certificate to be granted, which drew out cases for at least four months when both plaintiff and defendant needed to apply. High Court applications were reviewed by a panel of up to five board members, which was both expensive and time-consuming. Far better, argued the SLL, in much smaller and less costly cases, for this work to be done by the secretary of the committee, who decided on the spot in cases where less than £40 was involved. The requirement for applicants to have their means tested by the National Assistance Board – a drain on their resources as well as a further cost to the applicant in travel and lost earnings – could also be waived in favour of being dealt with by the secretary.[111]

The debate in June was wide-ranging. William Wells, the Labour MP for Walsall North, and a barrister, made a long intervention and at the end brought in one of the SLL's points, calling for the legal aid certificate process to be hastened.[112] David Weitzman, the Labour MP for Hackney North and Stoke Newington, and another barrister, raised the SLL's point about the cost of a county court action being £50, when legal-aided litigants were liable for costs up to £112, and called for the regulations to be revised in order for them to work in a meaningful way. Weitzman also called for the introduction of legal advice, as it was, he argued, a false economy not to fund advice that might prevent some cases from needing resolution in the county court.[113] The ensuing County Courts Act 1955 brought the changes of the jurisdiction into force, with provision of legal aid in the county courts enabled by a statutory instrument.[114] Legal advice, however, remained outside the scheme. The SLL had some success, therefore, in getting Labour MPs to raise their points about the workings of the legal aid scheme and to promote the issues at stake. Kilmuir and Manningham-Buller were sympathetic to their opposition colleagues, but the pace at which they were able to move on county court legal aid was slower than Labour would have liked.

Kilmuir was not averse to the political organisation of barrister colleagues. In 1947, he founded the Inns of Court Conservative and Unionist Society (ICCUS), becoming its chair in 1948. Its aim was to bring the thinking of Conservative barristers – not solicitors at this point – to bear on various questions of law and politics.[115] In 1955, ICCUS changed its name to the Society of Conservative Lawyers (SCL).[116] In the eyes of ICCUS, the Labour Governments of 1945–51 brought the state further into private business and life, thereby curtailing individual liberties. A particular threat was the power of ministers to requisition property or compel someone to serve in the armed forces. In 1951, ICCUS called for a new Magna Carta or Bill of Rights that would curb these excesses.[117] ICCUS continued this theme of wanting to review and keep a check on the power of government throughout the 1950s. As far as legal aid and advice were concerned, the emphasis was to be on ensuring that individuals could get a fair hearing against an expanding state. They were especially concerned with the growth of administrative tribunals and offered a twelve-page list of tribunals in force by 1955 at the end of their pamphlet, *Rule of Law*.[118] Although there were major political differences between the Conservatives and ICCUS and their Labour counterparts over the relationship of the state to the individual, there was broad consensus over the social function of legal aid. In 1954, for example, Ian McLeod and Enoch Powell listed legal aid and advice as one of the social services in modern Britain, alongside education, National Insurance and health services, amongst others.[119]

Law reform accelerated under Gerald Gardiner's tenure as Lord Chancellor from 1964.[120] Both the ICCUS/SCL and Haldane/SLL researched and published on law reform in the 1950s and 1960s, but legal aid and advice were not a major part of this agenda. Following their split from the Haldane Society, the SLL published two books that outlined their position of what reforms needed to be made. The first, *The Reform of the Law*, was edited by Glanville Williams, and – as it was prepared in the run-up to the split – it was published jointly with Haldane in 1951. The second, *Law Reform Now*, was edited by Gardiner and Andrew Martin and published in 1963. It made many radical suggestions for reforming the legal system, but it largely overlooked legal aid and advice. *The Reform of the Law* offered two paragraphs on legal aid, calling the 1949 Act a 'stop-gap', which would leave the 'legal service [...] still far behind the new national health service'. Haldane and the SLL were calling for a Ministry of Justice, which would have the responsibility for running such a national legal service or at least taking over legal aid from the Law Society. There was also a call for lay people, ideally those who had experienced the scheme, to be involved in the governance of the legal aid scheme.[121] Some twelve years later, *Law Reform Now* viewed legal aid and advice as a 'great success' and paid attention only to four issues that would serve as reforms or extensions of the scheme, one of which was the extension of civil legal aid to all administrative tribunals.[122] This was not dramatically out of line with ICCUS' position in *Rule of Law*, which was broadly concerned with the freedom of the individual in the context of an expanding state. In a letter to *The Times* in 1955, Benenson argued that ICCUS agreed with the SCL on the need to extend legal aid to tribunals and also for an administrative division to be set up to deal with tribunals; the differences lay in how suitable the two societies thought the existing court and tribunal structures were for handling reforms.[123]

Prior to the General Election of 1964, Gardiner was successful in getting law reform on to the Labour manifesto, and after the election, he accepted the role of Lord Chancellor on condition that he could set up a Law Commission. The Law Commissions Act 1965 set up a Law Commission for England and Wales and another for Scotland. Both commissions were tasked with considering and implementing law reforms and also looking at systems and practices in other countries, opening up a comparative, international approach. In the run-up to the election, Wilson was reported as having law reforms of his own in mind, which included laws against racial discrimination, removing the right of landlords to evict tenants with force, and amending the possibility of trade unions being sued for intimidation in the light of the *Rookes* v. *Barnard* case of 1964.[124] Gardiner introduced a range of reforms in addition to the creation of the Law Commission: a major restructuring of the criminal courts, the re-establishment of a vice-chancellor for the Chancery Division, the abolition of ex officio magistrates, and the creation of an ombudsman service in the Parliamentary Commissioner for Administration.[125] With a reform-minded Lord Chancellor, there was scope for the SLL in particular to set the agenda. The Lord Chancellor's Advisory Committee began to consider the question of why the legal aid and advice schemes were not widely taken up in around 1965 and asked the Law Society to explore the issue in 1967. The Law Society published a memorandum with a proposal to create a single scheme for advice, claims and aid, which would provide the same kind of experience as that of a fee-paying client. A solicitor would be able to approve work up to a ceiling of £25, which would speed up matters, as there would be no need for the Supplementary Benefits Commission to be involved in means-testing for the majority of work. They also called for liaison officers, lawyers who would be employed to work with the CABx, providing advice to the individual bureau when needed and helping to refer clients to a solicitor if needed.[126] In the meantime, the Advisory Committee had also been considering US experiments with 'neighbourhood law firms' as well as the option to extend facilities within the CABx, which they considered in their reports for 1966 and 1967.[127] As Bindman notes, interest in 'law centres' had been growing in the 1960s.[128] Such neighbourhood law offices or firms had been developed in the United States from the mid-1960s in the light of Lyndon Johnson's 'War on Poverty' and were beginning to prove successful in making legal aid and advice more accessible.[129]

In January 1967, the SLL held a conference on law reform, to which they invited Gardiner. Conrad Ascher, the secretary of the SLL, put to the conference the idea of adopting the US neighbourhood law firm model. This caught the imagination of the attendees, and a committee was set up to take the idea further.[130] This move to consider some form of salaried legal service – and the attendant possibility of a national legal service – attracted the attention of the Conservative Party. A few months later, in June 1967, Edward Heath gave a speech to their counterparts at the SCL, which called upon them to research and develop their own proposals into the accessibility of the justice system.[131] The SLL's work would result in the Fabian pamphlet *Justice for All*, whilst the SCL published *Rough Justice* through the Conservative Political Centre, both in December 1968.

The SLL's committee consisted of Morris Finer, Geoffrey Bindman, Benedict Birnberg, Roger Warren Evans, Anthony Lester, Michael Walker, Richard White and Michael Zander. Finer, the chair of the committee, then had a thriving practice as a commercial barrister.[132] Birnberg established a general practice solicitors' firm in London in 1962, but he was best known for civil rights work.[133] Bindman, a solicitor, was a partner in a law firm and was also the legal advisor to the Race Relations Board. Zander was then a lecturer in law at the London School of Economics alongside working as legal correspondent for the *Guardian* newspaper. He had also recently been in the United States, had seen law centres in action and would soon be involved with the first neighbourhood law centre in Britain.[134] Warren Evans had begun his career as an interviewer for Anglia Television but combined practice at the Bar with working as the legal correspondent for *New Society*.[135] From 1964, Anthony Lester served as the chair of the Campaign Against Racial Discrimination's legal subcommittee alongside his practice as a barrister.[136] White was then a lecturer at the University of Birmingham.[137] What was significant about this committee was its gathering not only of lawyers with an interest in social justice and radical practice but also their collective skill set, which brought experience of university-based social sciences research alongside journalism and public communication about the law.

In the first phase of their work, the committee met with witnesses and received evidence from stakeholders, such as the trade unions, free legal advice centres and CPAG. The SLL put special emphasis on how this research was driven by working with those who were actively engaged in work with the socially excluded.[138] One notable participant was Peter Kandler, who had, in the summer of 1967, worked on the Notting Hill Summer Project's legal programme.[139] The Summer Project emerged out of long-standing dissatisfaction with local government in the area, which was channelled into activism through those involved with the London New Left Club, the Campaign for Nuclear Disarmament and other leftist networks in the 1950s and 1960s.[140] Kandler was involved with the establishment in 1970 of the North Kensington neighbourhood law centre, which opened shortly after *Justice for All* was published.[141] The committee took the first draft of their report to an SLL conference on access to justice in August 1968, where delegates included stakeholders such as Seton Pollock, then in charge of legal aid at the Law Society, the free legal advice centres, CABx, social workers and Shelter, the last being then a newly founded housing action group, which had also come out of activism in Notting Hill.[142] The final draft of *Justice for All* reflected those concerns.

The question of the qualifying thresholds for the legal aid scheme, which had exercised the SLL throughout the 1950s, remained an important issue in *Justice for All*. The SLL also called for paid solicitors at CABx in order that people might be able to access legal advice easily – a point on which they were in agreement with the SCL, but the latter preferred the solicitors to be volunteers.[143] However, the SLL had a more radical suggestion to make: the setting up of 'local legal centres', which would be analogous to the American neighbourhood law centres, with salaried lawyers taking on cases. These would extend rather than replace the legal aid system. Shortly before the publication of *Justice for All*, the newly appointed President of the Law Society, Sir Edmund Sargant, criticised the idea of neighbourhood law centres, as they would open up the possibility of a national legal service – which in turn was a threat to the liberty of the individual. Silkin, then the Labour MP for Dulwich, retorted that the individual needed to be aware of what his or her rights were and to be able to take legal action to protect those rights without being prevented by the cost.[144] The Lord Chancellor's Advisory Committee was lukewarm on the question of neighbourhood law centres, preferring instead to improve awareness of legal aid services and to develop a liaison scheme with the CABx.[145]

The concept of a neighbourhood law centre was anathema to the SCL, who were vehemently opposed to a national legal service or any attempt to nationalise the legal profession. A nationalised legal profession would, in their eyes, necessarily act in the interests of the state, not the client.[146] *Rough Justice* raised again their concern about the proliferation of tribunals since the 1940s and also the difficulties in challenging a decision made by local government. Their proposed solutions were the extension of legal aid to administrative tribunals and the establishment of a regional ombudsman to tackle problems with local government decisions.[147] In terms of access to legal advice, the SCL thought that the legal aid scheme was a success, albeit for those who felt confident in going to a solicitor for help. The issue, as they saw it, was to address the problems of there not being enough solicitors to take on legal advice and aid cases, the public's lack of awareness of solicitors and what they could offer, and the sense that seeing a lawyer was a middle-class privilege. Rather than looking at a system of salaried solicitors working in a neighbourhood law centre, as the SLL had done, the SCL called for a market-based solution. They argued that the way to attract more solicitors into areas in which there were shortages was to offer grants to encourage the setting up of practices or to offer higher rates for legal aid work. The SCL also wanted qualified solicitors to be attached to CABx branches so that legal advice would be readily available to anyone who dropped in. All solicitors' firms that participated in the legal aid scheme would then send staff to the CAB on a rota basis, with the workload being shared over the firms in an area.[148]

Gardiner passed both *Justice for All* and *Rough Justice* to the Lord Chancellor's Advisory Committee for them to consider, which they did whilst looking also at a further memorandum from the Law Society, which revised its £25 scheme in the light of the new reports.[149] In the meantime, JUSTICE, an all-party group concerned with the fair administration of the law and justice, had convened a meeting of the authors of all three reports, and the ensuing discussion had led to revisions of the various original proposals.[150] This was most significant in the case of the Law Society, which now wanted to be able to set up and run local legal centres in places where there were difficulties in accessing private solicitors, some of which would concentrate on advice and assistance whilst others would offer to conduct cases. As the Advisory Committee noted, the Legal Aid and Advice Act provided for salaried legal officers in legal advice offices, and the Rushcliffe Report also called for a special office to work on divorce cases for people on lower incomes.[151] The Advisory Committee preferred the Law Society's proposals. To their mind, the SCL's proposals made unreasonable demands in terms of solicitors' voluntary service, and the state subvention to encourage solicitors to open firms in areas of legal need ran the risk of fragmenting the legal profession between private and publicly funded solicitors. Commenting on the SLL scheme, the Advisory Committee thought that US-style neighbourhood law firms were undesirable in England and Wales, and that the SLL's version of local legal centres would not be able to litigate as fully as their American counterparts. On balance, the Advisory Committee preferred the local legal centres as proposed by the Law Society to those outlined by the SLL.[152] The Advisory Committee made six recommendations to Gardiner. First, they recommended that research into legal need should be carried out. As they wrote, White, on the SLL committee, was about to start a major project at the University of Birmingham, funded by the Nuffield Foundation as part of its programme of research into legal needs.[153] It also funded a £150,000 research unit, directed by Pauline Morris and overseen by a committee chaired by Sir William Mansfield Cooper, the former vice-chancellor of Manchester University.[154] The Ford Foundation would fund Brian Abel-Smith, Michael Zander and Rosalind Brooke to work on unmet legal need in three London boroughs, with their research being published in 1973.[155] Second, they wanted the £25 scheme to be implemented as soon as possible. It was – through the Legal Advice and Assistance Act 1972. Third, they wanted eleven liaison officers to be employed to work with the CABx, whilst, fourth, there should be some 'voluntary experiments' in legal assistance to explore the pursuit of cases. Fifth, there should be an urgent and significant increase in publicising legal aid and advice, with such professionals as social workers being given suitable training. The Law Society set up a pilot in the Tyne Tees area to try out publicity in the local press and on commercial television; a nationwide television and newspaper campaign followed in April 1973, with outdoor advertising on buses and hoardings in July that year.[156] Sixth, they called for closer work between CABx and local government to better ensure the even distribution of their services.[157] With respect to the CABx work, the Government announced a grant of £1,300,000 over 1974–7 to improve existing bureaux and to set up new ones.[158] As will be seen in Chapter 6, the neighbourhood law centres pressed ahead on their own, patching funding together from the Lord Chancellor, local government and urban regeneration schemes.

Conclusion

The development of political groupings of lawyers was deeply connected to the imbalances between the Conservative and Labour Parties in terms of their access to the legal profession. For Labour, building up the party's access to professionals in a range of specialisms was key to being able to compete with the far older Conservatives. This began in the legal advice clinics of London by being useful to members of the public and thinking about the needs of women and other groups. In the early 1930s, the Haldane Society created a dynamic network that connected socialist lawyers with each other, which then gave them a space to develop ideas about legal reform. Although the Haldane Society and SLL split in 1948, the ultimate agenda of the Labour lawyers was set in 1942 in the call in *Law and Reconstruction* for a national legal service. This idea of a state-funded, salaried legal service for the working classes informed thinking in *Justice for All*. With the ICCUS/SCL in action from the late 1940s, there was the potential for dialogue about legal reform and access to justice. This was most fruitful in the late 1960s, when *Justice for All* and *Rough Justice* forced reform of the legal aid and advice system high up the political agenda. There was plenty of consensus between the Labour and Conservative lawyers that there was an urgent need to make sure that the law was accessible as possible, but they were absolutely divided on the question of whether a 'national legal service' was the best mechanism for achieving this. The Conservatives could not tolerate the idea of such state involvement, but the Law Society were starting to move in the direction of seeing how the state could take on elements of the work they had been doing since the early twentieth century. Whilst there was a greater will to put public money towards legal advice and aid work, it remained vulnerable to being deprioritised against other forms of welfare during times of economic stringency.

Labour and the Conservatives diverged on how access to the law could be used to promote citizenship. For the Conservatives from the 1940s, legal advice was one way of enabling citizens to deal with a state that was rapidly expanding into new areas of private life; for Labour, legal advice was rooted in problems with housing and landlords. As the 1960s progressed, Labour lawyers' thinking was influenced by the US civil rights movement and ideas about civil rights and community organisation. Philanthropic research foundations also joined this part of the policy arena, putting money towards social science research into the potential of innovative approaches in legal advice work. From the 1960s, the SLL and their associates were particularly involved in pointing out how a rules-based welfare state could steamroller the most vulnerable members of society and the need for lawyers, community and social workers to try to address this, ideally with the support of the state.

Notes

1 R. Egerton, *Legal Aid* (London: Kegan Paul, Trench, Trubner, 1945), p. 104.
2 J. Mervyn Jones, *Free Legal Advice in England and Wales* (Oxford: Slatter and Rose, 1940), pp. 7–8.
3 O. Blaiklock, 'Advising the Citizen: Citizens Advice Bureaux, Voluntarism and the Welfare State in England, 1938–1964' (PhD dissertation, Kings College London, 2012), p. 8.

4 V. Bogdanor, *The New British Constitution* (London: Bloomsbury, 2009); see especially chapter 3 in A. King, *The British Constitution* (Oxford: Oxford University Press, 2007); G. Vanberg, 'Establishing and Maintaining Judicial Independence', in G.A. Caldeira, R.D. Kelemen and E.K. Whittington (eds), *Oxford Handbook of Law and Politics* (Oxford and New York: Oxford University Press, 2008).

5 See, as an introduction, T.H. Marshall, *Citizenship and Social Class* (London: Pluto Press, 1992); M. Bulmer and A.M. Rees (eds), *Citizenship Today: The Contemporary Relevance of T.H. Marshall* (London: UCL Press, 1996); G. Finlayson, 'A moving frontier: Voluntarism and the state in British social welfare, 1911–1949', *Twentieth Century British History*, 1:2 (1990), pp. 183–206; *Citizen, State and Social Welfare in Britain 1830–1990* (Oxford: Clarendon, 1994).

6 A. Thorpe, *A History of the British Labour Party*, 4th edn (Basingstoke: Palgrave Macmillan, 2015).

7 C. Hall, K. McClelland and J. Rendall, *Redefining the Victorian Nation*; S.S. Holton, *Feminism and Democracy: Women's Suffrage and Reform Politics in Britain, 1900–1918* (Cambridge: Cambridge University Press, 2003); M. Joannou and J. Purvis (eds), *The Women's Suffrage Movement: New Political Perspectives* (Manchester: Manchester University Press, 1998).

8 See commentary in P. Norton, 'Roles and behaviour of British M.Ps', *Journal of Legislative Studies*, 3:1 (1997), pp. 17–18.

9 P. Cairney, 'The professionalisation of M.Ps: Refining the "politics-facilitating" explanation', *Parliamentary Affairs*, 60:2 (2007), pp. 212–33.

10 D. Howarth, 'Lawyers in the House of Commons', in D. Feldman (ed.), *Law in Politics, Politics in Law* (London: Hart, 2013).

11 G. McCulloch, 'Labour, the Left, and the British General Election of 1945', *Journal of British Studies*, 24:4 (1985), pp. 470–3.

12 D.D. Searing, *Westminster's World: Understanding Political Roles* (Cambridge, MA: Harvard University Press, 1994), pp. 122–3.

13 Ibid., p. 125.

14 P. Norton, 'The growth of the constituency role of the M.P.', *Parliamentary Affairs*, 47:4 (1994), pp. 708–10.

15 This remains the case at the time of writing, in 2017, although the processes of parliamentary salary review have forced some delineation of what MPs might do: *Senior Salaries Review Body*, Cm 4997-II (2001), www.publications.parliament.uk/pa/cm200607/cmselect/cmcomm/685/68520.htm, correct at 26 June 2017. There is also a Code of Conduct for Members, of which the most recent edition can be found at www.publications.parliament.uk/pa/cm201516/cmcode/1076/107602.htm, correct at 26 June 2017. Norton, 'Growth of the constituency role', p. 705.

16 Norton, 'Growth of the constituency role', pp. 706–8.

17 Ibid., pp. 710–13.

18 Ibid., pp. 714–16.

19 S. Fielding, P. Thompson and N. Tiratsoo, *'England Arise!' The Labour Party and Popular Politics in 1940s Britain* (Manchester: Manchester University Press,

1995), p. 49; A. Thorpe, *Parties at War: Political Organization in Second World War Britain* (Oxford: Oxford University Press, 2009).
20 Thorpe, *Parties at War*, p. 77.
21 *Committee on Legal Aid for the Poor – Final Report*, Cmd. 3016, pp. 18–19.
22 The National Archives (hereafter TNA), LCO 2/987, Letter E.A. Berthen to Sir Claud Schuster, 1 July 1925.
23 J. White, *London in the Twentieth Century: A City and Its People* (London: Vintage, 2008), p. 22.
24 A.M. Steel, 'Explaining Changes in Political Party Fortunes in Greater London, 1918–1931' (PhD dissertation, Queen Mary, University of London, 2005), pp. 35–6.
25 TNA, LCO 2/981, Finlay Committee 36th Day, Thursday 10 June 1926. Evidence of Frank Briant MP, p. 1.
26 TNA, LCO 2/983.
27 'Stallholders' Street Mourns Daddie-O', *Daily Herald*, 3 September 1934, p. 5; 'Mr Frank Briant MP', *The Times*, 3 September 1934, p. 17.
28 K. Young, *Local Politics and the Rise of Party: The London Municipal Society and the Conservative Intervention in Local Elections, 1894–1963* (Leicester: Leicester University Press, 1975).
29 Steel, 'Explaining Changes', pp. 9–15.
30 Ibid., p. 15.
31 M. Savage, *The Dynamics of Working-Class Politics: The Labour Movement in Preston, 1880–1940* (Cambridge: Cambridge University Press, 1987), p. 195.
32 T. Jeffrey, 'The Suburban Nation: Politics and Class in Lewisham', in D. Feldman and G. Stedman-Jone (eds), *Metropolis – London: Histories and Representations of London since 1800* (London: Routledge, 1987).
33 John Scurr was MP between 1923 and 1931; Dan Frankel was the Labour MP for Mile End between 1935 and 1945. See V.A. McClelland, 'Scurr, John (1876–1932)', *ODNB*; E.R. Smith, 'East End Jews in Politics, 1918–1939: A Study in Class and Ethnicity' (PhD dissertation, University of Leicester, 1990), p. 70.
34 S.L. Bird, *Stepney: Profile of a London Borough from the Outbreak of the First World War to the Festival of Britain, 1914–1951* (Cambridge: Cambridge Scholar, 2010), pp. 88–9; Smith, 'East End Jews in Politics', pp. 71–2.
35 See H. Srebrnik, 'Class, ethnicity and gender intertwined: Jewish women and the East London rent strikes, 1935–1940', *Women's History Review*, 4:3 (1995), pp. 283–99; Smith, 'East End Jews in Politics', p. 70.
36 See R.V. Steffel, 'The Boundary Street Estate: An example of urban redevelopment by the London County Council, 1889–1914', *Town Planning Review*, 47:2 (1976), pp. 161–73; M.J. Daunton (ed.), *Councillors and Tenants: Local Authority Housing in English Cities, 1919–1939* (Leicester: Leicester University Press, 1984); A. Olechnowicz, *Working-Class Housing in England between the Wars: The Becontree Estate* (Oxford: Oxford University Press, 1997); S. Pepper and P. Richmond, 'Stepney and the politics of high-rise housing: Limehouse Fields to John Scurr House, 1925–1937', *London Journal*, 34:1 (2009), pp. 33–54.
37 Young, *Local Politics*, p. 66; T.P. Linehan, *East London for Mosley: The British Union of Fascists in East London and South West Essex 1933–40* (London:

Routledge, 2012); P. Thompson, 'Liberals, Radicals and Labour in London 1880–1900', *Past & Present*, 27 (1964), pp. 73–101.

38 Linehan, *East London for Mosley*, pp. 65–8.

39 D. Wring, 'Political marketing and party development in Britain: A "secret" history', *European Journal of Marketing*, 30:10/11 (1996), pp. 94–7.

40 D.E. McHenry, *His Majesty's Opposition: Structure and Problems of the British Labour Party, 1931–1938* (Berkeley, CA: University of California Press, 1940), pp. 60–1.

41 LSE Archives (hereafter LSE), FABIAN SOCIETY/H H24 Minutes, 26 March 1926–2 July 1930, 1 June 1927.

42 See L. Goldman, *The Life of R.H. Tawney: Socialism and History* (London: Bloomsbury, 2013, 2014), pp. 44, 48, 81, 88–9, 188.

43 LSE, FABIAN SOCIETY/H H24 Minutes, 26 March 1926–2 July 1930, 1 June 1927.

44 Ibid., 5 July 1927.

45 Ibid., 5 October 1927.

46 Ibid., 14 February 1928.

47 Ibid., 7 December 1927.

48 H.C.G. Matthew, 'Haldane, Richard Burdon, Viscount Haldane (1856–1928)', *ODNB*.

49 LSE, FABIAN SOCIETY/H H24 Minutes, 26 March 1926–2 July 1930, 8 March 1929.

50 For an obituary note, see M. Grundy, 'This Week in 1960', *Worcester News*, 30 November 2010, www.worcesternews.co.uk/news/nostalgia/thisweekin/8710714.29_November_to_6_December__2010/, correct at 29 August 2017.

51 Thorpe, *Parties at War*, p. 108.

52 L. Beers, *Your Britain: Media and the Making of the Labour Party* (Cambridge, MA: Harvard University Press, 2010), p. 121.

53 'Questions answered', *Labour Organiser*, 18:202 (April 1938), p. 78.

54 Blaiklock, 'Advising the Citizen', pp. 27–8; J. Richards, *Inform, Advise and Support: 50 Years of the Citizens Advice Bureau* (Cambridge: Lutterworth, 1989), pp. 1–3.

55 'The Party at work in war', *Labour Organiser*, 20:219 (September–October 1939), pp. 167–8; 'Around the Parties: A bird's eye view of country-wide activities', *Labour Organiser*, 20:220 (November–December 1939), pp. 179; 'Party organisation in war-time', *Labour Organiser*, 20:223 (March 1940), pp. 43–4.

56 'General Notices', *Edinburgh Evening News*, 21 October 1939, p. 1.

57 'To-day's Bulletin', *Daily Herald*, 11 October 1939, p. 8.

58 'Advice Centres', *Middlesex Chronicle*, 22 March 1941, p. 5.

59 'A Blitzed agent tells his story and draws conclusions', *Labour Organiser*, 22:239 (October 1941), p. 16.

60 A. Thorpe, 'Conservative Party agents in Second World War Britain', *Twentieth Century British History*, 18:3 (2007), pp. 334–64.

61 R. Topping, 'Party organisation and the war', *Conservative Agents' Journal* (April 1940), pp. 42–3.

62 Thorpe, *Parties at War*, p. 165.

63 H.H. Little, 'Suggested duties of agents in war-time', *Conservative Agents' Journal* (July 1940), p. 66.

64 'Rent Acts Guide', *Labour Organiser*, 21:229 (Blitz 1940), p. 132. See also R. Toye, *The Labour Party and the Planned Economy, 1931–1951* (London: Royal Historical Society, 2003), pp. 127–8; G. Grant McKenzie was a member of the research department. Also, Smith notes that Grant McKenzie was taken from the LRD in May 1940 to work with Attlee. See H.L. Smith, *War and Social Change: British Society in the Second World War* (Manchester: Manchester University Press, 1986), p. 133.

65 See R. Dudley Edwards, *Victor Gollancz: A Biography* (London: Faber and Faber, 2012).

66 R. Page Arnot, *History of the Labour Research Department* (London: Labour Research Department, 1926), pp. 5–9.

67 For histories of the Fabians and their associates in the arena of social reform, see Goldman, *Life of R.H. Tawney*; L. Radice, *Beatrice and Sidney Webb: Fabian Socialists* (Basingstoke: Macmillan, 1984); R. Harrison, *The Life and Times of Sidney and Beatrice Webb: 1858–1905, the Formative Years* (Basingstoke: Palgrave Macmillan, 2000); N. MacKenzie, *The First Fabians* (London: Weidenfeld and Nicolson, 1979).

68 Page Arnot, *History of the Labour Research Department*, p. 19.

69 Ibid., pp. 21, 26.

70 See Labour Research Department, 'Our First 100 Years', www.lrd.org.uk/index.php?pagid=60, correct at 29 August 2017.

71 Page Arnot, *History of the Labour Research Department*, pp. 55–62.

72 Labour Research Department, 'Our First 100 Years'.

73 See M. Box, *Rebel Advocate: A Biography of Gerald Gardiner* (London: Victor Gollancz, 1983), p. 54; J. Platts-Mills, *Muck, Silk and Socialism: Recollections of a Left-Wing Queen's Counsel* (Wedmore: Paper Publishing, 2001), p. 92.

74 N. Blake and H. Rajak, *Wigs and Workers* (London: Haldane Society of Socialist Lawyers, 1980), p. 8; E. Durbin, *New Jerusalems: The Labour Party and the Economics of Democratic Socialism* (London: Routledge and Kegan Paul, 1985), p. 76; S. Brooke, 'Revisionists and fundamentalists: The Labour Party and economic policy during the Second World War', *Historical Journal*, 32:1 (2009), p. 159.

75 Box, *Rebel Advocate*, p. 54. However, the Inns of Court Conservative and Unionist Society, or the Society of Conservative Lawyers from 1971, was not founded until 1947: Bodleian Library, Conservative Party-affiliated Organisations – Fonds description, www.bodley.ox.ac.uk/dept/scwmss/wmss/online/modern/cpa/affiliated-groups.html, correct at 21 August 2017.

76 D.N. Pritt, *From Right to Left: The Autobiography of D.N. Pritt* (London: Lawrence and Wishart, 1965), p. 29.

77 See Bodleian Library Special Collections. MS.Eng.hist.d.315, Speech 22 April 1932, Niblett Hall, Inner Temple. LSE, HALDANE SOCIETY/59, Haldane Society Circulars, 1948, Bulletin No.1 June 1948.

78 Haldane Society, *Annual Report for the Year 1937–38* (London: Haldane Society, 1938), p. 4.

79 Ibid., pp. 1, 3.

80 Blake and Rajak, *Wigs and Workers*, pp. 8–9.
81 Ibid., p. 9.
82 Box, *Rebel Advocate*, p. 54.
83 N.S. Marsh, 'Gardiner, Gerald Austin, Baron Gardiner (1900–1990)', *ODNB*.
84 Platts-Mills, *Muck, Silk and Socialism*, p. 399.
85 F. Beckett, *Enemy Within: The Rise and Fall of the British Communist Party* (London: John Murray, 1995), pp. 43, 86.
86 'Obituary: Jack Gaster', *Morning Star*, 21 March 2007, p. 8.
87 Platts-Mills, *Muck, Silk and Socialism*, pp. 82–3.
88 M. Pottle, 'Kidd, Ronald Hubert (1889–1942)', *ODNB*.
89 R.C. Whiting, 'Attlee, Clement Richard (1883–1967)', *ODNB*; R.D. Pearce, *Attlee* (London: Longman, 1997); K. Harris, *Attlee* (London: Weidenfeld and Nicolson, 1982).
90 Platts-Mills, *Muck, Silk and Socialism*, p. 92.
91 Ibid., p. 86.
92 Haldane Society, *Annual Report 1942–3* (London: Haldane Society, 1943), p. 6; *Annual Report 1943–4* (London: Haldane Society, 1944), p. 5.
93 H. Samuels, *The Industrial Worker's Guide to His Rights and Duties* (London: Haldane Society and Pitman & Sons, 1943), p. 3.
94 J.L. Williams, *The Airman's Guide to His Rights and Duties* (London: Frederick Muller, 1942), pp. 7, 11.
95 Haldane Society, *Annual Report 1942–3*, pp. 5–6.
96 Ibid., p. 6.
97 Haldane Society, *The Law and Reconstruction*, p. 1.
98 Ibid., p. 3.
99 Blake and Rajak, *Wigs and Workers*, p. 21.
100 LSE, SLL/6/17, Letter Peter Benenson to Roland Brown, 28 May 1952.
101 *Hansard*, HC Debate, 26 October 1954, vol. 531, cols 1890–1.
102 LSE, SLL/6/17, Letter Michael Young to Jean Graham Hall, 9 August 1954.
103 T. Flower, *Trusting in Change: A Story of Reform* (York: Joseph Rowntree Reform Trust, 2004), p. 9.
104 LSE, SLL/6/17, Letter T.E. Chester to Jean Graham Hall, 24 August 1954.
105 'George Corbyn Barrow', *Independent*, 8 July 1998, p. 6.
106 *First Interim Report of the Committee on County Court Procedure*, Cmd. 7468, p. 2.
107 LSE, SLL/6/17, Letter George Corbyn Barrow to Jean Graham Hall, 21 March 1955, reply 30 March 1955.
108 LSE, SLL/6/17, Legal Aid in the High Court: Scale of Financial Contributions, 21 June 1955.
109 LSE, SLL/6/17, Letter R. Thesiger to J. Graham Hall, 23 June 1955, and Letter J. Graham Hall to the Lord Chancellor's Department, 21 June 1955.
110 LSE, SLL/6/17, Letter J. Graham Hall to membership, June 1955.
111 LSE, SLL/6/17, County Courts, June 1955.
112 *Hansard*, HC Debate, 24 June 1955, vol. 542, col. 1681.
113 *Hansard*, HC Debate, 24 June 1955, vol. 542, col. 1696.
114 See Legal Aid (General) (Amendment No. 2) Regulations, 1955, 1955/1829.

115 Conservative Party Archive, Bodleian Library (hereafter CPA), *A Giant's Strength: Some Thoughts on the Constitutional and the Legal Position of Trade Unions in England* (London: Inns of Court Conservative and Unionist Society, 1958), rear page; '250 on the House', *Daily Mail* (19 October 1948), p. 3. At the time of writing, the papers of the Inns of Court Conservative and Unionist Society and its successor body, the Society of Conservative Lawyers, are held by the Conservative Party Archive but have not been sorted and catalogued – they were therefore unavailable to researchers.

116 CPA, 'Conservative Party-affiliated Organisations', Bodleian Library, University of Oxford, www.bodley.ox.ac.uk/dept/scwmss/wmss/online/modern/cpa/affil iated-groups.html, correct at 8 August 2018.

117 'Industry Must Be Helped', *Financial Times*, 8 October 1951, p. 6; 'Threat to Liberty: Barristers Want New Magna Carta', *Manchester Guardian*, 8 October 1951, p. 4.

118 CPA Publications 165/20 Conservative Political Centre, *Rule of Law* (London: Conservative Political Centre, 1955), p. 62 and appendix.

119 CPA Publications; I. McLeod and E. Powell, *The Social Services: Means and Needs*, 2nd edn (London: Conservative Political Centre, 1954), p. 5.

120 R.F.V. Heuston, *Lives of the Lord Chancellors* (Oxford: Clarendon, 1987), p. 226.

121 G. Williams (ed.), *The Reform of the Law* (London: Victor Gollancz, 1951), p. 12, p. 32.

122 G. Gardiner and F. Elwyn Jones, 'The Administration of Justice', in G. Gardiner and A. Martin (eds), *Law Reform Now* (London: Victor Gollancz, 1963), pp. 22–3.

123 'Liberty of the Subject', *The Times*, 18 May 1955, p. 5.

124 'Lord Gardiner's Law Reform Bill Soon', *The Times*, 6 January 1965, p. 7.

125 Heuston, *Lives of the Lord Chancellors*, pp. 227–8; G. O'Hara, 'Parties, people and parliament: Britain's ombudsman and the politics of the 1960s', *Journal of British Studies*, 50:3 (2011), pp. 670–714.

126 *Report of the Advisory Committee on the Better Provision of Legal Aid and Assistance*, Cmnd. 4249 (London: HMSO, 1970), p. 5.

127 *Legal Aid and Advice: Report of the Law Society and Comments and Recommendations of the Lord Chancellor's Advisory Committee, 1966–17*, Seventeenth Report (London: HMSO, 1968), pp. 56–7.

128 G. Bindman, 'The British Legal Profession Has a Duty to Help Ensure Justice for All', *Shine a Light*, 17 May 2013, www.opendemocracy.net/shinealight/geoffr ey-bindman/british-legal-profession-has-duty-to-help-ensure-justice-for-all, correct at 8 August 2018.

129 See, for example, B. Garth, *Neighborhood Law Firms for the Poor: A Comparative Study of Recent Developments* (Alphen aan den Rijn: Sijthoff and Noordhoff, 1980), p. 17.

130 'More Legal Help for Poor Sought', *Guardian*, 23 January 1967, p. 16.

131 CPA Pub, *Rough Justice* (London: Conservative Political Centre, 1968), p. 5.

132 S. Cretney, 'Finer, Sir Morris (1917–1974)', *ODNB*.

133 P. Boateng, 'My Legal Hero: Benedict Birnberg', *Guardian*, 13 October 2010, www.theguardian.com/law/2010/oct/13/my-legal-hero-benedict-birnberg; L.

Tsang, 'Law: Farewell to a Non-Fat Cat', *Independent*, 25 February 1999, www.independent.co.uk/arts-entertainment/law-farewell-to-a-non-fat-cat-1073079.html, both correct at 15 August 2018.

134 'Bindman, Sir Geoffrey (Lionel)' and 'Zander, Professor Michael', *Who's Who*; P. Kandler, 'You thought that a really great society was going to come out of all of this', in H. Curtis and M. Sanderson (eds), *The Unsung Sixties: Memoirs of Social Innovation* (London: Whiting and Birch, 2004), p. 156.

135 'Warren Evans (John) Roger', *Who's Who*. Also, 'Roger Warren Evans', profile on Asylum Justice (2014), http://asylumjustice.org.uk/people/roger-warren-evans/, correct at 15 August 2018.

136 'Lester of Herne Hill', *Who's Who*; 'Lord Anthony Lester of Herne Hill QC', Jane Compton Management, www.comptonmanagement.com/?p=533, correct at 15 August 2018.

137 'White, Richard Hamilton Hayden', *Who's Who*.

138 LSE, SLL/6/77, Letter from S.C. Silkin, Chair of SLL to Secretaries of Constituency Labour Parties and Regional Councils, May 1969.

139 Society of Labour Lawyers, *Justice for All* (London: Fabian Society, 1968), p. 1.

140 See J. O'Malley, *The Politics of Community Action: A Decade of Struggle in Notting Hill* (London: Spokesman, 1977); J. Dearlove, *The Politics of Policy in Local Government: The Making and Maintenance of Public Policy in the Royal Borough of Kensington and Chelsea* (Cambridge: Cambridge University Press, 1973); S. Hall, 'Life and times of the First New Left', *New Left Review*, 61 (2010), pp. 177–96.

141 Kandler, 'You Thought That a Really Great Society', pp. 155–62.

142 See M. White, 'Obituary: The Reverend Bruce Kenrick', *Guardian*, 19 January 2007, www.theguardian.com/news/2007/jan/19/guardianobituaries.obituaries, correct at 15 August 2018; S. Younger, 'Kenrick, Bruce Henderson (1920–2007)', *ODNB*.

143 Kandler, 'You Thought That a Really Great Society', pp. 155–62.

144 'Legal Service', *The Times* (22 October 1968), p. 9; 'Sargant, Sir (Henry) Edmund', *Who Was Who*.

145 Society of Labour Lawyers, *Justice for All*, p. 55.

146 Ibid., p. 7.

147 Ibid., pp. 11–13.

148 Ibid., pp. 19–21.

149 *Report of the Advisory Committee on the Better Provision of Legal Aid and Assistance*, Cmnd. 4249, p. 3.

150 See JUSTICE, 'History and Achievements', https://justice.org.uk/about-us/history-achievements/, correct at 26 August 2018.

151 Ibid., p. 6.

152 Ibid., p. 7.

153 'University Study to Ensure Legal Services for Public', *The Times*, 27 October 1970, p. 3.

154 'Research to Help in Spreading Legal Aid', *The Times*, 7 January 1971, p. 4; one of the research avenues undertaken by Morris and colleagues was an investigation into neighbourhood law centres, published as A. Byles and P. Morris,

Unmet Need: The Case of the Neighbourhood Law Centre (London: Routledge Kegan Paul, 1977).

155 B. Abel-Smith, M. Zander and R. Brooke, *Legal Problems and the Citizen: A Study in Three London Boroughs* (London: Heinemann, 1973), p. xii.

156 *Report of the Law Society and Comments and Recommendations of the Lord Chancellor's Advisory Committee, 23rd Annual Report 1972–73*, HC 1 (1974) (London: HMSO, 1974), p. 35.

157 *Report of the Advisory Committee on the Better Provision of Legal Aid and Assistance*, Cmnd. 4249, pp. 11–12.

158 Ibid., pp. 36–7.

4

The trade unions and legal services

Trade union legal services emerged through the development of tort law in the nineteenth century as industrialisation led to new or different kinds of injuries that could be sustained in the workplace.[1] The trade unions responded to the impact of their members being injured at work or contracting major illnesses through the negligence of employers in three ways: first, through the collective push for legislation to improve conditions, such as the Workmen's Compensation Act 1867 and the Trades Dispute Act 1906; second, through collective action to tackle specific industries or employers; and, third, through legal support to individual members.[2] With mass membership from the early twentieth century, trade unions were the major provider of legal services to working people. Trade union membership grew rapidly in the first years of the twentieth century, with a peak in the early 1920s, before dropping dramatically in the 1930s. Membership grew again steadily between the 1940s and 1960s, before rapidly growing again in the 1970s, reaching an all-time peak in 1979. Whilst there was a further decline in raw numbers of members from 1979, proportionately more white-collar workers and women became union members from the 1980s.[3] Legal services were part of the friendly society-style benefits that unions offered their members as part of a package that – certainly before 1948 – included benefits to support members through unemployment, sickness and ill health, pensions and funeral payment. However, it was often the case that such legal support was limited to injuries or illnesses caused through work, or individual disputes with employers.

Trade unions as corporate bodies needed access to legal advice to operate as effective campaigning bodies. The Taff Vale Judgement of 1902 made trade unions liable, as corporate bodies, for damages arising out of strike action. The Trades Dispute Act reversed this through a combination of a sympathetic Liberal Government being elected in 1906 and the campaigning work of the early Labour Party.[4] For unions, legal advice and services mattered not only for managing their liabilities but also for supporting members at the point where industrial relations casework was not enough – or was not appropriate.

This was particularly the case in industrial accidents and in supporting members who were unable to work, either for a long period of time or permanently. The Workmen's Compensation Acts of 1897 and 1906 introduced and extended the principle of employers being liable for accidents, illnesses and disabilities their employees suffered because of the employers' negligence. This was an important lifeline for families who lost the earning capacity of their main or only breadwinner; yet establishing and winning a case were not necessarily straightforward.

As Roberts notes, the common law in the mid-nineteenth century provided precious little restitution for injuries or illnesses sustained at or through employment. Trade unions undertook sustained campaigning for the introduction of legislation to protect workers, from the Master and Servant Act 1867 to the Law Reform (Personal Injuries) Act 1948, but still needed the means of being able to support their members in upholding their rights in cases under these Acts. The introduction of the National Insurance (Industrial Injuries) and Law Reform (Personal Injuries) Acts in 1948 did not reduce the need for trade unions to run such departments but, rather, increased it.[5] Roberts, writing in 1956, observed that there was no fixed set of provisions offered by the trade unions, as this was determined by their rules – so some offered support only for matters arising out of work, whilst others were far more expansive in what could be covered.

By the Second World War, trade union legal departments were winning millions of pounds for their members in compensation, costs and damages, largely in relation to injuries and illnesses incurred through their employment. Despite this, the trade unions' legal departments were mostly overlooked by the major studies of access to advice on the civil law. The Finlay Committee focused mainly on the provision of pro bono legal advice at Poor Man's Lawyer evenings, though they included services by the political parties and a Trades Council.[6] Jones's 1940 survey of free legal advice replicated the same view of legal advice provision, although he mentioned briefly that both approved societies and the trade unions offered services.[7] Trade unions figured in passing in the study of legal aid and advice in three London boroughs undertaken by Abel-Smith, Zander and Brooke.[8] Why the lack of attention? Settlement houses, Councils of Social Service and other local providers of Poor Man's Lawyer work would have had a working knowledge of sources of advice – and the gaps in provision. On the other hand, Toynbee Hall in particular had close links to the labour movement and the Labour Party through its warden, J.J. Mallon, who worked on the development of the Trades Councils and remained closely linked into Labour networks.[9] Individual members of the Haldane Society were approached to do work on behalf of trade unions – as in the case of D.N. Pritt and the National Union of County Officers (NUCO).[10] Whilst the networks were there, the settlements, local Councils of Social Service and other proto-voluntary sector providers of legal advisory services were involved in trying to make the case for *their* work to attract state support. The key difference was that trade unions did not rely on voluntary work by lawyers but employed them, either through contracting the services of a solicitors' firm or by having solicitors on their salaried staff. Through paying their dues, trade union members were effectively paying for a form of legal insurance scheme, and the union would arrange for payment for the legal work. Unless otherwise agreed, there would be no additional cost to the member. The trade union legal departments may have been offering similar services to their counterparts at Poor Man's Lawyer evenings, but they were very different in both conceptual and practical terms.

Whilst trade union services were peripheral to the Poor Man's Lawyer and free legal advice centres, those studying trade unions *also* overlooked the role of the legal departments, as Latta and Lewis noted in their own survey of the field in the early 1970s.[11] Aside from mentions in institutional histories of individual unions, Latta and Lewis found that the only dedicated study of legal departments to that point was a short appendix in Roberts's 1956 study of trade union administration and governance.[12] Latta and Lewis did not explain this caesura, which persisted even in the thinking of the TUC's own survey into trade union legal services, which purposely did not examine the historical development of such provision.[13] It is possibly a reflection of the emphasis in trade unions on collective action, whilst their legal insurance tended to provide for individuals or small groups of members as a means of individual redress. G.D.H. Cole located legal services within the friendly society work of the trade unions, in which legal representation sat alongside unemployment, superannuation and funeral benefits.[14] Further to this, where legal services departments were provided in-house, as services supporting members, they were located on the administrative side rather than the negotiating and collective bargaining side.[15] In the 1930s, union spending on legal benefits was dwarfed by expenditure on unemployment, superannuation, and sickness and accident benefit. In Cole's 1939 survey of trade unions, legal benefits were in the 'other benefits' category, which included grant-making by unions and retirement lump sums. In 1930, for example, over £5 million was spent on unemployment benefit, whilst 'other benefits' accounted for £258,098.[16] However, this was money that went directly to the member rather than being paid by the union, and on this measure, the Transport and General Workers' Union's (TGWU) legal services had won £2,448,000 by 1939.[17] As state provision of unemployment and sickness benefits gradually took the onus off trade unions to support their members in this way, the ability of their legal services to secure compensation for their members became more apparent. Legal services were effectively an enforcement and application of the rights for which the unions had campaigned.

Trade unions and the Legal Aid and Advice Bill

The importance of legal services to the trade union movement was such that the TUC – the federation of British trade unions, founded in 1868 – sought to intervene in the development of what would become the Legal Aid and Advice Act 1949. As Taylor notes, the TUC sought from its foundation to represent the views of working people in Parliament; before the rise of the Labour Party, this took the form of sending deputations to government ministers. Through a combination of reorganisation in the 1920s, the growth of trade union membership and the emergence of Labour, the TUC grew in importance as a policy actor. From 1939 to the late 1970s, it exerted a powerful influence on the development of policy, particularly in relation to social welfare.[18] It also had an explicit interest in legal matters that impacted on the labour movement.[19] It was therefore unsurprising that the TUC took an interest in the Legal Aid and Advice Bill, though its concerns were not solely about the impact of the legislation on working people.

TUC deputations took place between the second reading of the Legal Aid and Advice Bill in the House of Commons on the 15 December 1948 and the third in the House of Lords on 19 July 1949.[20] During the second reading debate, trade union services figured as one of the forms of support that were available, along with Poor Man's Lawyer and Personal Service Societies. Whilst much of the debate around the Bill was uncontentious, concern was raised by Harry Wallace, MP for Walthamstow East. Drawing on his experience as a trade union official, Wallace had two main concerns. The first was whether the proposed scheme could be as responsive in practice as the trade unions' legal provision; the second focused on the Bill's Clause 4. Clause 4 concerned the 'Assessment of disposable capital and income and of maximum contribution'. Wallace's question centred on how payments to building society mortgages would be treated under the scheme. Clause 4 was key to how accessible the scheme was in practice, as it set the financial parameters in terms of who qualified for legal aid and advice. Whilst Jowitt would describe the 'controversy' on the passage of the Bill as 'extremely limited', this was not true of the relationship between the TUC and the LCO during this period. In early 1949, the TUC sent two deputations to the Lord Chancellor, Attorney-General and Solicitor-General, whilst Standing Committee A met regularly to review the Bill.[21]

Four affiliated unions – the National Union of Public Employees (NUPE), the National Union of Agricultural Workers (NUAW), the Birmingham Trades Council and the National Union of Tailors and Garment Workers (NUTGW) – raised concerns with the TUC that the Legal Aid and Advice Bill could have deleterious impacts on unions and their members. These concerns were laid out in a memorandum that formed part of the process of lobbying the Lord Chancellor over the Bill.[22] Whilst some concerns were about the funding of civil or criminal cases, or the potential for trade unionists to use the proposed legislation to sue their unions, the two most important issues were over the relationship of trade union legal provision to the proposed scheme. The unions were concerned that having recourse to trade union legal services could deny a member the chance to make use of the statutory scheme and that trade unions could become involved in administering legal aid. The potential denial of legal aid spoke to two fears. First, trade unionists might be denied civil rights that other citizens who were not members of unions could access. Second, the trade unions in question saw legal services as a critical benefit that members actively sought out and were worried that a state service would impact on membership. However, as the author of the memorandum noted, the means-testing of legal aid in terms of both income and capital meant that this was unlikely to be an issue in practice. In addition to this, the Confederation of Health Service Employees (COHSE) were also concerned that there was no lay representation on the local and area committees that would be granting aid.[23] COHSE included members who had administered the various means tests required in the Poor Law and Public Assistance frameworks, as well as hospital almoners, and therefore represented a number of professions whose members would have much to offer to the committees.

In response to these representations, the TUC sent two deputations to Jowitt, in January and March 1949, to put forward the trade unions' case. In preparation for the deputation of 28 January 1949, the General Council prepared three points to put to the Lord Chancellor. The first was about the potential for trade unionists who were otherwise eligible for legal aid to be denied it by virtue of being union members. The second was that the General Council felt that lawyers were not well suited to judging the merits of what were, essentially, social work cases. As their report put it, 'Lawyers were not always best fitted to take a humane view, nor were they necessarily qualified to evaluate the importance of working-class problems, grievances and injustices.' The third was the lack of ability to pay legal aid to trade unions as part of their work in brokering legal support for their members.[24]

The first deputation consisted of Arthur Citrine, as the TUC's legal advisor, Vic Feather, the assistant general secretary of the TUC, and a number of General Council members.[25] On this occasion, the General Council members on the deputation were Florence Hancock, then President of the General Council and chief women's officer of the TGWU, Andrew Conley, Lincoln Evans, then the chair of the Economic Committee, and Sir William Lawther, President of the National Union of Mineworkers.[26] Conley was general secretary of the NUTGW, one of the unions that had raised concerns about the Legal Aid and Advice Bill.

Lawther opened the meeting with the three recommendations: that trade unionists should be eligible for legal aid, regardless of what provision their union might make; that trade unions should be able to 'act as agents under the Legal Aid Scheme' where legal aid was available in the types of cases that trade unions dealt with; and that there should be lay members on the area and local committees who would decide on the merits of cases. Jowitt rebutted the recommendation on lay members, arguing that the decisions would be legal ones, requiring legal training. Further, the committees worked for the Law Society, which was administering the scheme, so it was important for this to be done by lawyers. Finally, the private and confidential nature of the cases to be brought also, in Jowitt's view, called for the committees to be constituted only of lawyers. He also thought that the legal profession would refuse to work with committees with lay members. Instead, Jowitt proffered, there would be an advisory committee to 'keep a check upon the operation of the Legal Aid Scheme'. This would be a lay committee, and the TUC would be able to nominate representatives to it. Union representatives would be able to accompany their members to meetings with the local and area committees. Jowitt also rejected the possibility of trade unions being agents under the scheme, as this would open up the potential for mutual insurance companies to claim the same status. The Solicitor-General, Sir Frank Soskice, felt that trade unionists had a distinct advantage in comparison to non-union members, seeing the weekly contribution to a fund that offered legal support to a non-unionist saving a similar amount each week – the latter would have their savings taken into account in the means test. Unsurprisingly, the TUC delegation disagreed with this, arguing that very little of the weekly membership contribution went towards legal funds. The meeting concluded with Jowitt agreeing to take the recommendations and a summary of the discussions to the Lord President's Committee and stating that the recommendations were more likely to become regulations rather than amendments to the Bill. Jowitt gave his 'assurance that no Regulation would be made without prior consultation with the TUC'.[27] In a subsequent letter, Jowitt conveyed the news that the cabinet was also against lay representation on the area and local committees, and also the impossibility of trying to discriminate positively on behalf of the trade unions in terms of both legal support and the ability to treat them as legal aid agents.[28]

The TUC returned to meet with Jowitt, Soskice and their team in March 1949, but prior to this, Jowitt spoke at a meeting of the National Council of Labour (NCL) at Transport House in February. Here, he spoke about his role and outlined issues with legal reform.[29] With a Labour Government in power, it was common practice for ministers to attend the NCL in order to discuss the work they had been doing.[30] As Lord Chancellor, Jowitt was part of the Government, but was a great officer of state rather than a minister. A meeting with the NCL meant that Jowitt had an audience with the TUC's General Council and the executive committees of both the Labour Party and the Parliamentary Labour Party; it was also the part of the TUC that worked most closely with advisory bodies and was involved in the coordination of policy between all the different bodies.[31] Jowitt pursued a dual career at the Bar and in politics in the interwar period, initially standing as a Liberal candidate before moving to the Labour Party in 1924. He served as Attorney-General under Ramsay MacDonald in 1931–2, and during the war, variously served in the Coalition cabinet as Solicitor-General, Paymaster-General, Minister without Portfolio, and then Minister of National Insurance. Jowitt was deeply involved with post-war reconstruction, with notable projects including a white paper on National Insurance that followed from the Beveridge Report's findings, and developing what would become the National Insurance (Industrial Injuries) Act 1946. With the Labour victory of 1945, Jowitt moved into the role of Lord Chancellor.[32] Jowitt led on the drafting and passage of what would be the Legal Aid and Advice Act, and he did so with considerable engagement with the TUC, the Labour Party and other organisations in the labour movement.[33]

The meeting with the NCL was well attended. Most of the TUC's representatives were present: its general secretary, Vincent Tewson; Arthur Deakin, the general secretary of the TGWU; Florence Hancock; Sir William Lawther; Tom O'Brien MP; and Frank Wolstencroft.[34] Sir Luke Fawcett and Dame Anne Loughlin were absent.[35] The Labour Party sent J.E. Corrin, George Daggar MP, Arthur Greenwood MP, James Griffiths MP, who replaced Jowitt as the Minister for National Insurance in 1945, and the party organiser, Morgan Phillips.[36] Present from the Co-operative Union were William Coldrick MP, chair of the Co-operative Party,[37] John Corina, chair of the union,[38] G. McAleese, H.M. Steel, H. Wilde, J.W. Blower, Lord Williams and Robert Southern, then the assistant general secretary of the Co-operative Union.[39] The Labour Lords were represented by Lord [George] Shepherd.[40] Also in attendance were R.T. Windle, the Labour Party National Agent,[41] Carol Johnson, the general secretary of the Parliamentary Labour Party,[42] George Woodcock, assistant general secretary of the TUC,[43] and Victor Feather, assistant TUC secretary.[44] Percy Cudlipp, the editor of the *Daily Herald*, was also there.[45]

The significance of this meeting can be seen in two ways. Jowitt was not just specifically talking about legal aid and advice but about his role and the need for legal reform in the Labour Party. As seen in Chapter 3, concerns about the legal capacity of the Labour Party led to the formation of the Haldane Society. The Haldane Society had split some months earlier, in 1948, over the question of communism, with some lawyers joining the rival and – critically – Labour Party-affiliated SLL. Jowitt, Soskice and the Attorney-General, Sir Hartley Shawcross, had all been members of the Haldane Society, but, given their senior positions in the Government, remaining in Haldane would have been untenable.[46] To a degree, Jowitt's visit was a reaffirmation of this role for lawyers within the Labour Party in the light of a highly acrimonious and politically charged split. The SLL and the Labour Party were, however, taking up much of the reform programme that the Haldane Society had developed. It was also an excellent opportunity to put legal reform on the agenda of the Labour Party and to influence the thinking of individuals and groups who could help. James Griffiths, the Minister for National Insurance, was a particularly important person to influence. Given his interests in trying to modernise the Labour Party by bringing more professionals into membership, Morgan Phillips was likewise a key contact.[47] Although Labour had a majority in the Commons, this was not true of the Lords, and here, Lord Shepherd had been instrumental in getting Labour bills through that stage of passing legislation.[48]

The second deputation went to meet with Jowitt, Shawcross, Soskice, Sir Albert Napier and their officials on 25 March 1949 in the House of Lords. Citrine attended, this time with Sir Luke Fawcett, J.G. Baty, H.L. Bullock, A.C. Dann, Albert F. Papworth and George Woodcock. Sir Luke Fawcett led the deputation. Fawcett was a major figure in the Amalgamated Union of Building Trade Workers, and he had been a member of the General Council for nine years by this point. He was also a member of the National Arbitration Tribunal.[49] This tribunal was set up in the summer of 1940 when Ernest Bevin, the Minister of Labour, ordered compulsory arbitration. Bevin appointed Mr Justice Simonds as the chair of the tribunal along with Sir Hector Hetherington and Sir John Forster. There were two representatives, one from the General Council of the TUC and the other from the British Employers' Federation – Fawcett was the TUC's representative on the tribunal.[50] Bullock was another important choice from the General Council. He was an official in the National Union of General and Municipal Workers. He also served on over twenty negotiation bodies and was on the National Arbitration Tribunal Panel.[51] Alfred Dann was general secretary of the NUAW. Dann began his career working in a legal firm, but a period of work on the land during the First World War changed his mind. After the war was over, he went to work for the NUAW, setting up their legal department.[52] Albert (Bert) Papworth was from the TGWU and also one of the few communists to be elected to the General Council.[53] J.G. Baty was a long-standing member and leader of the Associated Society of Locomotive Engineers and Firemen (ASLEF).[54] This deputation went to see Jowitt with a considerable wealth of expertise, not only in union matters but also in the running of legal departments and dealing with industrial disputes through mediation.

Fawcett opened the meeting by conveying the General Council's dismay at their recommendations not being taken forward, which was exacerbated by a new clause in the Bill. This new clause appeared to offer the possibility that a trade union member could seek legal aid to sue his or her union and, therefore, the possibility that the courts could serve as a route for the state and business owners to maliciously interfere in trade unions' domestic affairs. Fawcett pointed to Section 4 of the Trade Union Act 1871, which set up this exclusion. Woodcock said that the General Council had dropped their demand for lay representation in the light of Jowitt's vehement disagreement with this idea, and there was hence some expectation that their other recommendations might have been met. Clause 4 still appeared to offer the possibility of a trade unionist being denied recourse to the state legal aid fund: Woodcock argued that this was 'putting a premium on non-unionism'. The clause was removed from the Bill, but this meant that any trade unionist who was granted legal aid would see their entitlement transferred into the legal aid fund. In other words, the Law Society would be interfering with the right of the unions to administer their own business. Jowitt disputed this, arguing that trade union rule books would prevent members from being able to use the legal aid fund to sue their union and, further, that the rules also did not allow members to be indemnified for any legal expenses they incurred. Citrine was less confident in the ability of the rule books to prevent this, given variations amongst the unions, and also warned of the democratic threat of trade unions having public funds used to take action against them. Shawcross agreed that decisions on how a union should effectively use its funds should not be made by an external body and that this would come under intense scrutiny in Parliament. Woodcock returned to the democratic issue, stating that 'Trade unions had a long history of legal conflict and trade unions, not unnaturally, wished to keep out of the hands of the lawyers and of the law courts' and that this had been the point of the Trades Unions Act 1871. Therefore, the solution would be to exclude either trade unions in total or matters that related to a person doing their job. Jowitt continued to disagree with the need for this amendment but made a concession in offering to add text to the clause, with the opportunity for the General Council to approve it. Fawcett offered: 'Nothing in this Act shall empower the bringing of legal proceedings of any kind of by or on behalf of the Legal Aid Fund against a trade union in respect of any right or alleged right of an employee to legal assistance from that union.'[55]

By the time the Bill was enacted, either the offending passages had been removed or provision had been made in the accompanying regulations. Jowitt held firm on his promise to allow the TUC representation on the Advisory Committee that oversaw the operation of legal aid under the Act, with an invitation being issued in March 1950. The TUC first sought to appoint Arthur Citrine as the advisor, but this was rejected by the LCO on the grounds that the TUC representative needed to be a lay member. The TUC instead nominated Sir Luke Fawcett. The day after submitting Fawcett's nomination, the TUC received a copy from the LCO of the draft regulations that would be used to operationalise legal aid when the Act came into force in August 1950. In this draft, there was an instruction that a member of an organisation that offered legal support, such as a trade union, would be able to use the legal aid scheme provided that they had been refused support by that organisation. It also required that 'any ex-gratia payment made to the member by the organisation on account of the costs should be handed by him to the Legal Aid Fund'.[56] By the time the ensuing statutory instrument was released in August 1950, the applicable regulation made having sought and been rejected from a scheme like that offered by the trade unions a requirement for a local committee to consider an application.[57] This regulation, therefore, made trade union legal services the first port of call for members before they could be considered for the state-funded legal aid scheme – but they were not precluded from it. This dealt with the concerns of the NUPE, NUAW and NUTGW, and the presence of Fawcett on the Advisory Committee partially addressed the concerns of the COHSE and the Birmingham Trades Council.

The TUC kept a watching brief of the implementation of the Act throughout the 1950s. The Legal Aid and Advice Act 1949 was not fully implemented due to the devaluation of sterling in 1950. Whilst legal aid was supported, legal advice was not. As will be seen in Chapter 6, this had major implications for settlement houses and other charities that offered Poor Man's Lawyer services in terms of funding for their work. In December 1953, Fawcett wrote to Towson enclosing a paper from the NCSS that outlined the cost of running free legal advice centres at Cambridge House and Mary Ward Settlements and the precarity of their funding. It also highlighted the emphasis on volunteers providing a legal advisory service despite the provision made in law for this by the Legal Aid and Advice Act 1949.[58] The question of implementing Section 7 of the Legal Aid and Advice Act had been raised with the TUC from early 1952, when the Birmingham Trades Council wrote calling for this.[59] The Civil Service Clerical Association likewise wrote to Towson in September 1952, demanding the immediate implementation of the advice part of the Act.[60]

Despite these concerns, the catalyst for implementing more elements of the Act was the Housing Repairs and Rent Act 1954. The Economic Committee of the TUC considered the issue in October 1954. The devaluation of sterling had prevented legal aid being available in the county courts – where, arguably, most civil cases involving people on lower incomes would be dealt with. The Housing Repairs and Rent Act would also mean more working-class people needing legal advice to ensure that landlords complied with the Act and dealing with the implications of being rehoused. As Fawcett reported, the Advisory Committee was pushing for the full implementation of the Act, but the Conservative Government then in power did not see this as a priority. The TUC resolved to make representations on the matter to the Lord Chancellor, Lord Kilmuir.[61] Kilmuir (previously known as Sir David Maxwell Fyfe) took over the role from Lord Simonds within days of the Economic Committee meeting.[62] Tewson wrote to Kilmuir, reporting on the General Council's consideration of the Legal Aid and Advice Act 1949, in the light of the new legislation on rents and leaseholds coming into force; Tewson noted that the Advisory Committee had also been calling for the full implementation in its reports to date. He also suggested that, should it not be possible for the Act to be implemented in full, legal aid in county courts should be the first priority, followed by legal advice, and legal aid in all remaining courts.[63] Kilmuir responded in late November, stating that he agreed with the need for this to happen but that it was impossible for the Government to do this. He offered, however, to work on a priority area.[64] In early December, the Attorney-General, Sir Reginald Manningham-Buller, announced the introduction of legal aid in the county courts.[65]

As the autumn progressed, the question of legal advice rose up the agenda of the General Committee and through the grass roots of the labour movement, in part through the intervention of the NCCL issuing a circular calling for the full implementation of the Legal Aid and Advice Act. The Bermondsey Trades Council and the Beckenham, Penge and District Trades Council both wrote to Tewson in late 1954 and early 1955 calling for this on behalf of their members.[66] The Letchworth and District Trades Council wrote to Towson on 19 April 1955 calling for the Labour Party to adopt a pledge for the full implementation of the Act when it was next returned to Parliament – the General Election of 1955 was a little more than a month away at that point. The Trades Council wrote: 'the complexities of life today demand more than ever before, "the freedom of Justice" to all citizens'.[67]

As Towson laid out in correspondence with the Estimates Committee, the official position of the General Committee was for full implementation of the Act, and if that was not possible, for legal aid in the county courts to be prioritised, then for the provision of funding for legal advice, followed by legal aid being available in all remaining courts.[68] Sub-Committee D of the Estimates Committee of the House of Commons wrote to Len Murray, head of the TUC economic department, requesting trade union views on legal aid.[69]

The involvement of the TUC continued throughout the 1950s, keeping this watching brief on the full implementation of the Act. Sir Luke Fawcett remained on the Advisory Committee throughout the 1950s and until his death in 1960, when G.F. Green replaced him.[70] Sydney Robinson of the National Union of Boot and Shoe Operatives replaced Green in 1963.[71] Robinson – a direct TUC representative – remained on the Advisory Committee until 1968, when Professor Oliver R. McGregor took over his place.[72] McGregor was an important and timely choice in the light of the influence of the CPAG and interest in the rights and needs of families. McGregor was an expert on divorce and the experiences of separated couples and families; he served on the Finer Committee on One-Parent Families, which commenced its work in November 1969.[73] The next time that the TUC had a member of its General Council on the Advisory Council was 1974, when Geoffrey Drain, the general secretary of the National and Local Government Officers' Association (NALGO), was appointed; unusually for a union leader, he was a barrister by training.[74] However, the moment was lost for the TUC and the labour movement more generally, as appointees were increasingly drawn from the academic, philanthropic and practitioner community around the provision of legal advice. Trusts and foundations that funded both legal services and research into legal services were represented instead, first in the form of Lewis Waddilove and then by Patricia Thomas of the Nuffield Foundation.[75] The debates around legal advice shifted, first with the publication of *Justice for All* and *Rough Justice* and second in the light of Abel-Smith's two major books, so that attention was paid to those groups who were delivering or campaigning for improved legal services. Although they had lost their place on the Advisory Committee, the TUC remained engaged with the campaigning world around legal advice.

Surveying trade union legal support

In the 1980s, Annual Congress passed numerous resolutions calling for greater coordination of legal services in the trade union movement. In 1984, General Council decided to launch a study of legal services through its working party on legal services. Nine unions were involved in the survey: the Amalgamated Union of Engineering Workers (AUEW), COHSE, the Fire Brigades Union, the *General, Municipal, Boilermakers and Allied Trades Union* (GMBATU), NALGO, the National Communications Union (NCU), the Society of Civil and Public Servants (SCPS), TGWU and the Union of Shop, Distributive and Allied Workers (USDAW). The survey did not ask the unions for any historical information but rather, surveyed them on their position in the 1980s. The survey found that legal services were still very valuable to members, and that a good legal service could be important leverage when trying to head off competition from breakaway unions. The report argued that the reason why union legal services had survived the state legal aid scheme was that union schemes were free at the point of use and did not have the same demands in terms of means-testing or financial contributions. Union legal services were also part of a framework that was already familiar to a union member. Where cases and claims related to employment, union legal services were in a better position than, for example, a free legal advice centre lawyer to draw upon the collective bargaining and convening powers of a trade union. The report argued that the importance of legal services to members correlated with the inherent risks in the industry, with members in the heavier industries placing a greater premium on them than those in office-based professions; but this was further influenced by the specific services offered. The report found that there was a strong case for unions to publicise their legal services work as an essential function of recruiting and retaining members. It argued that, whilst greater publicity could lead to a rush of applications for legal services, this would be offset by the usual tests applied by the legal teams and also in terms of the benefits of maintaining membership in the longer term.[76]

The report noted that union rulebooks differed in the flexibility of services that they could offer. The report also noted the discretionary basis of this legal support, which prevented union legal services from being drawn into cases without any hope of resolution or vexatious litigation. The nature of legal provision also related to the risks that could be run by members, which could include criminal issues, such as driving offences, or defamation for NALGO members. Most of the unions also offered a general legal advisory service, which members could use for a wide range of personal issues for free or for a small fee, and which usually offered the chance to be introduced to another solicitors' firm if appropriate. With the pressures on unions in the 1980s – rising unemployment and deindustrialisation – expanding legal services had to be balanced against costs to the union and therefore, to members. Eligibility for membership and therefore, for legal services was an important issue. One risk that unions did face was of people joining purely to seek help with a significant legal matter. Although they would be required to pay subscriptions to access this, they would not have contributed to the cost of their case through years of earlier subscriptions – in a sense, they were acting as free riders on the scheme. Some unions required a qualifying period before the legal services could be used. Members in arrears also posed a similar risk, though the unions often wrote in the flexibility to treat members whose arrears were not necessarily their fault with discretion. One major issue was how to deal with members who moved to other unions during the conduct of a case as well as those who left the union altogether. Unemployed and retired members were usually able to access the legal services offered by their union.[77]

The survey also brought out the differences in terms of structure and the implications these had for union members. Most of the unions centralised their legal services through a specialist legal department or dedicated officer. GMBATU and TGWU had a central legal office, but a lot of work was dealt with by regional offices. The purpose of the central or regional team was to assess and triage cases to either a solicitors' firm, the union solicitors or the case officers. NALGO directly employed five solicitors and two legal executives and effectively acted as a firm of solicitors; GMBATU and USDAW both employed a single solicitor. Most of the other unions instructed external firms. Although cases were sent out to other firms, the legal departments did a lot of work in-house. Relatively minor injury cases and claims against employers, for example, were negotiated by the legal departments, as they were uncontentious. Solicitors would be consulted on the agreement of compensation and damages. Legal department staff could also work on and support members at employment and social security commission tribunals or triage the work between the executive officers of the union and an external legal firm. The legal department was also a source of legal advice in general, usually in response to officials contacting them on behalf of members. The departments were expected to be a source of support in developing union policy, as well as exploring potential test cases, and to deal with actions taken against the union itself. In terms of engaging external firms, most of the unions had one specific firm that they used; some used a couple of firms; whilst the larger ones used a wider number, employing firms based around the country rather than sending all their work to one place. The firms used often had a long-standing arrangement with the union and had built up the necessary expertise, and the unions were also more than willing to challenge bills from solicitors' firms and to shop around for a better deal.[78] The survey did not probe how this diversity in the unions' practice had come about – but we can gain a sense of this through looking more closely at a range of unions and their legal services.

Accessing trade union legal support

Practice varied between unions regarding how members could access advice and support, with some offering this through a service administered by the union's head office and others allowing it to be brokered by branches. The latter was the case with the TGWU in the 1950s, which arguably benefited members, as branches had more discretion in terms of what could be sent to a solicitor's office.[79] Such legal services could be offered either through a contracted solicitors' firm or through in-house teams. Some solicitors' firms developed trade union work as a specialism. Morrish and Company added trade union work to their portfolio around 1906, whilst Thompsons Solicitors were established in 1921 to work on trade union matters when their founder, W.H. Thompson, defended the Poplar councillors during their rebellion against increasing rates.[80] Thompson was imprisoned for being a conscientious objector during the First World War and was strongly left-wing in his political views by the early 1920s.[81] He was also an associate of the Haldane Society and one of the founders and an early chair of the NCCL.[82] Unions would offer their legal services work to specific firms, which would then take up the cases that were forwarded to them. For example, the National Union of the Footwear, Leather and Allied Trades (NUFLAT) contracted Morrish and Co. to undertake their members' legal work in the 1980s.[83]

The TGWU offered legal services through an in-house team from its foundation. The TGWU was formed in 1922 through the merger of fourteen unions, some of which represented transport workers – a broad definition, including dockers as well as road hauliers – and others 'general' workers, which included clerks in ports and local government workers.[84] In the 1940s, the secretary of the legal department was Frank Stillwell, who oversaw the central team, with regional offices in Finsbury Park, Southampton, Bristol, Cardiff, Birmingham, Salford, Glasgow, Newcastle, Leeds, Hull, Dublin, Liverpool and Shotton (for North Wales).[85] Stillwell was not, however, a lawyer – he started his working life as an office boy for Ben Tillett, whose union, the National Transport Workers' Federation, merged with others to form the TGWU in 1922.[86] A TGWU leaflet for prospective members from the mid-1940s was blunt in its portrayal of the risks some of its members faced, with an artist-drawn cover image of a crate falling onto a worker at the dockside and a photograph on the inside of a man being rescued after falling through a roof. The leaflet was also clear about how the legal department had secured over £4,500,000 in damages and compensation since 1922 and how members would be eligible for this legal support 'par excellence' from the moment of joining.[87] Within a couple of years, and with the introduction of the National Insurance (Industrial Injuries) Act 1946, the emphasis changed. A TGWU leaflet from the later 1940s was at pains to point out that claims still needed to be made with expert guidance in order to be successful – and that the legal department would support members in pursuing cases to the House of Lords, if necessary. The leaflet also pointed to a widening of the scheme, which offered advice on a range of personal matters, such as housing, superannuation schemes and income taxation, the latter two being areas that had become a concern of thousands of workers in the light of the welfare reforms of the 1940s.[88] A further leaflet from the later 1940s expressed the legal services support as an opportunity for members to 'Complete the Protection Between Parliament and the Home', emphasising the role of the legal department in *securing* the provision that members were entitled to by right.[89] In this way, the TGWU and other trade unions could ensure that the state delivered on its promises to union members.

With a high proportion of its members involved in heavy labour involving machinery, it was unsurprising that the TGWU would emphasise its legal services' ability to deal with injuries sustained at work. The precise offer and the importance of legal services were shaped by the concerns of the industry or professions served. NUCO ran a legal committee, whose primary task was to review applications for legal support. In the case of NUCO, the legal services offer was very closely related to its negotiating and campaigning work, largely because of the changes wrought to the environments in which its members worked. NUCO was originally founded in 1918 as the Poor Law Workers Trade Union, becoming the Poor Law Officers' Union in 1922.[90] The Local Government Act 1929 abolished the system of Poor Law Unions and transferred the responsibility for public welfare from the Boards of Guardians to county councils and county boroughs. The union changed its name to better reflect its membership, becoming NUCO. In 1943, it became the Hospital and Welfare Services Union, and it merged with the Mental Health and Institutional Workers Union to form COHSE in 1946.[91] Shifting the responsibility for public assistance from the Boards of Guardians to county governance also involved moving thousands of employees between employers. The Act required such 'transferred officers' to be given the exact terms and conditions of service that they had had right up to the point of transfer to their new employment. This was not necessarily a straightforward process. In many of the cases that came before the committee in the 1930s, problems caused by the transfer emerged only when the member had reason to call upon a specific condition of service or benefit. Sick pay was one example of this, as it was something which a member might have broad awareness of at the time of transfer but would not necessarily need until much later.[92] Other types of complication also arose. In a case reviewed in February 1932, a married couple whose posts were terminated claimed for compensation under the Local Government Act, but the couple's length of service was left out of the package. The general secretary reported that an appeal was lodged with the Minister of Health.[93]

The union's legal services were also able to broker changes of type of contract and conditions for its members. Members at the Dudley Road Hospital in Birmingham were moved from the City Council's manual to its non-manual pay scale. The members were in a variety of attendants' jobs, in the operating theatre, mortuary or baths, and whilst they may not have been doing the highly skilled medical work undertaken by doctors and nurses, they were not technically doing 'manual' work. The change of contract brought with it a more generous holiday allowance. The local correspondent wrote: 'It is causing quite a hubbub among the younger men of the Hospital Staff. They want to know why they cannot have the same. I have told them to join the Union and see what might happen to them.'[94] In this instance, union legal services directly benefited union members but created an inequality between non-union and union staff.

Lawyers were also able to intervene in cases that would have been difficult to solve otherwise. A charge nurse at a Public Assistance Institution hospital in Kent had a period of ill health in the summer of 1937 following an upsetting incident at work. She was given medical leave of ten days by the Medical Officer at the hospital, but she took a longer period of leave from the institution, going to Dorset for seven weeks. The nurse returned to work with two letters confirming her fitness to do so, one from a doctor in Dorset and the other from the Public Assistance Officer. The nurse continued to work without incident at the hospital until January 1938, when she requested holiday leave, which was granted. However, whilst on leave, she received a letter informing her that her employment had been terminated. The hospital subsequently provided a letter from the Medical Officer stating that she was not fit for work. The Medical Officer's letter had sufficient power to terminate her employment despite the other medical evidence – and the Medical Officer was also of high standing in the wider community. The legal opinion of the solicitor working for NUCO was that the member had a case for libel against the Medical Officer and one for wrongful dismissal against her employer.[95] In this instance, the intervention of the union solicitor had given leverage to a female employee who was at risk of being overruled and her career being damaged by a powerful professional.

Union members' engagement with legal services varied. One case dealt with by NUFLAT involved a member who was considering taking out a claim through the union's legal scheme but was also trying to engage the services of a private solicitor, apparently in order to play them off against each other. The branch officer was extremely frustrated, as he felt that the member was trying to unfairly exploit the union's legal services and was making false claims about how he was treated by the union.[96] Another NUFLAT member was delighted at how the union's legal services helped his daughter – also a member – with an injury claim. He wrote: 'I have told [her] that she was a very lucky girl to listen to me, in keeping her union dues up, once again thanking you for all the help you gave us.'[97] Whilst there was plenty of anxiety about 'ambulance-chasing' solicitors before the Second World War in any discussion of legal advice and aid reform, it would be wrong to assume that members of the public were oblivious to the financial gains that could result from successful cases or that they were passive in their dealings with solicitors. In the first of the two cases outlined here, the member was presented as problematic and ungrateful by the branch official because he was attempting to seek a better deal by hedging his bets between the union and a private solicitor; in the second, the member's pleasure on behalf of his daughter was acceptable insofar as it was framed in terms of good, citizenly behaviour in paying subscriptions and working with the union. Despite the ways in which unions advertised how much they had won for their members, notions of greed and selfishness informed behaviour around making claims.

Unlike some of the other unions in this section, the Banking, Insurance and Finance Union (BIFU) had different motivations for promoting its legal services. As a leaflet from the mid-1990s was at pains to point out, BIFU was not affiliated to the Labour Party, and strikes were an absolute last resort.[98] Although BIFU was open to members in all parts of these industries and at all levels, in the 1990s, its promotion of its legal work focused on the types of problems encountered by front-line staff in branches. In addition to the issues common to clerical work – such as repetitive strain injury cases – the union was particularly concerned with supporting members who had been injured or traumatised during bank raids. Bank raids became more commonplace after the Second World War as service weapons found their way onto the black market. Armed robbery of banks increased in the 1970s and 1980s before declining in the 1990s.[99] BIFU began monitoring raids in 1989, as the number of these attacks was rising dramatically, as well as lobbying for better safety for staff.[100] According to BIFU figures, the annual number of raids on banks and building societies doubled from 1989 to 1993; bank branches suffered 842 attacks and building societies 940 in 1993, with raids being most common in highly urban areas such as London, Greater Manchester, the West Midlands and the Bristol area.[101] BIFU launched a campaign called Raidwatch, with members reporting raids that took place in branch or targeted delivery vans.[102] This spike was believed by the banks to be driven by the wider recession of the late 1980s and early 1990s, as criminals saw it as a means of making money. The cost of the raids was ultimately high for employees in branches, as raid losses and the cost of putting in deterrents such as CCTV were used as justification for closing high-street branches.[103] From the early 1990s, armed robberies on banks declined, first, because of the deterrent technologies and second, because of the impact of massive branch closures across the sector.[104] Whilst BIFU pushed for collective solutions to the problems faced by its members – improved safety in branches, protecting members from the impacts of closures – its legal services were a means of trying to address impacts as experienced by individuals. A 1996 leaflet highlighted the union winning £15,000 for a worker after she had been injured in a raid, on the grounds of the bank's negligence.[105]

Legal services were also an area in which trade unions could potentially make money. A proposal put to the National Union of Teachers (NUT) in the late 1980s called for a radical development of the legal services provision.[106] Trade union membership was in decline in the 1980s, with the power of the unions dramatically weakened through the policies of Margaret Thatcher.[107] The NUT was restructuring its headquarters, and part of this included looking at services such as legal support.[108] The NUT paper pointed to the commercial potential of its legal services provision as a means of shifting its income from a reliance on subscriptions. Its author argued that a considerable amount of legal work was being done by lawyers working for trade unions, charities and other public interest groups as a 'service' to both the organisations and their members. With this market in mind, the author argued that a white-collar trade union like the NUT was well placed to offer an employment law service delivered through a set of computer software packs.[109] This drew upon recent developments in the field, such as LAWTEL, an electronic law database. By offering a basic service on employment law, the NUT thought that it would have a product with wide market appeal and could also draw upon its status as an 'articulate profession'. The author also recommended allowing the union solicitors to form a law firm to undertake work that would attract fees, which could involve offering services in relation to personal matters or the option to work for other trade unions.[110]

This particular plan for exploiting the potential of the legal services work did not come to pass, though the union gave careful thought to the role that legal services could play. Legal services were seen to be a means for developing a strong profile through drawing attention to the rights of teachers.[111] The union also considered ways of making legal support more accessible to members. Some of this came down to the appearance of an accessible service. A brochure was planned, which would show the legal department staff going about their daily business, and attention would also be paid to the physical environment: 'People must come out from behind desks. Walls need pictures. Chairs and tables should cease to be used as file depositories.'[112] As with other legal services, the aim was for the union member to see their union solicitor as a valuable part of what they signed up for – and a reason to keep paying their subscriptions.

Conclusion

Given their mutual basis, trade unions tended to limit the actions that they would consider to workplace matters, though they would offer advice more broadly. The Legal Aid and Advice Act 1949 was a potential threat to the trade unions insofar as it initially appeared to offer something that reduced the appeal of a trade union, and lay people with suitable expertise – who were members of a TUC-affiliated union – were excluded from sitting on the panels that decided upon eligibility. In the 1940s and 1950s, the TUC used its considerable political and economic power to ensure that the LCO engaged with its concerns and then to take a place on the Lord Chancellor's Advisory Committee. The threat of the Legal Aid and Advice Act receded, and concerns arose over ensuring that working-class concerns had a suitable remedy – such as in the case of needing support with getting repairs done to a rented property. Compensation for an injury was part of the citizenship of being a union member, a material gain for months and years of making payment and complying with the rulebook. Union legal services differed in how they were arranged, largely because of the nature and scale of the risks that their members faced and the demands this placed on their legal services. Risks were dynamic, and it was not necessarily easy to predict them or to anticipate how they would impact upon union members. Advocacy that was agile and connected with a responsive trade union team was important.

Trade union legal provision was markedly different from other forms of voluntary-run legal services, largely because trade unions raised funds through members' subscriptions. Funds supported numerous mutual aid functions, of which legal advice and aid were one. As members contributed, the issues about state funding of legal advice simply did not figure; rather, unions had degrees of gatekeeping over new members getting legal funding far in excess of what they had paid in and also about whether members were acting fairly in their expectations of the service. These were not unlike the concerns raised about the use of state funding to pay for legal aid and advice, though the emphasis here was on the earmarking of funds for use by those who had acted as good trade union citizens. Trade unions were a form of associational culture that emerged to protect workers during industrialisation, taking the shared workplace or trade as a starting point, and like friendly societies, they operated as a mutual form of welfare alongside both the Poor Law and the welfare state, though the latter took away the need for many union mutual services. In this way, the other things that unions could offer – such as legal support – became more important to both unions and members after 1948. In terms of upholding citizens' rights, the link between trade union legal services and this aim was clear: to ensure that employers and the state gave members fair treatment.

Notes

1 M. Lobban and J. Moses, 'Introduction', in J. Moses and M. Lobban (eds), *The Impact of Ideas on Legal Development, Comparative Studies in the Development of the Law of Torts in Europe* (Cambridge: Cambridge University Press, 2012).
2 The classic general text is H. Pelling, *A History of Trade Unionism* (Harmondsworth: Penguin, 1992).
3 D. Gallie, 'The Labour Force', in A.H. Halsey and J. Webb (eds), *Twentieth-Century British Social Trends* (Basingstoke: Macmillan, 2000), pp. 308–11; Department for Business, Energy & Industrial Strategy, *Trade Union Membership 2017: Statistical Bulletin* (London: Department for Business, Energy & Industrial Strategy, 2018), pp. 5–6, https://assets.publishing.service.gov.uk/government/uploads/system/uploads/attachment_data/file/712543/TU_membership_bulletin.pdf, correct at 18 June 2018.
4 See J. Thompson, 'The genesis of the 1906 Trades Disputes Act: Liberalism, trade unions and the law', *Twentieth Century British History*, 9:2 (1998), pp. 175–200.
5 B.C. Roberts, *Trade Union Government and Administration in Great Britain* (London: G. Bell and Sons, 1956), pp. 543–5.
6 *Committee on Legal Aid for the Poor – Final Report*, Cmd. 3016 (London: HMSO, 1928), pp. 14–19.
7 J. Mervyn Jones, *Free Legal Advice in England and Wales* (Oxford: Slatter and Rose, 1940), p. 7.
8 B. Abel-Smith, M. Zander and R. Brooke, *Legal Problems and the Citizen: A Study in Three London Boroughs* (London: Heinemann, 1973), pp. 58–60.
9 On Mallon and links: K. Bradley, *Poverty, Philanthropy and the State: Charities and the Working Classes in London, 1918 – 1979* (Manchester: Manchester University Press, 2009); S. Blackburn, 'Ideology and social policy: The origins of the Trade Boards Act', *The Historical Journal*, 34:1 (1991), pp. 43–64; J.M. Lee, 'The Romney Street Group: Its origins and influence – 1916–1922', *Twentieth Century British History*, 18:1 (2007), pp. 106–28; S. Blackburn, 'A very moderate socialist indeed? R. H. Tawney and minimum wages', *Twentieth Century British History*, 10:2 (1999), pp. 107–36.
10 Modern Records Centre, University of Warwick (hereafter MRC), MSS.229/NU/1/2/14 Minutes 1 September 1945.
11 G. Latta and R. Lewis, 'Trade union legal services', *British Journal of Industrial Relations*, 12:1 (1974), pp. 56–70.
12 Ibid., p. 57. See also Roberts, *Trade Union Government*, pp. 343–8.
13 MRC, 547/FLA/L/1/2, 'TUC Sample of Union Legal Services Report', Chapter 2.

14 G.D.H. Cole, *British Trade Unionism To-day* (London: Victor Gollancz, 1939), p. 17.
15 H.A. Clegg, A.J. Killick and R. Adams, *Trade Union Officers: A Study of Full-Time Officers, Branch Secretaries and Shop Stewards in British Trade Unions* (Oxford: Basil Blackwell, 1961), p. 19.
16 Cole, *British Trade Unionism*, p. 201.
17 Ibid., p. 323.
18 R. Taylor, *The T.U.C.: From the General Strike to New Unionism* (Basingstoke: Palgrave, 2000), pp. 2–3, 7, 9–10.
19 Cole, *British Trade Unionism*, p. 181.
20 *Hansard*, HC Debates, 15 December 1948, vol. 459, cols 1221–327; HL Debates, 19 July 1949, vol. 164, cols 142–4.
21 Standing Committee A, *Minutes of Proceedings on the Legal Aid and Advice Bill*, 5 April 1949 (London: HMSO, 1949).
22 MRC, MSS.292/850/3, Memorandum on the Position of Trade Unions with Regard to the Legal Aid and Advice Bill, 1949.
23 '378 Legal Aid and Advice Bill', TUC, *Annual Report 1949*, p. 279.
24 MRC, MSS.292/850/3, 'Report on Legal Aid Bill', attached to General Council Report, 1949.
25 T. Buchanan, 'Citrine, Walter Mclennan, First Baron Citrine (1887–1983)', G. Goodman, 'Feather, Victor Grayson Hardie, Baron Feather (1908–1976)', *ODNB*.
26 'Section L (376) Obituary, Andrew Conley', TUC, *Annual Report 1952*, p. 306; 'Sir Lincoln Evans', *Guardian*, 4 August 1970, p. 5; J. Saville, 'Lawther, Sir William (1889–1976)'; Buchanan, 'Citrine'; Goodman, 'Feather'; J. Hannam, 'Hancock [Married Name Donovan], Dame Florence May (1893–1974)', all *ODNB*; K. Walker, 'Hancock, Dame Florence (1893–1974)', in C. Hartley (ed.), *A Historical Dictionary of British Women* (London: Europa Publications, 2003).
27 MRC, MSS.292/850/3, 'Trades Union Congress, Legal Aid and Advice Bill, Minutes of the Deputation Received by the Lord Chancellor at the House of Lords on Friday 28th January 1949, at 11.00am'. See also '(365) National Council of Labour', TUC, *Annual Report 1949*, p. 273.
28 MRC, MSS.292/850/3, 'Report on Legal Aid Bill', attached to General Council Report, 1949, p. 3.
29 MRC, MSS.292/850/3, Minutes of National Council of Labour meeting at Transport House, 22 February 1949.
30 'Section K: Miscellaneous (365) National Council of Labour', TUC, *Annual Report 1949*, p. 273.
31 MRC, University of Warwick, 'The Trades Union Congress, 1936–1939: Its History and Organisation', https://warwick.ac.uk/services/library/mrc/explore further/digital/scw/more/tuc/, correct at 24 June 2018.
32 'The Lord Chancellor: The career and personality of Viscount Jowitt', *American Bar Association Journal* 33:9 (1947); T.S. Legg and M.L. Legg, 'Jowitt, William Allen, Earl Jowitt (1885–1957)', *ODNB*; Minister for Reconstruction, *Social Insurance, Part I*, Cmd. 6550 (London: HMSO, 1944); R.F.V. Heuston, *Lives of the Lord Chancellors, 1940–1970* (Oxford: Clarendon, 1987).

33 Legg and Legg, 'Jowitt'.
34 'Frank Wolstencroft', TUC, *Annual Report 1952*, p. 308; 'Deakin, Arthur (1890–1955)', *ODNB*.
35 'Section K: Miscellaneous (365) National Council of Labour', TUC, *Annual Report 1949*, p. 273.
36 'George Daggar Dies at 71', *Observer*, 15 October 1950, p. 1; 'Phillips, Morgan Walter (1902–1963)'; K.O. Morgan, 'Griffiths, Jeremiah [James] (1890–1975)', 'Greenwood, Arthur William James [Anthony], Baron Greenwood of Rossendale (1911–1982)', *ODNB*. Greenwood had also been a member of the Haldane Society, pre-split. N. Blake and H. Rajak, *Wigs and Workers: The Haldane Society of Socialist Lawyers 1930–1980* (London: Haldane Society of Socialist Lawyers, 1980), p. 21.
37 'Coldrick, William (1896–1975)', *Who Was Who*.
38 L. Black and T. Spain, 'How Self-service Happened: The Vision and Reality of Changing Market Practices in Britain', in D. Thackeray, A. Thompson and R. Toye (eds), *Imagining Britain's Economic Future, c.1800–1975* (Basingstoke: Palgrave Macmillan, 2018), p. 164; J.F. Wilson, A. Webster and R. Vorberg-Rugh, *Building Co-operation: A Business History of the Co-Operative Group* (Oxford: Oxford University Press, 2013), p. 226.
39 'Southern, Sir Robert (1907–1999)', *Who Was Who*.
40 D. Howell, 'Shepherd, George Robert, First Baron Shepherd (1881–1954)', *ODNB*.
41 A. Thorpe, *Parties at War: Political Organization in Second World War Britain* (Oxford: Oxford University Press, 2009), p. 59.
42 A. Roth, 'Obituary: Carol Johnson', *Guardian*, 15 August 2000, www.theguardian.com/news/2000/aug/15/guardianobituaries1, correct at 24 June 2018.
43 G. Goodman, 'Woodcock, George (1904–1979)', *ODNB*.
44 Goodman, 'Feather'.
45 G. Goodman, 'Cudlipp, Percival Thomas James [Percy] (1905–1962)', *ODNB*.
46 Blake and Rajak, *Wigs and Workers*, p. 21.
47 'Phillips, Morgan Walter (1902–1963)', *ODNB*.
48 D. Howell, 'Shepherd, George Robert, First Baron Shepherd (1881–1954)', *ODNB*.
49 'Sir Luke Fawcett', TUC, *Annual Report 1961*, p. 290.
50 'Trade Disputes in War-time', *The Times*, 20 July 1940, p. 2; The Industrial Court, www.industrialcourt.gov.uk/, 2018, correct at 27 June 2018.
51 'Section K (437) Obituary', TUC, *Annual Report 1967*, p. 436.
52 'Alfred Dann', TUC, *Annual Report 1953*, p. 288.
53 J. Eaden and D. Renton, *The Communist Party of Great Britain since 1920* (Basingstoke: Palgrave, 2002), p. 98; F. Beckett, *The Enemy Within: The Rise and Fall of the British Communist Party* (London: John Murray, 1995), p. 109.
54 'Section K (392) Obituary', TUC, *Annual Report 1959*, p. 319.
55 MRC, MSS.292/850/3, 'Report of the Deputation received by the Lord Chancellor at the House of Lords on Friday 25th March 1949'.
56 MRC, MSS.292/850/3, 'History of Case: Legal Aid and Advice Act Advisory Committee'.

57 'The Legal Aid (General) Regulations', Statutory Instrument 1950/1359, Duties of Local Committees Regulation 4, section 6.
58 MRC, MSS.292/850/3, Letter from Fawcett to Towson, 18 December 1953, and insert NCSS, 'Notes on the Voluntary Legal Advice Service', 7 December 1953.
59 MRC, MSS.292/850/3, Letter from Birmingham Trades Council to TUC, February 1952.
60 MRC, MSS.292/850/3, Letter from L.C. White of the Civil Service Clerical Association to Towson, 10 September 1952.
61 MRC, MSS.292/850/3, TUC Economic Committee, 1/5 13 October 1954.
62 D.J. Dutton, 'Fyfe, David Patrick Maxwell, Earl of Kilmuir (1900–1967)', *ODNB*.
63 MRC, MSS.292/850/3, Letter from Tewson to Kilmuir, 19 November 1954.
64 MRC, MSS.292/850/3, Letter from Kilmuir to Tewson 24 November 1954 and Letter from Tewson to Kilmuir, 29 November 1954.
65 MRC, MSS.292/850/3, Extract from Minutes of Economic Committee, 8 December 1954.
66 MRC, MSS.292/850/3, Letter from Bermondsey Trades Council to Tewson, 21 January 1955.
67 MRC, MSS.292/850/3, Letter from Letchworth and District Trades Council to Tewson, 19 April 1955.
68 MRC, MSS.292/850/3, Memo on Legal Aid to Sub-committee D of the Estimates Committee of the House of Commons, 28 February 1955, including Letter from Towson, 19 November 1954.
69 MRC, MSS.292/850/3, Internal Departmental Communication from L. Murray to George Woodcock, 25 February 1955.
70 '(344) Legal Aid Advisory Committee', TUC, *Annual Report 1961*, p. 286.
71 '(431) Legal Aid Advisory Committee', TUC, *Annual Report 1964*, p. 360; 'Robinson, Sydney Allen (1905–1978)', *Who Was Who*.
72 Lord Chancellor's Office, *Legal Aid and Advice: Report of the Law Society and Comments and Recommendations of the Lord Chancellor's Advisory Committee*, 1968–69, HC 283, p. 43. For Bragg, see A.M. Glazer and P. Thomson, *Crystal Clear: The Autobiographies of Sir Lawrence and Lady Bragg* (Oxford: Oxford University Press, 2015).
73 R. Pinker, 'Obituary: Lord McGregor of Durris', *Independent*, 12 November 1997, www.independent.co.uk/news/obituaries/obituary-lord-mcgregor-of-durris-1293591.html, correct at 11 June 2018; 'McGregor of Durris (1921–1997)', *Who Was Who*; *Final Report of the Committee on One-Parent Families*, Vol. 1, Cmnd. 5629 (London: HMSO, 1974), p. iii.
74 G. Goodman, 'Obituary: Geoffrey Drain', *Independent*, 6 April 1993, www.independent.co.uk/news/people/obituary-geoffrey-drain-1453676.html, correct at 5 July 2018.
75 For example, LCO, *25th Legal Aid Annual Reports [1974–75]* HC 629, p. 83; *29th Legal Aid Annual Reports [1978–79]* HC 309, p. 83.
76 MRC, 547/FLA/L/1/2, 'TUC Sample of Union Legal Services', ca. 1987, pp. 1, 3–4.
77 Ibid., pp. 10–12.
78 Ibid., pp. 14–18.

79 Roberts, *Trade Union Government*, pp. 545–6.

80 Leeds-based Morrish Solicitors LLP (name at the time of writing), whose first trade union client was the National Master Farriers', Blacksmiths' and Agricultural Engineers' Association in 1906. Morrish Solicitors LLP, 'Our History', www.morrishsolicitors.com/about/our-history/ (2016), correct at 5 June 2018; Thompsons Solicitors, 'Our Work with Trade Unions', www.thompsonstradeunion.law/about/our-work-with-trade-unions, correct at 24 June 2018. On Poplarism, see N. Branson, *Poplarism, 1919–25: George Lansbury and the Councillors' Revolt* (London: Lawrence and Wishart, 1979).

81 Ibid., pp. 37–8.

82 C. Moores, 'From Civil Liberties to Human Rights?: British Civil Liberties Activism' (PhD dissertation, University of Birmingham, 2010), pp. 43–4.

83 MRC, 547/FLA/L/1/1, Letter from Assistant General to Morrish and Co., 16 December 1981.

84 A. Murray, *The T&G Story: A History of the Transport and General Workers Union 1922–2007* (London: Lawrence and Wishart, 2008), pp. 39–43.

85 'To-day's Labour Personality', *Daily Herald*, 13 April 1938, p. 13; MRC, MSS.126/TG/507/1/6, 'Complete the Protection between Parliament and Home', n.d.

86 MRC, MSS.74/7/8/1–3, see http://mrc-catalogue.warwick.ac.uk/records/TLT/16/2, correct at 11 June 2018; 'Family Union', *Observer*, 2 January 1976, p. 36.

87 MRC, MSS.126/TG/507/1/5, 'This Might Have Been You', n.d.

88 MRC, MSS.126/TG/507/1/4, 'Don't Be Caught Out When an Accident Happens', n.d.

89 MRC, MSS.126/TG/507/1/6, 'Complete the Protection between Parliament and Home', n.d.

90 See M. Carpenter, *Working for Health: The History of the Confederation of Health Service Employees* (London: Lawrence and Wishart, 1988).

91 Ibid.

92 MRC, MSS.229/NU/1/2/6, Harold B. Williams and Geoffrey M. Wilson, Legal opinion on Public Assistance Order 1930, Sick Pay to Senior Poor Law Officers, 1937.

93 MRC, MSS.229/NU/1/2/1, Minutes 13 February 1932.

94 MRC, MSS.229/NU/1/2/2, Minutes 11 February 1933.

95 MRC, MSS.229/NU/1/2/8, T.A. Harrison, Legal Opinion, 4 March 1938.

96 MRC, NUFLAT, Letter from J.E. Dodds, Kendal, Furness and Lancaster Branch, 26 September 1983.

97 MRC, NUFLAT, Letter from G. Belben to G.G. Stewart, 3 November 1981.

98 MRC, MSS.56/BIFU/box 20/2, 'BIF-WHO?' n.d. (1990s).

99 R. Matthews, *Armed Robbery* (London: Willan, 2002), pp. 128–30.

100 International Labour Organization – Sectoral Activities Programme, *Social Effects of Structural Change in Banking* (Geneva: International Labour Office, 1993), p. 62.

101 'Bank Raids up by 20%', *Independent*, Wednesday, 28 April 1992, www.independent.co.uk/news/uk/bank-raids-up-by-20–1457847.html, correct at 11 June 2018.

102 'Bank–Building Society Robberies up, Union Reports', Press Association release, 27 April 1993.
103 J. Freeman, 'Bank Staff Face More Organised Criminals', *Herald*, 3 December 1993, p. 36; D. Connett, 'Armed Raids Blamed for Bank Closures', *Independent on Sunday*, 1 March 1992, p. 10.
104 D. Campbell, 'Where Did All the Bank Robbers Go?' *Guardian*, 4 July 2014, www.theguardian.com/commentisfree/2014/jul/04/where-did-bank-robbers-go, correct at 11 June 2018.
105 MRC, MSS.56/BIFU/box 20/2, 'BIFU Legal Services', March 1996.
106 MRC, MSS.880/36/7, 'A Self-Financing Union Legal Service?' n.d. (1980s).
107 E. Evans, *Thatcher and Thatcherism* (London: Routledge, 2013).
108 MRC, MSS.880/36/7, 'Legal Services', n.d. (1980s).
109 MRC, MSS.880/36/7, 'A Self-Financing Union Legal Service?' n.d. (1980s).
110 Ibid.
111 MRC, MSS.880/36/7, 'Legal Services', n.d. (1980s).
112 MRC, MSS.880/36/7, 'The Development of Union Legal Services, Phase II', n.d. (1980s).

5

Technology, access and education

As we have seen, the problems with accessing legal or any other kind of advice in person were well noted by the legal profession, voluntary organisations, the political parties and the various commissions tasked with investigating the matter. However, the intersection of the legal profession with the various media and communication technology industries offered new opportunities for combining widening access to legal knowledge with preserving restricted access to the more technical issues. This work took a range of forms, from educating the public and professionals about areas of law to providing a means of overcoming distance for those seeking advice. Calder draws our attention to the need to understand how print culture has enabled people to learn how to manage their money.[1] The same is true for legal advice and print culture. Financial and legal advice overlapped in such areas as guidance on faulty consumer goods, writing a will or dealing with a hire purchase contract; all the situations in which people on lower incomes and with less economic power needed to be able to make suitable judgements about what to do – and to be able to find help if things went wrong. Financial advice – in the form of consumer columns in magazines and newspapers or in radio or television programmes – was as much a form of legal rights education as it was about money and financial products. However, it was not just financial-legal advice and information that made use of new technologies. Print culture had a range of applications in developing legal knowledge, and emerging technologies – such as telephony – could also make direct advice more accessible for people who faced a range of practical obstacles to seeking advice by removing the need to visit a service in person. These technologies allowed communities of identity spread across the country to share information and support in new ways, often whilst maintaining privacy.

Print culture: books

The growth of the legal profession generated spin-off industries of legal publishing and librarianship. Some of the major legal publishers and imprints were founded during the eighteenth and nineteenth centuries in London, as was the case with Shaw and Sons (1750), Sweet and Maxwell (1802) and Butterworths (1818).[2] Publishing was vital, as both branches of the legal profession needed daily access to Acts of Parliament and statutory instruments, as well as the journals and texts that outlined cases and the established precedents. Librarianship was another profession that serviced the informational needs of working solicitors and barristers, providing reference materials as well as managing the inward flow of materials on the latest developments and practice.[3] Librarianship was also key within the Houses of Parliament and Whitehall for organising the legislation in the first place.[4] For legal practitioners, publishing was part of sharing professional knowledge as well as having benefits as a sideline that could provide some protection against the vagaries of self-employment. Books were an important business expense for trainee lawyers as well as for established professionals, being a form of information capital that acted as a back-up and expansion to human knowledge of the law.

The advent of compulsory elementary education to at least the age of twelve from 1870 was intended to improve Britain's competitiveness in industry and trade through improving the literacy and numeracy of the nation; it also provided further stimulus to the growing publishing industry. Books became more affordable to greater numbers of Britons during the nineteenth century. Some of this can be attributed to the business practices of firms like W.H. Smith, which branched out into selling cheap 'yellow back' books at Euston railway station in 1848, as well as the work of J.M. Dent and Sons in launching affordable versions of classic texts. The growth of public libraries, stimulated to a considerable degree by the work of philanthropists like Andrew Carnegie and J. Passmore Edwards, made books, newspapers and magazines available to those who visited them.[5] As Black notes, libraries were an important resource for the community; a source of information that could be consulted and for 'self-help' more generally.[6]

These technical and economic processes both responded to and stimulated new markets for legal books. In addition to the legal publishers publishing more generalist or popular texts, other publishers ventured into the arena. Waterlow and Sons, whose main business involved printing banknotes, also published various editions of books on the law of distress for rents – or claiming tenants' possessions in place of rent – as well as volumes on how to navigate patents in the light of new legislation and the intricacies of selling alcohol.[7] Book publishing was an appropriate format for the information to be conveyed. Such books were intended to be either read in depth or regularly dipped into and were comprehensive in their coverage. Unlike magazines and newspapers, paperback books were sufficiently robust to tolerate being carried around or regularly thumbed through. The information contained in the books would be current for a couple of years in many cases, meaning that the relatively low price of the book would be justified by its regular use, and it would not be prohibitive to buy an updated version.

That books were being published and updated regularly on particular areas of the law indicates, to a point, the degree to which those areas of the law were at the cutting edge of social, political and economic change. An example of this can be seen in the books that were published in relation to the expansion of state or charitable intervention into welfare at home or at work. May Tennant, appointed as one of the first female factory inspectors in 1893, published a book on *The Law Relating to Factories and Workshops, Including Laundries and Docks* that ran to several editions with Eyre and Spottiswoode between 1896 and 1908. Tennant was at the heart of reform of working conditions and thus had both the expert insight into the emerging legislation and the reputation to make this an important book for civil servants, lawyers, employers and trade union representatives.[8] Other guides to the law were pitched at paid and voluntary social workers, such as *The Workhouse Officers' Handbook* of 1907, the *Guide to the Law and Administration of the Needs Test* (1933) and *The Relieving Officers' Handbook* of 1930.[9] These books provided succinct guidance on the various applicable laws as well as pointers on best practice. They served as introductions to the complex world of the workhouse or needs-testing, as preparatory reading for a training course at university or college, and for updating experienced staff.

Other publications were more clearly aimed at the home library market. The 1910 *Householder's Guide to the Law with Respect to Landlord and Tenant, Husband and Wife, Parent and Child, and Master and Servant* clearly pitched itself to the middle-class male householder and the navigation of a series of (apparently) subservient relationships, as did the *Householder and the Law* (1949).[10] From the later 1950s, a growing number of publications were aimed at the motorist and the family or householder as both car and home ownership grew. Titles such as *The Motor Guide to the Law, Homeowner's Guide to the Law, The Law and You: Everybody's Guide to Everyday Problems, The Reader's Digest Family Guide to the Law* (including a version of this published by the Automobile Association (AA)), *Your Guide to the Law, The RAC Drivers' Guide to the Law*, and *The Law and You* could join a household library including such items as a dictionary, a thesaurus, religious texts, an encyclopaedia, cookery books, manuals and medical reference books.[11] Or these titles might sit usefully in a public library for consultation. The market could also include titles on law and everyday life that were becoming more culturally prominent, such as books on cohabitation from the 1970s.[12] Common to all these titles was the distillation of technical process and language into short, accessible pieces, which either provided a standard, common-sense answer to a problem or suggested that a legal or other professional – such as trading standards or a social worker – should be consulted. Having the wherewithal to spend money on a set of reference volumes was a status symbol, speaking to affluence and education.[13]

Several of the publications mentioned earlier were published by trade publishers working with consumer or subscription organisations with a strong 'reader offer'. The Royal Automobile Club (RAC) and the AA were both founded at the start of the twentieth century to support the predominantly upper- and middle-class motorist community. The RAC was concerned with the development of breakdown assistance, whilst the AA was intended to help drivers to avoid being caught speeding or driving recklessly and was involved with providing road signage until the 1930s.[14] In their own ways, both were concerned with protecting the rights of drivers and ensuring that they received affordable and reliable services, be that in terms of mechanical work or the administration of insurance. They also acted as a buffer between the driver and the state, promoting 'good' driving to try to avoid drivers being treated punitively on account of those who were 'bad' drivers.[15] Guides on the law around motoring sat very comfortably within their offer to their members and could be given to new members as a gift on joining or offered at a discount. The *Reader's Digest* was founded in the United States in 1922, offering a collection of feature articles and an abridged fictional or autobiographical article to close. It launched in the United Kingdom in 1938 and reached the peak of its popularity in the 1960s.[16] In addition to its subscription magazine, it offered volumes of condensed books alongside affordable reference works, including guides to the law. *The Law and You* was published with the Consumers' Association (later better known as *Which?* after the name of its magazine) and edited by lawyer and broadcaster Marcel Berlins. The Consumers' Association was founded in 1957 to educate consumers about their rights and responsibilities as well as campaigning for better product safety and service.[17] *The Law and You* was part of the Consumers' Association's offer to its members, being a volume for a home library in an affordable format. Offering a reference guide with basic legal principles and guidance was a method of 'soft' campaigning, giving the individual a source of information that could be called upon when needed – and that came with the Consumers' Association's branding.

Publishing by campaigning groups was increasingly important in the second half of the twentieth century, as seen in the discussion of the Haldane Society. Book publishing was a means of getting more specialised advice either into the pockets of those who needed it or into libraries, and it often fell to the organisations to publish these titles themselves or in conjunction with community presses. The Ramblers' Association published books such as *Right of Way: Footpath Law for Everyman* for planning routes or keeping in a rucksack ready to argue a case with a recalcitrant farmer or gamekeeper.[18] Similar publications were issued by the Commons, Open Spaces and Footpaths Preservation Society and the Scottish Rights of Way Society, whilst the British Museum and the Scottish Natural Heritage Society published books on wildlife and the law.[19] Concern with a wider range of rights was taken up by the publishing activities of the NCCL. The NCCL undertook research into the law on a regular basis and viewed publishing pamphlets on aspects of the law and civil liberties as a central part of its work.[20] Its more generalist book publishing included *Handbook of Citizens' Rights: A Guide to the Law for the Man in the Street* of 1954.[21] Whilst business publishers like Business Books released employers' guides to the racial and sexual equalities acts of the 1970s, the NCCL also published *Race Relations Rights: A Practical Guide to the Law on Race Discrimination*, providing guidance for individuals and advocacy groups.[22] Likewise, *The Travellers' Handbook*, published by Interchange in 1985, was aimed at supporting traveller communities as well as the statutory and voluntary social services working with them.[23] The defence of the rights of young people in Northern Ireland was central to *Rights and Responsibilities*, published by the Community of the Peace People in 1983.[24] Charitable and public sector umbrella groups could also use their collective expertise and convening powers to publish directories of use to their member bodies, such as the many editions of the legal guides for charities published under the auspices of the London Voluntary Service Council.[25] These were titles that would be unlikely to be profitable enough to attract the attentions of the trade publishers, but they addressed the needs of their members or service user groups, often being prepared and written by peers on behalf of their peers. In addition to seeking social justice ends for a specific group, the act of publishing through a community press could also put money and opportunity back into the community. It also gave the community control over what was published, how it was published and who could access it in ways that commercial publishing could not always provide.[26]

Innovations

Whilst book publishing provided a means for individuals to build up a personalised library of reference books or access to a range of generalist and specialist texts in a local library, newspaper coverage of 'problems' offered a different means of accessing guidance on legal and similar problems. Sales of daily newspapers were in the millions throughout much of the twentieth century, with their actual readership higher still. Radio also provided a mass medium for reaching the British public. The major development in terms of the accessibility of information on the law was the rise of the tabloid and the growth of the 'human interest' story as well as campaigning or service journalism. From the 1890s, Alfred Harmsworth (later Viscount Northcliffe) successfully revamped the content and style of a series of newspapers and periodicals to rapidly increase their readership and market share, creating the 'tabloid' in the process; other newspaper owners and editors followed suit in order to protect their own business.[27] The advent of the BBC radio programmes also added further competition in terms of where breaking news and interesting features could be found.[28] The 'tabloidisation' of some national newspapers entailed increasing engagement with readers and the 'human interest' story. Whilst major broadsheet newspapers like *The Times* had printed letters to the editor since 1785, such letters were written in a very formal style, often presenting a rebuttal or support of a specific point by individuals or groups with expertise in relation to an issue.[29] In contrast, the new letters pages for readers provided a forum for writing in with responses to the issues of the day or providing their own funny, sad or outrageous stories. Conboy describes the letters page as offering as an 'epistolary bridge' between the reader and the newspaper, as the letter provided the point at which the reader of the newspaper and the producers of the newspaper converged, creating a community around the publication.[30] The epistolary bridge is an important concept for understanding the way in which the tabloid newspapers in particular developed advisory services for their readers during the mid- and later twentieth centuries, as will now be seen.

Letters to the editor provided something of a means of capturing the public mood, and the *Daily Mail* employed this to full effect during the First World War. The paper set up a letters page to deal with the problems faced by soldiers but also allowed their families to write in.[31] The paper also published a range of booklets dealing with issues around military life, including 'Joining the Army' and 'Pensions, Allowances etc'. Readers could write in for a copy of the booklets, which cost 3 d with free postage. Those whose problems could not be solved through the booklet were invited to write into the 'Soldier's Friend' column and would receive a reply in the post; the answer to their question might, in addition, be included in the column.[32] By March 1918, the paper was using the term 'Soldier's Friend' as its strapline.[33] The column and the service of providing answers to the problems of those in the forces did not end with the Armistice but continued up to 1925, becoming the 'Soldiers' and Sailors' Friend' in September 1921.[34] Demobilisation was often a slow process, as was the individual's transition back into civilian life, particularly if there were issues of physical disability and psychological trauma involved.

The advice column and 'human interest' format grew in popularity during the interwar period as newspapers became more aware of what their readers wanted. During the 1930s, the development of market research approaches and the findings of the Mass Observers fuelled this process.[35] The 'agony aunt' emerged in this period, with Ann Temple at the *Daily Mail* and Dorothy Dix at the *Daily Mirror* providing advice and moral guidance to those who sent in personal questions.[36] For those interested in trying to change people's behaviour for the 'better', for moral or public health ends, the advice column and the documentary film were powerful ways of trying to educate the public.[37] 'Human interest' features could provide titillation, but this arguably arose because the people involved in the stories were 'just like us' and the scenarios could be readily imagined. Advice columns and letters pages added to this sense of 'just like us' by providing an articulation of these scenarios happening, albeit on a much smaller scale.

The epistolary bridge between newspaper staff and readers created a specific space for airing personal problems. In one sense, writing to an 'agony aunt' was easy; easier than personally seeking down professionals face to face. Yet the writing of a letter was not an easy matter. First, it required the literacy skills and confidence to be able to express a complicated and potentially deeply embarrassing problem effectively. Second, it also required a presentation of self to an unseen and imagined other. The projected or imagined audience was a kindly, sympathetic agony aunt or advice columnist, whereas the reality was – particularly after the 1940s – a member of a large team of specialist letter answerers, whose responses were highly likely to be passed through the typing pool en route to being returned to the answer seeker.[38] The letter answerers and their typists were not necessarily any less empathetic or effective than the imagined reader of the letter, but they were not the addressees in the writer's imagination. The letter-writer was positioning him- or herself as a wronged or confused party, needing to sort out a complex situation, often riven with deep emotions, into a simpler narrative. The agony aunt in turn selected the most newsworthy letters and wrote them up into the highlighted topic of the day or week, providing guidance and support in accordance with the prevailing moral outlook of the newspaper.[39]

Letters that fell into the realm of financial, legal and consumer problems could be driven by emotion and confusion on the part of the letter-writer as much as any letter seeking help in a romantic or sexual matter. Such letters also spoke to the positioning of the specific newspaper as being the 'voice' of 'the people'. The letter-writers were the victims of an uncaring or overly bureaucratic state, which either took its time or did not differentiate enough in applying its policies on the ground; they could also fall foul of sharp practices by companies and traders, being sold shoddy goods or talked into buying things they did not need. The newspaper was something that millions of readers bought each day; they were fundamental to its survival and success. The 'reader offer' emerged as a way of providing readers with an incentive to buy the newspaper and to feel ownership of it as well as being a member of the newspaper community. With millions of readers, national newspapers had fantastic leveraging powers, with the power to name and shame those who were wronging members of their community. The same was also true of the nascent BBC, though its campaigning values were filtered through the public service broadcasting principles and constraints imposed by John Reith, its director-general. The newspapers could occupy a trusted space that was neither part of the state nor a charity, and whilst they were profit-making (at least in intention, and on the backs of the readers), they offered a product that cost little and provided much. For people with little power of their own, this granted the mass media an important space in the mixed economy of welfare.[40]

The social and economic problems of the 1920s and 1930s provided opportunities for the mass media to explore their power in terms of providing services for the newly enfranchised masses. Voluntary organisations were early adopters of new media technologies and employed innovative techniques to better reach potential donors or to raise awareness of issues.[41] One example was the attempt to tackle the social impact of long-term unemployment in special areas. In 1935, the NCSS's chief advisory officer for the Midlands, Richard Clements, made twelve broadcasts on BBC radio entitled 'Question Time for the Unemployed'.[42] Listeners wrote in to the BBC with their personal questions and then received a reply from the NCSS staff. Clements' role was to explain the legislation that impacted on the lives of the unemployed, and how to navigate it, in the space of a twenty-minute programme. The service was popular, with 1,500 letters being received at the BBC in the first ten days.[43] This programme used the model set up by John Hilton, Professor of Industrial Relations at the University of Cambridge, in aiming short radio programmes to first inform the nation about its rights and responsibilities and then later, to entertain and engage people at clubs for the unemployed. Hilton had presented 'Talks for the Unemployed' and the 'National Stocktaking' in 1933, with 'This and That' the following year. He developed an evening broadcast on legal and similar issues in 1934, called 'This Way Out'. From 1936 until 1939, Hilton also wrote a column on ordinary people's issues and a readers' questions forum in the *News Chronicle*.[44]

The work of Clements and Hilton took the epistolary bridge in a new direction by quite literally speaking to audiences through the radio on the mantelpiece or sideboard. A surviving broadcast of Hilton's 'This Way Out' programme reveals a speaker with a clear, engaging tone outlining his commitment to the 'common people [...] Tom, Dick and Harry, and [...] Peggy, Joan and Kate'.[45] Hilton also had firm 'common person' credentials, having started his working life in the cotton mills of Bolton, and regularly drew upon conversations he had with people whilst he was out walking. Unlike reading a newspaper column and imagining the voice of the agony aunt during a tea break or after an evening meal, the radio broadcast brought Hilton into the room and alive to the listener.

Clements and the NCSS were effectively providing a write-in advisory service, with the broadcasts and listings in the *Radio Times* serving as a call for the public to write in. Hilton's broadcasts were equally interactive. Following the outbreak of the Second World War, Hilton resumed his broadcasts for the BBC in the form of the 'John Hilton Talking' series of programmes. This also elicited a flood of letters from the public, as did a leading article in the *News of the World* in March 1942 on the problems of the war. A thousand letters were sent to Hilton via the newspaper, which prompted the creation of the John Hilton Bureau in 1942. Hilton died in 1943, but the bureau remained in operation until the early 1970s, offering a major advisory service to the public for free in combination with publishing problems and their solutions in the newspaper.[46]

The *News of the World* was not the only national newspaper to attempt to solve the public's problems. From the late 1930s, the *Daily Herald* offered a 'free advice bureau' to any reader who wished to write in for personalised advice from one of its panel of experts. Legal advice was on offer along with guidance on poultry-keeping, politics, films, pensions and unemployment insurance.[47] Between 1943 and 1946, the *Daily Mirror* offered three columns that dealt with the problems of life during the Second World War. Mary Ferguson was recruited from the BBC to write a column entitled 'Home Service'. Ferguson was already known for her 'Women's Wartime Problems' radio programme on the BBC Home Service.[48] Ferguson saw her role as 'helping others to get justice, to find happiness, to cope with all the problems that afflict us in our daily lives'.[49] Ferguson's concept of 'justice' was a broad one, encompassing the minutiae of relationships between individual family members as well as failures of the forces or the Government to honour their responsibilities. Her column, which ran from 5 November 1943 until 29 May 1945, was concerned with daily experience on the home front. From 12 October 1944 until 31 May 1945, Barbara Betts wrote a sister column for those in the forces, 'Question-time in the Mess'. The two columns merged in 1945 to become 'Help Yourself by Asking Us', which ran until 21 August 1946. Initially, both Betts and Ferguson wrote the 'Help Yourself …' column, although Betts resigned in the summer of 1945 to take up her seat as a Labour MP in her married name of Castle.[50]

Twenty-one articles – almost one-third of the articles – in the various columns were concerned with demobilisation and the return to civilian life, with a further fourteen centred upon family finances and ten on workplace rights and responsibilities. Stability and financial security were at the centre of the letters sent in, largely about the individual negotiating the world around them. One young man feared that war work in the mines would prevent him from 'tipping up' his wages to his mother as he had long done: Ferguson advised him to tell his employment exchange so that he could make the necessary arrangements that would enable him to continue to support his mother.[51] Questions of workplace relations and pay disputes also figured prominently, such as part-time workers who wanted the same holiday entitlement as full-time workers in order to catch up with the demands of family life and war work but were advised by Ferguson that they could not have this.[52] Other cases involved people being thrown up against bureaucracy never encountered in peacetime, and the newspaper was able to give individual complaints a boost that they might not otherwise have had. Ferguson helped a serviceman who had returned home to find his wife was finding it impossible to get the paperwork she needed for necessary furniture to go directly to the Board of Trade, bypassing obstructive local officials.[53] Ferguson also took up the case of demobbed Land Girls who were routinely given shabby demob clothes, unlike women in the auxiliary services, having questions raised in Parliament and publicly challenging the leaders of the Women's Land Army.[54] Ferguson's and Betts's approach combined common sense with an ability to translate dense regulations into clear, everyday English and could encompass direct action when necessary. The national newspaper or radio programme, with its readership or audience in the millions, could exert powerful leverage over Whitehall or local government departments or private enterprises that were treating the ordinary person unfairly.

Newspaper advisory services remained an important feature of the advice landscape into the 1970s, when they merged into consumer journalism sections. In the mid-1960s, research by the solicitor and legal correspondent Michael Zander found that the caseload of the John Hilton and *Mirror/People* bureaux dwarfed the legal advice work of both private law work and settlement house legal advice centres. The two newspaper bureaux handled 150,000 cases each in 1964–5, whilst in London 23,000 people were helped by private law firms, and the London legal advice centres at Toynbee Hall, the Mary Ward Centre and Cambridge saw a total of 14,000 people.[55] Although there was a geographical limitation on the settlement houses and (to a degree) the private law firms, and there were restrictions on the types of advertising any free legal advice centre or law firm could do, it was clear that there was popular demand for an advisory service that was free and did not require a visit in person.

The position of the legal advice bureau work at the *Daily* and *Sunday Mirror* newspapers was somewhat different from that at the *News of the World*. The *Daily Mirror* launched the 'Philip Wright Readers' Service' in July 1954, which operated on the same model as the John Hilton Bureau: readers wrote in with their problems, and the Philip Wright team provided advice, sometimes taking up cases. The service cost readers nothing, and the act of passing a problem on to the service could mean that a rogue trader could be put out of business.[56] 'Philip Wright' was not an actual individual but a name used to give the sense of there being a crusading journalist at the helm of the readers' service.[57] The Philip Wright team very rarely came up with any stories that were particularly salacious; rather, the stories that they chose to highlight in their calls for readers to write in were very recognisable, everyday scenarios. They gave examples of getting the taxman to cough up a refund or of getting money back on holidays that had gone wrong.[58] These were the problems of an increasingly affluent working class, but one that was not affluent enough to be able to shrug off a late tax refund or other expense and did not have the financial resources to threaten legal action on their own. In 1955, the Readers' Service branched off once again into dealing with the problems of men in the armed forces, though this was subsumed within its standard reader offer by the end of the decade.[59] The Readers' Service was present in short articles pointing out a victory in a relatively small matter for a reader, which were placed in many cases on the same page as the popular Marjorie Proops problem page or on the teen page.[60] These articles or advertorials were close enough in their content to catch the eye of the reader and provide them with a course of action that might work for them.

Other calls to action were even more direct. In 1966, the paper combined the work of Proops, Robert Head, the city editor, and Philip Wright to offer a free financial advisory service for under-twenty-five-year-olds.[61] This age group – the putative 'teenage consumers' of Mark Abram's 1959 market research – were deemed to have more money than previous generations, along with the inability to spend it wisely.[62] Articles were accompanied by a cut-out form to structure the reader's response, which asked for details about income, marital status and hire purchase commitments. The articles were pitched at helping young people with problems and giving them advice on contracts for hire purchase and services but were still redolent of attempts from the later nineteenth century to encourage the young to rein in their spending and to think of their futures.[63] In 1969, the paper positioned itself as the 'Crusading Mirror' and presented a series of exposés about the ways in which the welfare state was not reaching out to Britons in need. Readers wrote in with tales of their own difficulties in securing tenancies or wholly inappropriate and cramped housing conditions, with other contributions from Frank Field, then director of the CPAG, a representative of the Archbishops' Council and the head of Community Transport, then a charity operating in Birmingham with needy families. A text box highlighted the services of the Philip Wright Bureau, noting that they had handled around 8,000 individual enquiries the previous year in relation to housing.[64]

Newspaper advice bureaux struggled to retain their format and purpose in the 1970s. The John Hilton Bureau was streamlined and then eventually shut down in favour of premium-rate phone lines for advice-seekers after Rupert Murdoch acquired the paper in 1969. Although the bureau was popular with readers, it was expensive to run and did not bring in sufficient income to justify its existence to managers keen to make savings at the paper.[65] The last hurrah for the Mirror Readers' Service as an advice bureau came with the three-day week, when the service provided advice on how to cope with the national state of emergency. The paper offered a cut-out guide on page 11, with a summary of how to get help with unemployment benefits, healthcare, rate relief and taking a break from mortgage payments, along with some answers to questions from readers and instructions on how to seek advice from the Readers' Service Crisis Line.[66] The advent of the 'Let off steam' column in the *Sunday Mirror* in late 1973 marked a splitting-off of reader criticism of bureaucrats and businesses into a more 'Old Codgers' format rather than going wholly into the advisory service postbag.[67] By 1974, the Readers'

Service was scaled back into the Help! Consumers' Service, which ran under Margaret Jones's byline. Jones worked as a general reporter at the *Mirror* from the early 1970s, developing expertise in consumer and women's affairs as the decade progressed. The consumers' service under Jones did not promise to answer all questions that came in but to print responses to selected queries: a much less labour-intensive way of organising the work, though one that was also less personal. As the 1970s and 1980s progressed, Jones's work straddled consumer affairs reporting – such as her 1979 report on the National Consumer Council's findings on the ways in which poorer families were being financially hammered by tallymen and inefficient heating – and women's features. In some cases, she highlighted the work of women in ensuring consumer standards, such as her feature on a twenty-three-year-old county trading standards officer.[68]

Jones's byline was used on a series of 'Square Deal' team articles written in conjunction with the Consumers' Association in 1972 and 1973. These articles sought to demystify manufacturers' and retailers' practices before providing a stinging critique. One article, printed in February 1972, outlined the huge variations permitted in the amount of orange that should be present in various types of orange drinks before going on to criticise the unclear labelling of fruit cocktail to juice or syrup ratios in various brands of tinned fruit.[69] These articles reproduced the message of the Consumers' Association through the *Mirror*'s pages, and the mutual benefits of this enterprise were considerable. As one of the bigger tabloids, the newspaper provided the Consumers' Association with a far greater platform than it had on its own; for the *Mirror*, teaming up with the Consumers' Association offered it added authenticity in getting to the heart of the things that impacted on its readers' lives. Whether the items in question were tinned food or insurance policies or white goods, the articles united against these attempts to maximise profits through a process of fudging the facts. The articles were rooted in the everyday, relatable experience of a housewife in the supermarket or department store or with a pushy salesman on the doorstep. These were highly gendered issues, with the articles explicitly using the language of 'housewife' and 'salesman' regardless of who was doing the shopping (or making or selling) or the contexts in which decisions were made at home. This structured the housewife as a woman taken up entirely by the concerns of the household, with a horizon bounded only by the drained weight of tinned fruit. It emphasised the threat to the home as a female space from devious males. Salesmen and dentists were the everyday manifestations of much larger processes of intensely detailed market research and sales targets, of the need to make profits for shareholders as the costs of transporting goods and running factories and supermarkets rose. The 'Square Deal for You' articles turned these macroeconomic processes and business practices into an everyday drama and placed them on a human scale. They also attempted to educate

Daily Mirror readers in how to protect themselves from unscrupulous practices as well as aiming to embarrass the brands in question.

By the 1970s, newspaper advice bureaux and the related columns had evolved from a service that aimed to both educate readers and tackle their problems in a range of areas to having a more specific focus on consumer affairs. By the 1970s, the print cultures of financial advice and legal advice overlapped, as educating a young person about hire purchase was as much about negotiating a binding legal contract as about appreciating the advantages or disadvantages of a deal. It also constructed those with problems as the 'little man' against the big state or big business, and the housewife, who needed to be educated and enlightened as a means of protecting the household, against an exploitative world. On the one hand, this shift reflected the newspapers' inability to afford to offer a generalist legal advisory service; on the other, more specialist providers of advice on the problems of poverty were emerging. Whilst consumer pieces were not a form of advertising, insofar as they drew out the weaknesses of a product as much as its strengths, they sat more readily within the commercial model of the newspaper. Consumer matters appealed to a much wider demographic than welfare issues might have done and also pitted the individual against big firms. The format also lent itself well to moving on to television, with programmes such as *That's Life* (1973–94) and *Watchdog* (from 1980) showing problems with products or services to the nation. This did not mean, of course, that the media lost their interest in the problems of the most vulnerable – but their ability to pay for practical help and advice in legal matters was a casualty of newspaper finances by the 1970s.

Dialling in for advice

Developments in telephone technology in the 1960s and 1970s made it possible for voluntary organisations and charities to run phone lines for advice-seekers to contact them. Phones were more readily available in British homes by the late 1960s, and there was a widespread network of call boxes; calling across distances was easy and instantaneous. With the introduction of 999 in 1939, the talking clock and a directory enquiries service in 1954, the precedent of using the telephone as a source of help and information was set.[70] In December 1953, the Samaritans launched their '999 for the suicidal', which allowed people to speak in confidence to a trained volunteer who would listen to them without judgement.[71] Subscriber Trunk Dialling (STD) from 1958 meant that callers could place calls without having to speak to an operator at the exchange.[72] This offered many possibilities for charities and voluntary organisations to reach people in new ways. First, the availability of relatively cheap calling meant that, rather than having to find time to visit an advisory service in person, an advice-seeker could make a telephone call. The telephone call might be enough to resolve the matter or it could serve as a form of triage, with the caller being directed to visit in person or to another service. Second, the telephone allowed discreet calling, with the caller phoning when their family or flatmates were asleep or out, or they could drop into a phone box at their convenience. The Samaritans provided a model for this, with callers being connected to volunteers, but the charity – set up before STD – adopted a local model, with callers ringing into their local branches.[73] Third, the ability to phone across the country without having to speak to a telephone operator meant that people could access at least initial advice from services in a different part of the country. This opened up the geographical reach of advisory services and also helped to connect those in rural areas with support.

The ability to offer discreet advisory services without geographical impediment was important for legal advisory services, which were themselves part of wider initiatives to engage with minority groups. The CABx considered a twenty-four-hour telephone service for advice in the late 1960s, with calls being routed either to advice workers' homes or to an automated answering service. They rejected this, as they did not think they should be expected to give advice at any time of day or night and also because they placed the greatest emphasis on face-to-face interviewing with the ability to turn to a well-equipped reference library. They did, however, recognise that there were cases in which being anonymous through making a phone call was important to the advice-seeker.[74] For gay men and women, phone services could offer discreet support with a reduced risk of exposure to the caller. Phone lines were also helpful to groups supporting immigrant rights as well as groups supporting students, as this allowed the advice line to support people who were spread across the country. In all cases, legal advice, or the possibility of accessing legal advice, was part of a broader package of advice. Advice lines began to proliferate in the late 1960s and early 1970s.

One of the first initiatives was the Student Advisory Centre, which was an offshoot of Richard Branson's *Student* magazine, both founded in London in 1968. Branson set up the Student Advisory Centre after experiencing trouble with trying to find reliable information when he got his then girlfriend pregnant. The advisory centre offered help on a wide range of matters, from sexually transmitted diseases, to issues with rent, to helping to connect young gay and lesbians, as Branson and his friends found that students often felt unable to confide in their parents about the things that troubled them. It offered a phone line that students could call to gain information and guidance on where to go with their problems rather than having an office to which advice-seekers would come.[75] A similar model was offered by BIT, the underground information service, founded in 1968 with a Gulbenkian Foundation grant. In its earliest days, BIT ran from a house in Notting Hill, open for people to drop in between 10.00 a.m. and 10.00 p.m. for information in person, and the phone line was open twenty-four hours a day, seven days a week, with information being given out by volunteers. BIT largely offered free information and advice on a range of topics, including legal issues, as well as free photocopying, clothes and food. In 1973, it received 1,000 phone calls a week, 300 visitors in person and 90 letters.[76]

ADVISE: Immigrant Advice Centre opened in the summer of 1970 in an office on Upper Street in Islington. ADVISE offered telephone access to its services twenty-four hours a day, seven days a week, with legal and other advice provided by black lawyers and social workers. In a 1970 *Sunday Telegraph* interview, the founder, Brother Louis, spoke of his frustration at how cases that went to the Race Relations Board took several months to go through before complainants discovered that their cases were unfounded.[77] Brother Louis – also known as Louis Nwaogu – was a journalist before setting up the ADVISE project and worked alongside three other activists: Rene Webb, Gerlin Bean and William Bloom. Rene Webb came to Britain from Jamaica in 1947, after serving in the RAF, and took paid employment in the Post Office. Webb was also instrumental in establishing a number of black community organisations and in civil rights work, including supporting the United Coloured People's Association, part of the Black Panther movement – in which Bean was also involved. Bean was also born in Jamaica and came to Britain as a child before becoming a Black Power activist in the 1960s and being heavily involved in black women's groups in the 1970s and 1980s.[78] One of the aims of the United Coloured People's Association was to provide legal aid to all black and Asian people who found themselves being racially persecuted and oppressed by the state.[79] William Bloom worked as an editor at Macmillan publishing before joining ADVISE.[80] In the interview, Brother Louis spoke of how ADVISE was going to work with a wide range of partners, from Release (a charity with expertise in drugs and drugs law) to the Government, BIT and Branson's Student Advisory Centre. The connection to BIT presumably came through Bloom, who had been involved with the *International Times*. ADVISE aimed not only to provide a free legal service to black Londoners but also to educate black people as to their rights and to offer mediation between black communities and the police, the Government and other bodies. A specific part of their offer was free legal advice to black people in dispute with their landlords or local council. The group also wanted to have a campaigning element to their work and to this end, wanted to undertake research into the conditions faced by the community.

ADVISE did not just offer help on the phone but also offered practical education and reference points. In a similar way to the Haldane Society publishing pocket-sized guides to the law for those in the services, ADVISE offered cards on common legal issues of a size that would fit easily into a pocket or wallet. One offered advice on arrest. The arrestee was advised to be 'calm, patient and polite'; that they could remain silent without penalty, but anything they did say should be polite. The card-holder was advised to insist on being able to make a phone call to their solicitor or ADVISE. If they were unable to speak to a solicitor before going to the magistrates' court, then they were advised to plead not guilty, to ask to be remanded and for legal aid, and to be bailed: this would provide the arrestee with sufficient time to get their legal advice together before going to trial. Another card offered advice on dealing with landlords. This card pointed out how landlords expected their tenants *not* to know much about the law and their rights. Tenants were advised not to permit themselves to be evicted by a landlord who had not got a court order for their eviction and to ensure that they were accompanied by a solicitor to any court proceedings. The card advised on where to take a complaint about the level of the rent and how to complain about a nuisance landlord. Both cards pointed out that ADVISE was also available in case of any doubt.[81] The cards did not prevent someone from being arrested or harassed by a landlord, but they offered just enough information to avoid that person acting against their own best interests in a very stressful situation. The points they made were clear and easy to remember, as well as quick to read in an emergency.

The line between wanting information and needing advice – potentially legal advice – was a fine one. The London Gay Switchboard was founded in 1974 as a solution to the problem of callers phoning the *Gay News* offices to ask for information or advice. It began as a seven-days-a-week phone line for its first year, moving to a twenty-four-hour service in its second.[82] By 1980, it had taken half a million calls, and it hit the million mark in October 1982.[83] There were calls to the switchboard seeking information on a wide range of topics, from the opening times of a nightclub to where to find a suitable flat share, as well as calls looking for help with civil and criminal legal matters. In 1981, the switchboard published a report on its legal work that year. Of 1,496 calls that had a legal dimension, 21 per cent related to the legal position of gay people, 9 per cent to migration, 7 per cent to employment, 9 per cent to divorce and custody of children, 9 per cent to housing, 6 per cent to being a victim of theft or assault, 6 per cent to blackmail, 10 per cent to domestic matters, 3 per cent to complaints against the police and the final 20 per cent included drugs, libel and slander, and the Mental Health Act. Legal support for gay people crossed both criminal and civil law. That the legal position of gay people accounted for the largest number of calls was unsurprising. The Sexual Offences Act 1967 decriminalised homosexual acts between men, but only in specific circumstances. As the report noted, the Act had a variable impact depending on what part of the United Kingdom a man lived in, and it could, depending on his situation and living arrangements, render any form of sex life illegal. Other Acts and by-laws could be used arbitrarily to harass, as in the case of the Public Order Act 1936 being used to harass transgender people. Homosexual activity by either men or women was illegal in the armed forces, and the switchboard offered advice to those who had joined thinking that they might find more freedom than they had experienced in civilian life. Migration law mattered for those who had left countries in which being gay could result in persecution or death. The discovery of someone's sexuality could lead to them losing their job or home or being blackmailed by someone. Being a victim of crime – for example, being attacked or robbed after leaving a gay club – was traumatic and distressing, but it could also lead to the revelation of someone's sexuality to family members or colleagues. There was also the risk, either as a victim of a homophobic crime or as someone arrested under the Sexual Offences Act or other law, of brutal and disrespectful treatment by the police.[84] The Information Group amassed a considerable amount of information on the law that the volunteers could use when responding to calls, but it still needed the capacity to refer callers on to known sympathetic solicitors, the NCCL or Gay Legal Advice (GLAD).[85]

GLAD was a legal support group established in 1977 with the aim of combatting harassment through the criminal law. GLAD aimed to support men shortly after their arrest by giving them timely advice and reassurance. GLAD also established a network of solicitors who were both sympathetic and expert in the relevant areas of law, to whom advice-seekers could be referred. In addition to dealing with the consequences of arrest and prosecution, GLAD was concerned with educating people about their rights.[86] GLAD's first three months of operation were given over to trying to assess the demand for the service. During this period, without any publicity, they received thirty-five referrals from other agencies, which convinced them that there was a pressing need for the service. They had been able to obtain free publicity through BBC Radio London and articles in *Gay News*, but they needed funding to run advertisements in gay newspapers and magazines. They also needed funds for the telephone service, which cost £270 a year. GLAD did not need an office, as callers were directed to the home of the person on duty. In 1978, when the service was in full operation, the telephone line ran between 7.00 p.m. and 11.00 p.m. with volunteers triaging the cases that came in – and at no charge to the caller. The volunteers committed to two shifts a week. They offered a combination of reassurance and immediate legal advice. All volunteers received a copy of the GLAD Manual, a folder that gave them guidance on the main types of offences with which men could be charged. This manual gave details of the maximum penalty in each case and legal notes on what the prosecution needed to prove. The manual also gave guidance on what to do if arrested. The GLAD guidance also stressed the importance of being polite. The reader was counselled to go to the police station with the officer only if they had been arrested and to ask, again politely, what the arrest was for. Pressing for the right to make a phone call was also emphasised. The manual ran through various police strategies, from trying to encourage a guilty plea for a swifter conclusion to the matter to threatening to leave the arrestee in the police cell until they were ready to talk. It also gave advice on the importance of the arrestee writing their statement, rather than the police officer, and the niceties of bail conditions – including how to apply for legal aid in the criminal court. As with the cards issued by ADVISE, the aim of the manual was to enable the volunteer to give the caller just enough information to avoid them getting into more trouble than they were already in. Although ADVISE, London Gay Switchboard and GLAD were part of the wider civil rights and liberation movements of the later 1960s and 1970s, and therefore part of attempts to alter power imbalances, all groups were acutely aware of how little power the individual on the end of the phone line had. Politeness was a way of not giving the arresting officer a reason to assault the person or concoct other charges against them; it did not necessarily mean that the individual was completely compliant with the officer. Politeness and an awareness of rights could buy someone precious time and the ability to phone ADVISE, GLAD or another organisation to get further support.

Conclusion

Emerging media technologies – from book publishing to advances in telephone exchanges – offered different types and methods of engagement with the law. Print culture could encompass everything from books for legal libraries to cards that could be slipped into a pocket or wallet to help someone at the point of arrest. Such materials could be used not only as part of an individual's education but also for rapid access to information as it was needed. Between the 1930s and the 1970s, newspapers were able to combine the educational – the weekly articles and letters that highlighted problems and solutions – with the emergent, as readers could write in for tailored help. As the 1960s progressed, developments in telephone technology offered a similar means for the individual to access help through phoning in to a volunteer who could either give them what they needed or put them in touch with the right person or service. Newspapers and radio and television programmes advertised their advisory services to millions each week, whilst London Gay Switchboard, GLAD and ADVISE were advertised through more specialist media, such as *Gay News*. Yet the principle of offering swift connection through a trusted and valued source to someone who could provide at least initial advice remained the same.

Although newspaper advice bureaux regularly provided legal and other advice, their position as an arm of the social or welfare services was increasingly untenable in the course of the 1970s. They provided a service that had a national, even international, reach and did not depend on the relative availability of lawyers volunteering their time and services. There was no need to take time off work or away from caring for relatives to chance queueing up to see a lawyer at a free legal advice centre. The Philip Wright Bureau came with the air of a crusading journalist fighting for the rights of the ordinary *Daily Mirror* reader, which it was, to a large degree. Yet it was also part of the operations of a newspaper group that needed to make money in order to survive, and this money had to be made from the readers and advertisers. Thus, scaling back from a full advice bureau that took on all cases to specialist journalists who dealt with selected queries through the consumer or finance pages made financial sense, though it limited the potential for the paper to act as a further arm of the welfare state. In a far looser way than the mutualism of trade unions, a newspaper reader bought a small stake through buying their daily copy; but newspapers needed to attract those readers their advertisers wanted to attract. As state funding for legal advice grew – however imperfectly – newspapers paying for the legal needs of their least affluent readers became harder to justify.

Book publishing and the media serviced the need for lay information to be out there and to educate the public on their rights and responsibilities. As much as the Philip Wright Bureau could take direct action, the *Daily Mirror* and the Consumers' Association could also educate readers in how to shop effectively. This was also an education for the new consumer-citizen in navigating different types of social interaction, providing protection from feeling intimidated by a salesperson. Books in the library and the potential for help from the media also came from a quarter that was not part of the state – often an antagonist – and was not a charity, which made it more palatable to many. Although the papers took advertising money from some of the companies they criticised, they were not, on the surface, part of the market that so disadvantaged the consumer. They were very much a part of the post-war welfare state in a consumerist society, helping individuals find traction against state or company bureaucracy. Yet they were also highly dependent on the advice-seeker being literate and sufficiently confident in their literacy to use a letter to articulate their problems and seek a resolution. Although they could provide a mass media solution to many problems of the masses, the lack of personal contact was insufficient for some cases that urgently needed support and guidance.

ADVISE, GLAD and the London Gay Switchboard were not necessarily educating *consumer*-citizens, or educating consumer-citizens in the same way, but they were concerned with increasing knowledge of rights. These phone lines made use of technological developments to instantly connect an advice-seeker with someone who could help them, regardless of the time or the distance involved. Their concern was with protecting vulnerable citizens, directly giving them the information they needed, and giving the landlord or police officer a warning that the person could call upon knowledgeable support. They offered strategies of politeness as a means of buying time for a lawyer to support the individual and protecting them in the meantime. The welfare state and its officers could be supportive or antagonistic, depending on the situation the advice-seeker was in. ADVISE, GLAD and the London Gay Switchboard sought to help people who belonged to a minority, whilst mass media radio programmes and newspapers aimed to address the broadest range of people. Both harnessed advice as a means to act as an advocate for people in need, using technology to make connections across time, space and place. The switchboards' activism and the newspapers' reports also drew attention to the limitations of the welfare state and legislation, pressing for change in the longer term whilst defending individual citizens in the short term.

Notes

1 L. Calder, 'Saving and Spending', in F. Trentmann (ed.), *Oxford Handbook of the History of Consumption* (Oxford: Oxford University Press, 2012). See also The History of Financial Advice project, led by Nicky Marsh and funded by the Arts and Humanities Research Council (https://gtr.ukri.org/projects?ref=AH%2FN003241%2F1, correct at 2 August 2018). Publications from the project were still forthcoming at the time of writing (August 2018).

2 Shaw and Sons, *A Good Name Endureth: The Story of Shaw and Sons Ltd.* (London: Shaw and Sons, 1950); Sweet and Maxwell, 'Company History: A Short History of Sweet and Maxwell and GEE Publishing', http://web.archive.org/web/20060822230430/, www.sweetandmaxwell.co.uk/about/history.html, correct at 13 August 2016; H. Kay Jones and W. Gordon Graham, *Butterworths: History of a Publishing House*, revised edn (London: Butterworths Law, 1997).

3 Although it refers to the United States, see C.A. Brock, 'Law libraries and librarians: A revisionist history; or more than you ever wanted to know', *Law Library Journal*, 67:3 (1974), pp. 325–61.

4 See J. Greenwood, 'Library Note: History of the House of Lords Library', House of Lords Library, Library Note 2014/041, 3 December 2014. Available via http://researchbriefings.parliament.uk/ResearchBriefing/Summary/LLN-2014-041, correct at 6 August 2018.

5 J. Feather, *A History of British Publishing* (London: Croom Helm, 1988).

6 A. Black, *A New History of the English Public Library: Social and Intellectual Contexts, 1850–1914* (Leicester: Leicester University Press, 1996), p. 116.

7 R.T. Hunter, *A Guide to the Law of Distress for Rent* (London: Waterlow and Sons, 1898); H.B. Hemming, *A Practical Guide to the Law of Patents, with Special Reference to the Patents Act 1902, and the Patent Rules, 1903 and 1905* (London: Waterlow and Sons, 1905); B.S.S. Foster, *A Guide to the Law of Licensing, so Far as It Affects the Sale by Retail of Intoxicating Liquors in England and Wales* (London: Waterlow and Sons, 1898).

8 See V. Markham, *May Tennant: A Portrait* (London: Falcon, 1949); S. Kelly, 'Tennant, Margery Mary Edith Josephine Pia (1869–1946)', *ODNB*.

9 W.H. Dumsday, *The Workhouse Officers' Handbook* (London: Hadden Best, 1907), *The Relieving Officers' Handbook* (London: Hadden Best, 1930); C.H. Exley, *The Guide to the Law and Administration of the Needs Test* (Liverpool: Meek, Thomas, 1933).

10 J.A. Slater, *The Householder's Guide to the Law with Respect to Landlord and Tenant, Husband and Wife, Parent and Child, and Master and Servant* (London: Pitman and Sons, 1910); R.M. Lester, *The Householder and the Law* (Oxford: Pen-in-hand, 1949).

11 *The Motor Guide to the Law* (London: Temple Press, 1958), P. Douglas, *Homeowner's Guide to the Law* (London: Homefinders, 1960); A.H. Thrower, *The Law and You: Everybody's Guide to Everyday Problems* (London: Thorsons, 1963); M. Zander (ed.), *The Reader's Digest Family Guide to the Law* (London: Reader's Digest, 1971); M. Molyneux (ed.), *Your Guide to the Law* (London: Secker and Warburg, 1981); R.H. Lawrence, *The RAC Drivers' Guide to the Law* (Plymouth: Macdonald and Evans, 1980 and 1981); M. Berlins (ed.), *The Law and You* (London: Hodder and Stoughton, 1987).

12 B.B. Hirsch, *Living Together: A Guide to the Law for Unmarried Couples* (London: Houghton, 1976); A. Bottomley, *The Cohabitation Handbook: A Woman's Guide to the Law* (London: Pluto, 1981).

13 See J. Rose, *The Intellectual Life of the British Working Classes* (New Haven: Yale, 2001).

14 See H. Barty-King, *The A.A.: A History of the First 75 Years of the Automobile Association* (Basingstoke: Automobile Association, 1980); P. Brendon, *The Motoring Century: The Story of the Royal Automobile Club* (London: Bloomsbury, 1997).

15 See S. O'Connell, *The Car in British Society: Class, Gender and Motoring, 1896–1939* (Manchester: Manchester University Press, 1998).

16 Reader's Digest, *The Story of Reader's Digest* (London: Reader's Digest Association, 1981).

17 See M. Hilton, *Consumerism in Twentieth-Century Britain: The Search for a Historical Movement* (Cambridge: Cambridge University Press, 2003); 'The duties of citizens, the rights of consumers', *Consumer Policy Review*, 15:1 (2005), pp. 6–12; L. Black, '*Which?* craft in post-war Britain: The Consumers' Association and the politics of affluence', *Albion*, 36:1 (2004), pp. 52–82.

18 H. Overton and H.W. Stephens, *Right of Way: Footpath Law for Everyman* (London: Ramblers' Association, 1956).

19 I. Campbell, *A Practical Guide to the Law of Footpaths* (London: Commons, Open Spaces and Footpaths Preservation Society, 1968); *Right of Way: A Walker's Guide to the Law of Right of Way in Scotland* (Edinburgh: Scottish Rights of Way Society, 1972); *Wildlife, the Law and You: An Explanation of the Wild Creatures and Wild Plants Act 1975* (London: British Museum, 1975); J. Rowan-Robinson, *Public Access to the Countryside: A Guide to the Law, Practice and Procedure in Scotland* (Edinburgh: Scottish Natural Heritage, 1993).

20 NCCL, *The Record of a Decade of Work for Democracy and Civil Liberty, 1934–1945* (London: NCCL, 1945), pp. 3, 10–11.
21 NCCL, *Handbook of Citizens' Rights: A Guide to the Law for the Man in the Street* (London: NCCL, 1954).
22 E. Mitchell, *The Employer's Guide to the Law on Employment Protection and Sex and Race Discrimination* (London: Business Books, 1976); P. Gordon, J. Wright and P. Hewitt, *Race Relations Rights: A Practical Guide to the Law on Race Discrimination* (London: NCCL, 1982).
23 B. Forrester, *The Travellers' Handbook: A Guide to the Law Affecting Gypsies* (London: Interchange, 1985).
24 *Rights and Responsibilities: A Young Person's Guide to the Law and Emergency Legislation in Northern Ireland* (Belfast: Community of the Peace People, 1983).
25 See R. Hayes and J. Reason, *Voluntary but Not Amateur: A Guide to the Law for Voluntary Organisations and Community Groups* (London: London Voluntary Service Council, 1985).
26 B. Jones, 'The uses of nostalgia: Autobiography, community publishing and working-class neighbourhoods in post-war England', *Cultural and Social History*, 7:3 (2010), pp. 355–74.
27 K. Williams, *Read All About It! A History of the British Newspaper* (London: Routledge, 2010), pp. 127–9.
28 Ibid., p. 152.
29 See 'We've Got Mail: The Greatest Letters Sent to *The Times*', *The Times*, 24 October 2017, Times 2, www.thetimes.co.uk/article/weve-got-mail-the-greatest-letters-sent-to-the-times-nkznwqw9f, correct at 6 August 2018.
30 M. Conboy, *Tabloid Britain: Constructing a Community through Language* (London: Routledge, 2006), p. 20.
31 J.L. Thompson, *Politicians, the Press and Propaganda: Lord Northcliffe and the Great War, 1914–1919* (Kent, OH: Kent State University Press, 2000), p. 183.
32 See, for example, 'Boys of 18: How They Stand under the New Service Act', *Daily Mail*, 14 June 1916, p. 6; 'Soldier's Friend: Rejected Men's Rights', *Daily Mail*, 27 July 1916, p. 2; 'Joining-up Worries: Service Act Problems Explained', *Daily Mail*, 15 June 1916, p. 6.
33 See 'In the Shipyards', *Daily Mail*, 6 March 1918, p. 2.
34 'Soldiers' and Sailors' Friend', *Daily Mail*, 29 September 1921, p. 4; 'Soldier's and Sailor's Friend', 1 October 1925, p. 13.
35 Williams, *Read All About It!* p. 160; E. Lebas, '"When Every Street Became a Cinema". The film work of Bermondsey Borough Council's Public Health Department, 1923–1953', *History Workshop Journal*, 39 (1995), pp. 42–66.
36 A. Bingham, *Family Newspapers? Sex, Private Life and the British Popular Press, 1918–1978* (Oxford: Oxford University Press, 2009), p. 75.
37 See Ibid.; Lebas, '"When Every Street Became a Cinema"'.
38 See Lord Ardwick, 'The press as an arm of the social services', *Journal of the Royal Society for the Encouragement of Arts, Manufactures and Commerce*, 119:5177 (1971), pp. 302, 308.
39 Bingham, *Family Newspapers?*; C. Langhamer, 'Sexual politics in mid twentieth-century Britain', *History Workshop Journal*, 62 (2006), pp. 87–115; *The English in*

Love: The Intimate Story of an Emotional Revolution (Oxford: Oxford University Press, 2013); 'Everyday advice on everyday love: Romantic expertise in mid-twentieth century Britain', *L'Homme: Europäische Zeitschrift für feministische Geschichtswissenschaft*, 24:1 (2013), pp. 35–52.

40 K. Bradley, 'Becoming Delinquent in the Post-war Welfare State: England and Wales, 1945–1965', in H. Ellis (ed.), *Juvenile Delinquency 1850–2000: East-West Perspectives* (Basingstoke: Palgrave, 2014).

41 See, for example, discussion of Save the Children's advertising campaigns in E. Baughan, '"Every Citizen of Empire Implored to Save the Children!" Empire, internationalism, and the Save the Children Fund in inter-war Britain', *Historical Research*, 86:231 (2013), pp. 116–37.

42 M. Brasnett, *Voluntary Social Action: A History of the National Council of Social Service, 1919–1969* (London: National Council of Social Service, 1969), p. 76.

43 'To the Unemployed: Question Time: A Service of Information', *Radio Times*, 1 February 1935, p. 25.

44 E. Nixon, *John Hilton: The Story of His Life* (London: George Allen and Unwin, 1946), p. 161; M. Hilton, 'Hilton, John (1880–1943)', *ODNB*.

45 National Sound Archive, British Library. 'This Way Out', 3 December 1936, from 3 m 23 s.

46 See Bradley, 'Becoming Delinquent'.

47 See 'Ask Us', *Daily Herald*, 18 February 1939, p. 15.

48 L. Forster, *Magazine Movements: Women's Culture, Feminisms and Media Form* (London and New York: Bloomsbury, 2015); K. Murphy, *Behind the Wireless: A History of Early Women at the BBC* (Basingstoke: Palgrave, 2016).

49 'Mary Ferguson Is Going to Give You a New Home Service', *Daily Mirror*, 18 October 1943, p. 4.

50 A. Howard, 'Castle, Barbara Anne, Baroness Castle of Blackburn (1910–2002)', in *ODNB*.

51 '24/6 Goes to Pit Boy's Mother', *Daily Mirror*, 4 February 1944, p. 7.

52 'There's a Lot of Arguing Going on', *Daily Mirror*, 18 August 1944, p. 7.

53 'Home on Leave and No Bed', *Daily Mirror*, 13 September 1945, p. 7.

54 'The Land Girl Is Getting a Shabby Deal', *Daily Mirror*, 13 December 1945, p. 7.

55 M. Zander, *Lawyers and the Public Interest: A Study in Restrictive Practices* (London: Weidenfeld and Nicolson, 1968), p. 243.

56 'Introducing a New Friend', *Daily Mirror*, 12 July 1954, p. 7.

57 Ardwick, 'The press', p. 302.

58 'The Helping Hand', *Daily Mirror*, 29 March 1960, p. 8; 'Stamped with Success', *Daily Mirror*, 13 April 1961, p. 8.

59 'The Sergeant Says Thank You', *Daily Mirror*, 27 October 1955, p. 6.

60 'Just the Job', *Daily Mirror*, 16 April 1960, p. 11; 'When the Corporal's "Civvies" Just Vanished', *Daily Mirror*, 14 December 1955, p. 9.

61 'How to Use Your Money Wisely', *Daily Mirror*, 25 April 1966, p. 1 and 26 May 1966, p. 4.

62 M. Abrams, *The Teenage Consumer* (London: London Press Exchange, 1959); 'How to Use Your Money Wisely', *Daily Mirror*, 25 April 1966, p. 1.

63 S. Olsen, *Juvenile Nation: Youth, Emotions and the Making of the Modern British Citizen* (London: Bloomsbury, 2014).
64 'We Don't Want a Palace, but …' *Daily Mirror*, 16 October 1969, p. 9.
65 See K. Bradley, '"All human life is there": The John Hilton Bureau of the *News of the World* and access to free legal advice, c.1938–1973', *English Historical Review*, 129:539 (2014), pp. 888–911.
66 'Crisis Line – at Your Service', *Daily Mirror*, 11 January 1974, p. 11.
67 'Let off Steam', *Sunday Mirror*, 28 October 1973, p. 9.
68 'Her Day', *Daily Mirror*, 26 March 1979, p. 9.
69 'Is the Answer Really an Orange?' *Daily Mirror*, 4 February 1972, p. 19.
70 See E. Moss, '"Dial 999 for Help!" The three-digit emergency number and the transnational politics of welfare activism, 1937–1979', *Journal of Social History*, 52:2 (2018), pp. 468–500.
71 'The History of Samaritans', www.samaritans.org/about-us/our-organisation/history-samaritans, correct at 7 August 2018.
72 D.A. Barron, 'Subscriber trunk dialling: The scheme for full automation of the telephone service in the United Kingdom', *Proceedings of the Institution of Electrical Engineers, Part B*, 106:28 (1959), pp. 341–60.
73 By the early 2000s, the Samaritans offered a non-geographical number that connected callers to their local branch; see J. Pollard, 'It's Good to Talk', *Guardian*, 9 June 2002, p. G69. By the mid-1990s, they had diversified the methods of contact, including the use of post, text, email and visit in person: see D. Brindle, 'A New Age of Sympathy', *Guardian*, 29 March 1995, p. 4.
74 *Report of National Citizens Advice Bureaux Council to National Standing Conference of CABx, 1966–68* (London: NACABC, 1968), p. 11.
75 R. Branson, *Losing My Virginity: The Autobiography* (London: Virgin, 1998), pp. 68–70.
76 See M. Arundale, 'Budget Rent-a-Country', *Guardian*, 30 March 1990, p. A3; C. Atton, 'The infoshop: The alternative information centre of the 1990s', *New Library World*, 100:1146 (1999), pp. 24–9; P. Shipley, *Revolutionaries in Modern Britain* (London: Bodley Head, 1976), pp. 206, 242.
77 London Metropolitan Archives (hereafter LMA), ACC/1888/250/010, Text of 'Atticus Blackhearted', *Sunday Telegraph*, 5 July 1970.
78 C. Goodwin, 'Obituary: Rene Webb', *Independent*, 17 January 2006, www.independent.co.uk/news/obituaries/rene-webb-6111501.html, correct at 11 July 2018; N. Thomlinson, *Race, Ethnicity and the Women's Movement in England, 1968–1993* (Basingstoke: Palgrave, 2016), p. 221; P. Ohene-Nyako, '*The Heart of the Race*: Black women contesting British imperialism and whiteness', *Tijdschrift voor Genderstudies*, 21:3 (2018), p. 250.
79 A.M. Angelo, 'The Black Panthers in London, 1967–1972: A diasporic struggle navigates the Black Atlantic', *Radical History Review*, 103 (2009), pp. 17–35.
80 W. Bloom, 'About', http://williambloom.com/about/, correct at 26 August 2018.
81 LMA, ACC/1888/250/010, ADVISE Leaflet and cards.
82 L. Power, 'Voices in My Ear', in B. Cant and S. Hemmings (eds), *Radical Records: Thirty Years of Lesbian and Gay History, 1957–1987* (London: Routledge, 1988), p. 146.

83 London Gay Switchboard, *1980 Report* (London: London Gay Switchboard, 1980); *1983 Report* (London: London Gay Switchboard, 1983).
84 London Gay Switchboard, *1981 Legal Report* (London: London Gay Switchboard, 1981).
85 Ibid.; *1982 Report* (London: London Gay Switchboard, 1982).
86 'New Aid Line for Gays', *Guardian*, 13 June 1977, p. 9.

6

Advisory services in the post-war welfare state

The Legal Aid and Advice Act 1949 offered much in principle to advice-seekers and the legal profession by making it possible for solicitors to undertake work on behalf of the less affluent without this being totally at their expense and without the upheaval of the profession. Unlike their medical and dental professional counterparts, legal professionals were not required to join a universal, nationalised system whilst maintaining private practice. However, the Legal Aid and Advice Act was not fully implemented until the late 1950s, and despite the efforts of the Advisory Committee, the limits on income and capital meant that only the very neediest were able to access legal aid. Critically for Poor Man's Lawyer volunteers and the organisations offering these services, the advice provisions of the Legal Aid and Advice Act were not implemented due to the devaluation of sterling in 1950. Although qualifying members of the public could use public funds to take a case to court, getting the advice in the first place meant going to a volunteer.

Advising the citizen

The lack of funding for advice work was at odds with the growing emphasis on advising the citizen on his or her rights, a governmental activity that sat between voluntary and statutory organisations. A national network of CABx was established in 1939 when it became apparent that war was brewing. This was located primarily within the non-governmental sector, with the NCSS using its national and local networks to help coordinate activity at the local level. The CABx were initially coordinated by the NCSS before the National Citizens' Advice Bureaux Committee (NCABC) took over this role. During and after the Second World War, the CABx collectively offered a mixture of voluntary activity and work funded by grants from central and local government. The Ministry of Health funded the CABx and gave support to the NCSS until 1945. A Ministry of Health circular (197/45) and the Local Government Act 1948 empowered local authorities to provide an information service, which could be through their own offices or through a CAB or other voluntary organisation.[1] This legislation was passed partly to continue the work of the CABx and partly to tackle the long-standing problem of the public not knowing as much about the offerings of local government as they might.[2] Providing information to the public, whether that was in the aftermath of a bomb strike or to involve people in planning schemes or to raise awareness of a new service, was an increasingly important part of the work of local government and led to the development of public relations departments.[3] As will be seen in this chapter, the Local Government Act 1948 was instrumental in providing a route to funding an array of different activities, and it was supplemented in due course by the creation of the urban aid fund in the late 1960s. The national network of CABx grew after the Second World War, particularly in the 1960s. Whilst individual CABx were autonomous organisations, they were linked to the National CABx Council. In addition to bringing the individual CABx together for events such as the National Standing Conference, the Council was also the point at which branches gained access to the information service and the like. The different levels of the CABx attracted different types of funding. The central services were funded by the NCSS and central government grants, usually from the Ministry of Housing and Local Government. Individual CABx, on the other hand, sought funding from their local authority through the Local Government Act 1948. Fundraising was important at all levels for topping up government grant funding.[4] In the light of the Molony Committee's report on consumer protection, published in 1962, the CABx were given additional funding from the Board of Trade to help them grow their network.[5] As a result, there were 488 individual CABx by 1968.[6]

The CABx were not established to provide *legal* advice, although some branches were able to call upon the services of a solicitor or worked closely with a Poor Man's Lawyer service. Funded through a combination of local authority grants, fundraising and voluntary action, the CABx were a means by which members of the public could be referred on to organisations that could provide them with extra support – a Poor Man's Lawyer, a free legal advice centre, the Marriage Guidance Council or the Family Discussion Bureaux. Given the inability of CABx to provide legal advice, the NCABC went to considerable lengths to ensure that the free legal advice centres their branches used were able to continue running, and they were also represented on the Lord Chancellor's Advisory Committee. The NCABC and the CABx would also become key figures in terms of ideas about how legal advice might be delivered in the future.

Bleed and consolidation: consumer and housing advice

As the work of Hilton, Robertson, Black and others has shown, supporting the consumer-citizen was a major area in post-war Britain and built on the development of co-operativism and governmentality from the nineteenth century.[7] Consumer activism intersected with free legal advice at the point at which consumers needed education on their legal rights in transactions or practical legal assistance with asserting their rights. As seen in Chapter 5, consumer rights journalism had developed alongside rights journalism in the same period, offering as it did the opportunity for the newspaper to be on the side of the 'little' man or woman.

The Board of Trade set up the Molony Committee in 1959 to look at the practice of merchandise marks and certification trademarks, largely to see what, if any, improvements could be made in law or practice to better protect consumers from shoddy goods.[8] Whilst much of the Molony Committee's work was taken up with the practicalities of industry-wide standards, labelling and testing, it was also concerned with what civil redress there might be for consumers. The Molony Report pointed to the need for 'consumer education', beginning at school, to improve consumers' understanding of their rights and responsibilities and those of retailers and manufacturers. It acknowledged that there were instances that could not be simply dealt with by taking a shoddy product back to the retailer. The committee rejected the idea of directing such complaints to a consumer council as well as a proposal to set up local tribunals for such cases. From enquiries made by the Law Society, they found that legal advice tended not to be used for consumer matters apart from in the case of issues with motor cars – which would be the largest purchase an individual or family made except for buying a property. What did meet with the committee's approval was extending consumer work to the CABx, which already dealt with a growing number of consumer matters and could absorb this work within their existing provision. The CABx would also be able to obtain the expert testing and reports that might be needed in some cases. The Consumer Council would therefore work in partnership with the national CABx on dealing with emerging issues.[9] Indeed, in addition to granting the CABx additional funding in order to help expand their reach, the Board of Trade also set up a working group with representatives of both the NACAB and the Consumer Council, with analyses of consumer issues brought to the CABx passed to this group.[10] The Consumer Council was set up in early 1963. The CABx saw their work in relation to consumer advice falling into five distinct categories: development work, in terms of expanding and developing individual branches; training; individual bureaux educating the public about their rights; enhancing the information that was available to individual CABx on consumer matters; and working with specialist bodies.[11] That the CABx would want to expand in order to discharge a national service and to build up their expertise was not surprising, and this offered an opportunity for them to further entrench their position as the premier advice provider.

However, it was not just the CABx that took on the role of providing consumer advice. As Citron notes, this area of work boomed in the 1960s, as local authorities were enabled to spend money on their own advice and information services. In addition to the consumer advice centres that were set up in many towns and cities, the National Consumer Council was set up in 1975. However, in 1979, funding for consumer advice centres was instead redirected to CABx.[12] Before this, however, levels of enthusiasm and the ability to spend money on information and advice centres differed between councils. Those that did embrace consumer and housing advice centres were keen to foreground their offer and to entice people in to use their services. Hounslow Housing Aid Centre proudly stated that it 'will tackle **any** housing problem for **you**' (original emphasis) on the cover of a booklet advertising its services. It offered statutory support on issues with landlords and arrears, with the option of using the council's solicitors. The centre would help people to get on to the council waiting list and help with exchanging council properties through offering an exchange bureau. It also offered support to people in private rented accommodation and to those considering a move out of London. Those whose homes were up for repair or demolition under the 1950s Housing Acts were also able to find support in the centre. The booklet presented the housing aid centre as pleasant and welcoming, drawing attention to a comfortable waiting room, accessible and informal discussion cubicles, a convenient board for browsing properties wanted or up for exchange, and 'before and after' photographs of houses and streets that had been improved.[13] On the one hand, the housing aid centre aimed to enable Hounslow residents to make informed, empowered choices about housing; on the other, it also provided legal support on issues with private landlords. It was not clear how those who were in dispute with Hounslow, as a landlord in its own right, were handled by the centre.

The London Borough of Lambeth ran a consumer advice centre on Electric Avenue in Brixton, right in the heart of the main shopping area and keeping the then standard shop opening hours of 9.30 a.m. to 4.30 p.m. in the week and 10.00 a.m. to 4.00 p.m. on Saturday. The centre offered the chance for consumers not only to find out about what the best options in the shops would be for them but also to access support. The centre would also support shopkeepers who were dealing with customers making unreasonable or illegal demands.[14] By offering advice on the best choices for a consumer, the consumer advice centre was competing with the burgeoning work of the Consumers' Association's *Which?* magazine, founded in 1957 by Michael Young, and *Good Housekeeping* and its Good Housekeeping Institute, as well as other consumer pages in the press. Whilst the others could take up the cases of individuals or groups, the advice centre offered advice on the high street on aspects of consumer law and trading standards – minutes away from the shops where purchases were made.

Advice centres of these types offered the public the chance to drop into a physical location to discuss an issue that concerned them without necessarily having to go out of their way. In both examples here, the publicity materials took pains to point out that this was a convenient and helpful service and one that was free. These centres were funded through the same legal mechanism that empowered local authorities to fund legal advice centres. But if there was an emerging area of advice that was provided directly by local government, or funded by the state, voluntary providers had a different experience.

The settlement houses, advice and the post-war world

For those legal advisory services running since the 1890s, there were two critical challenges in the post-war period. The first was repositioning themselves as 'Free Legal Advice Centres' rather than 'Poor Man's Lawyers'. 'Free legal advice centre' was a perfect description of what was provided for the majority of people who used it, as only a small proportion needed more substantial work done on their behalf. 'Poor Man's Lawyer', in contrast, was not particularly clear about what was offered other than couching it in terms of the status of the advice-seeker – and it implied that there was something lacking about both the lawyer and the client.

The name changes began with the outbreak of the Second World War, in tandem with the launch of the CABx. The Family Welfare Association (FWA) supported the existing Poor Man's Lawyer services at three settlements to expand their services to full-time, beginning with Cambridge House in September 1939, Mary Ward Settlement in August 1942 and Docklands Settlement in August 1945.[15] Both Mary Ward and the Cambridge House had long-standing and popular Poor Man's Lawyer evenings. The other large and long-standing Poor Man's Lawyer, Toynbee Hall, was referring to its service as a legal advice centre by 1955.[16] However, it was still using 'Toynbee Hall Poor Man's Lawyer' in late 1953, and the NCSS used this as a generic term for a volunteer-run legal service.[17] The three settlements had close ties with CABx, either in their neighbourhoods or with one on site, as was the case with Toynbee Hall. As CABx could not offer legal advice, renaming the service as a 'Free Legal Advice Centre' was a way of clearly outlining what was on offer.

The FWA was established as the COS in 1869, changing its name in 1946. As seen in Chapter 2, the COS had been involved in the development of professional social work, pioneering the use of casework with families and individuals and trying to provide tailored yet efficient support to people. The COS philosophy was to use knowledge of the family and the local social work context to its most efficient effect. The social worker would draw on his or her expertise or direct the family to an external agency.[18] Many of its cases had legal disputes as a compounding factor in the multitude of problems faced by a family. One case study in the FWA's 1954 annual report painted a picture of a man who was devoted to his family but who had such chronic financial and legal problems that he wanted to run away from them to make their lives easier.[19] The central FWA was keen to support legal advice work because of its importance to its staff, volunteers and clients – hence its interest in good access to advice.

The FWA was not involved in the day-to-day running of the centres but instead, took on the role of applying for and administering grant money to run them into the 1960s. Benjamin E. Astbury, the general secretary of the FWA, was particularly involved in this work.[20] Astbury was head of the FWA from 1938 until 1956 and had been responsible for its change of name as well as the increasing focus of the organisation on family casework at the expense of trying to build the voluntary sector.[21] During the early stages of the Second World War, Astbury set up the CABx in Inner London. He was later on the Lord Chancellor's Advisory Committee, as well as other committees in relation to the law and charities, such as the National Executive of the NCSS.[22] Astbury had a deep commitment to the provision of legal aid and advice, and he made considerable efforts on behalf of the three free legal advice centres.

During the war and into the immediate post-war period, the free legal advice centres were funded by grants from the City Parochial Foundation and the Pilgrim Trust alongside money from US donors channelled through the British War Relief Society. By the summer of 1947, the American money had stopped, and the two grant-making trusts were about to come to an end. This prompted Astbury to write to *The Times* calling either for the Rushcliffe recommendations to be passed into legislation or for foundations like the City Parochial and Pilgrim to be enabled to continue their support.[23] As seen in Chapter 1, the drafting and passage of the Legal Aid and Advice Bill began in the months after Astbury's letter. Once the Bill was enacted, however, the problems for the free legal advice centres did not come to an end. From the 1950s until the 1970s, the two legal advice centres – the Docklands Settlement left the agreement by 1949 – continually had to fight to make their case for why they should be funded through grants to do this work when there was a government scheme.

As the summer of 1948 progressed, funds were made available for the legal advice centres by a grant from the LCC.[24] This grant was contingent upon the Legal Aid and Advice Bill being enacted in its entirety, meaning that there would be provision for paying for legal advice; it became apparent in late 1949 that this would not be the case. The LCC was therefore keen to remind the centres that the grants were only available until the full legal aid and advice scheme came in, and they wanted the centres to accept a reduction in the grant in the meantime.[25] This was not out of line with the thinking of the settlements with regard to the Act and its provision. J.V. Alexander, then sub-warden of Mary Ward Settlement, had been working on the assumption that its centre would have come under the provision of the Act by the end of the financial year – and that it would have to shut down without any support.[26]

The centres were able to make their case to the LCC for grant funding in early 1950 and also successfully sought financial support from both of their earlier funders, the Pilgrim Trust and the City Parochial Foundation.[27]

However, in August 1951, the centres' funding was in question again. A crisis meeting was held between staff and councillors of the LCC, the FWA and the two settlements at County Hall on 1 August 1951 with the aim of setting the council's policy towards the two centres. Henry Brooke, the leader of the opposition, raised the concern that the centres were seeking permanent, full-time funding for work that had previously been done by volunteers.[28] He was rebutted by Kenneth Nunn of Mary Ward. Nunn stated that whilst volunteer lawyers continued to provide legal advice at the settlement, legal advice was only effective when it was possible to take the cases to the lower courts, and that this required lawyers on the payroll. With the position clarified, the meeting proceeded to discuss plans for reducing the cost of the centres and keeping an eye on what could be provided through the Act.[29] The LCC grants were substantial, in the region of £5,500 per annum, and provided at least half of the centre's income.[30]

The remaining money, on the Mary Ward side of the operation, was patched together from various sources. The advice centre applied each year to the Society for the Discharge and Relief of Persons Imprisoned for Small Debts for regular annual grants of around £40 to £50, whilst donations from the Poor Box Funds of London police courts, such as that at Bow Street Magistrates' Court, also provided sums in the region of £5 to £10.[31] Leopold Spero, one of the centre's solicitors, also made approaches to potential funders, including Montague Burton of the Burton clothing company.[32] Burton was not able to make a major donation to the centre, but he did make a contribution of £5.[33] Other donations came from companies, such as the Oxford Street department store, Selfridges, which enclosed a cheque with a note thanking the centre for the support it had offered their staff.[34] Other examples of donations included £50 in 1953 from Martins Bank, a private banking firm, and £4.4.0 from Gestetner Limited, a maker of copying machines in Edmonton.[35] In these cases, the local link – be that in terms of employees and their families using the centre or through the professional and trade networks that existed between businesses – was important. An approach to the Nuffield Foundation in 1953 not only resulted in a rejection but also revealed the precariousness of the centres' funding, as some foundations and trusts had stopped making grants to them, and the LCC was adamant that the centres were not its 'special liability'.[36]

In March 1951, Astbury and the two settlement wardens, Eric E. Deuchars (Cambridge House) and C.C. Walkinshaw (Mary Ward), wrote to the editor of *The Times* newspaper to make an appeal for a sum of £2,500 to keep the centres afloat between the end of the LCC grant in May 1951 and the end of the following financial year in March 1952. They drew attention to how the Legal

Aid and Advice Act 1949 funded cases that would go to the High Court, but provision for the kinds of welfare-related advice work that the centres did had not been made available due to financial constraints.[37] Whilst this brought in some offers of help, the precarity meant that, in May 1951, all the solicitors working at the Mary Ward legal advice centre were put on a month's notice of redundancy.[38] Likewise, both of the legal advice centres had to strictly manage their resources. Cambridge House opened on Mondays, Tuesdays, Wednesdays and Fridays between 10.30 a.m. and 12.45 p.m. and 2.15 p.m. to 4.45 p.m., with a Thursday evening session for new callers who could not make a daytime session only. They were at pains to point out to the voluntary and statutory organisations that referred people to them that the evenings were solely for those who could not attend in the daytime. The Cambridge House centre accepted cases where the total income was £4.10s per week or less, allowing an extra 5s per week per child.[39] The Mary Ward legal advice centre was slightly more generous than its counterpart in Camberwell, allowing a single person £3.10s or less a week and couples £4.10s, with a 10s allowance per child under 16 years of age.[40] It was also open each weekday as well as having one weekly session in the evening.[41] Its clients were very clearly not the affluent working classes but those who were dependent on a rapidly evolving welfare state and those who were essentially the working poor. Demand was high. The first half of 1951 saw 2,534 new cases come to the Mary Ward legal advice centre – which meant around 90 to 100 new cases each week. The work was undertaken by three full-time, paid solicitors, assisted by four full-time and one part-time member of clerical staff, with the ability to instruct twenty or so barristers in a part-time and voluntary capacity.[42]

High demand and precarity meant ever more measures to try to bring income in. A letter to supporters of the Mary Ward Settlement and the legal advice centre in March 1953 was at pains to highlight the work that the settlement had done since the start of the century:

> Free legal advice has been available at the Mary Ward Settlement since the early 1900's and it seems incredible that this service to the lowest wage earners and Old Age Pensioners should be coming to an end. Many have been saved eviction from their homes, others have had their compensation claims properly handled, others still have unburdened themselves and many have been advised where necessary against court action.

Yet the letter then went on to discuss the need to introduce a registration fee of 2/6 d for all new clients because the financial situation had reached a breaking point.[43] The settlement sought the permission of the Law Society's legal advice committee to do this under the terms of the Legal Aid and Advice Act, emphasising that this was purely to reduce their overheads and not to benefit the solicitors.[44] In August 1953, Howard Roberts, the clerk of the LCC, wrote to inform the FWA and the two settlement centres that the council would award a further £1,445, and in December, he confirmed a further year's grant for the year 1954–5.[45]

The situation of the Mary Ward and Cambridge House advice centres became the focus of activity across a number of organisations as the 1950s progressed. Kathleen Oswald, the secretary of NACAB, led on much of this. Oswald had joined the NCSS in 1929, working for it until 1937, when she joined the National Fitness Council before working for the Ministry of Health as a regional welfare officer during the Second World War. She rejoined the NCSS in 1945 before moving to its CAB department in 1946.[46] Oswald did a considerable amount of networking and lobbying behind the scenes.

In October 1956, staff of the free legal advice centres, the Law Society and the NCSS met to discuss how best to implement the advice part of the Legal Aid and Advice Act. The meeting noted how the two main political parties had committed themselves to the full implementation of the Act in their manifestos for the 1955 General Election. The Conservatives were readying the provision of legal aid in the county courts, and they further wanted to bring the legal advice scheme in during the life of the next Parliament.[47] The meeting concurred that any national scheme for legal advice that used voluntary organisations to deliver it would need financial support from the Government. The NACAB noted that they had set up a standing committee to watch the development of the legal advice scheme.[48]

In November 1956, Oswald wrote to Sir George Haynes about the two centres. Like Oswald, Haynes was a long-standing member of staff at the NCSS, having served as its director since 1940.[49] Oswald commented that the centres offered support for those whose legal needs extended only to having a letter prepared for them but who would be unlikely to be able to easily afford to pay for this service at market rate and yet would not qualify for the statutory scheme. Oswald also noted the importance of understanding foreign legal questions, given the diverse communities in London. She also pointed to how the Poor Man's Lawyer centres valued the CAB staff for the work they did in preparing clients for referral to their services, which could include compiling paperwork and undertaking research.[50] The LCC remained conflicted regarding funding the two centres. The LCC was clear that it did not have any responsibility or requirement to provide legal advice, but it also valued the work done by the centres and did not wish to see them collapse. However, its funding was only to serve as a stopgap.[51]

In early November 1958, Oswald wrote to the Permanent Secretary of the Lord Chancellor's Department, Sir George Coldstream. Oswald drew upon a letter she had also sent to the Law Society. Oswald made the point clear to Coldstream that Section 7 of the Act needed to be implemented and also drew his attention to the point that cases often needed more than pure oral advice. There was often a need to do research around the cases, and therefore, more than one meeting was required. Oswald also called for the need to continue to support the three legal advice centres in London as well as to look at how there could be cooperation between social work agencies, such as the NACAB, the National Marriage Guidance Council and the FWA, and the legal profession. Oswald felt that it was essential for the legal profession to have access to professionals with better insight into the needs of working-class advice-seekers. The problem, as she saw it, was the combination of people who were not used to approaching lawyers for help with their problems and the extent to which their legal problems were mixed in with social problems.[52]

In December 1958, Sir George Coldstream replied to Oswald.[53] Coldstream was then the Permanent Secretary to the Lord Chancellor and Clerk of the Crown in Chancery, replacing Sir Albert Napier in 1954.[54] Some weeks earlier, Coldstream had welcomed Oswald, the chair and vice-chair of the NACAB, and the chair of the London CAB to a meeting at the House of Lords, where they had put to him ideas about the future of the CAB.[55] As was his standard practice, Coldstream had taken the representations to the Lord Chancellor, Kilmuir, for his consideration, reminding him also that the Advisory Committee was raising similar issues. Coldstream had also informed the Advisory Committee about the discussions he had had with the NACAB representatives. Kilmuir listened to the representations of NACAB, the Advisory Committee and the Law Society and made a number of decisions. First, he believed that Sections 5 and 7 of the Legal Aid and Advice Act 1949, which covered legal aid in matters not concerning litigation and the right to and nature of legal advice, respectively, would not reduce the need for the Poor Man's Lawyer centres that were attached to CABx. Kilmuir also stated that he was happy to speak to the LCC about the need to continue to support free legal advice centres. The NACAB also asked how the statutory and voluntary social services would communicate with each other in relation to Section 7. Kilmuir confirmed that the Law Society would circulate to all the voluntary organisations information about the statutory scheme for legal advice and their voluntary version of the scheme, and would send all the forms. Likewise, the Law Society would see to it that all solicitors would be given details of all voluntary and statutory social services in their area so that they could refer a client on as appropriate. Kilmuir also reassured the NACAB that the solicitors would recognise the value of the social service agencies in dealing with the more holistic – and often not legal – issues that impacted on the lives of working-class clients. He pointed out, however, that confidentiality rules meant that the solicitors could not report back to the referring social service agencies without the express permission of the client.

This precarity became the norm in the 1950s and 1960s for the two settlement legal advice centres and the FWA, as the LCC – and the Greater London Council (GLC) after 1965 – granted them a series of three-year grants to cover their work. The council generally accepted that the centres had a very important role in the community but regularly raised queries about the work, largely on the grounds of cost. Some of this was due to concern to avoid replicating work that could be covered by the governmental legal aid scheme, as was reported by W.O. Hart of the LCC to the FWA and centres in their 1963 round of case-making.[56] A meeting between the LCC, the FWA and the centres at the LCO in June 1963 also raised the same issue, with the LCC pointing out that only one-sixth of the cases that came to the centres were outside the remit of the legal aid scheme – and that the funding of the centres should be adjusted accordingly. Hume Boggis Rolfe,[57] then assistant solicitor in the Lord Chancellor's Department, wanted to know what was the justification for the two advice centres in those two parts of London when similar provision was not available in other parts of London or indeed, in other British towns and cities.[58] In 1967, when a meeting was convened, this time at County Hall and between Sir William Hart of the GLC, the FWA and the centres, the same question was raised.[59] The query was a reasonable one – if the centres were so important and so special, why weren't they being replicated elsewhere?

The rationality of the legal aid scheme did not necessarily meet the needs of those who might need legal advice. In a letter to Alexander, Nunn wrote how he felt that the solicitors at the free legal advice centres did things that their counterparts in private practices 'could not entertain'.[60] What the legal advice centres had was the time to listen properly and at length to the people who came to them with their legal problems, because they were not trying to work to the imperatives of a busy commercial office. When consulted as part of the 1967 case-making, E.A.L. Watts of the London Marriage Guidance Council (LMGC) wrote to Mary Ward, stating that he felt that the legal advice centres were to solicitors what the LMGC was to doctors in general practice: professionals with the time to listen and to engage with the emotional needs of the client.[61]

The need for the two legal advice centres at Cambridge House and the Mary Ward Settlement was not doubted. A report by the warden of Cambridge House, R.L.L. Guthrie, argued that the people of Lambeth and Camberwell – its main constituency area – had a resident to legal aid scheme lawyer ratio of 1:8,300 in comparison with a national rate of 1:2,600. Guthrie noted that the three main authorities involved in overseeing legal advice in this case – the LCC, the LCO and the Law Society – all believed that the work met an important need but that the work needed to 'cost less'. The annual cost of the centre in 1964 was just under £4,000, but if funded fully through the official legal aid scheme, it would have cost £15,000. The only rational solution in Guthrie's eyes was to close the scheme or reduce the demand for it.[62]

The LCC continued its support of the centres up until its dissolution in 1965, despite the eventual implementation of advice provision under Section 7 of the Legal Aid and Advice Act. The LCO wrote to Sir William Hart, the clerk of the LCC, in early February 1965 in response to a letter from Justice about the Cambridge House grants in the next three years. The view of the office was that whilst there was a case to be answered about a service that only ran in one part of the country and that potentially duplicated the statutory service, Gardiner, now the Lord Chancellor, 'appreciates the valuable work that the three centres have done and would consider very sympathetically giving his support to any proposal to continue the payments'.[63]

In 1965, W.O. Hart and W.L. Abernethy, the clerk and treasurer to the Council, respectively, produced a report for its General Purposes Committee on the funding of the centres. They noted the extent of the work undertaken by the centres, picking up cases that came from 'borough councils, probation officers, hospital almoners, citizens advice bureaux, Rent Tribunals, and the National Assistance Board', helping them with oral advice, writing letters and, if necessary, providing representation at court or in tribunals. Hart and Abernethy drew attention to the scale of the work, with 6,000 cases being dealt with at Cambridge House and Mary Ward Settlement and 1,260 at University House Bethnal Green, which had joined the group. The LCC was happy that the three centres were working as economically as they could and that they had exhausted all other sources of funding. Hart and Abernethy noted that the legal advice scheme had come into force in 1961, and whilst the centres had been supposed to scale back at this point, it had not been practical to do so:

> [T]he centres took the view that it would not be practicable simply to halve their organisation. They also made a strong plea to be allowed to continue full-scale operation as a worthwhile social service which went considerably beyond purely legal advice. They argued the difficulties in the kind of cases they deal with, of disentangling the legal from the social elements of the problem. It is apparent that the centres fulfil needs for legal advice that are not met by official schemes.[64]

Hart and Abernethy had articulated what the centres had been arguing since the early 1950s: that working-class advice-seekers were not necessarily well served by the 'normal' model of seeking advice from a solicitor. Absent from Hart and Abernethy's report – and, indeed, the others – was any direct engagement with what advice-seekers themselves might have wanted. Their views were implicit, taken from the thousands of people who made visits to the free legal advice centres each year.

In a second report, Hart and Abernethy stated that the LCC would take on the provision of the centres with the FWA, with increases in the funding over the following three years to be decided.[65] The successor body to the LCC would fund the free legal advice centres into the 1980s, when they came under pressure to pass the funding for free legal advice centres and the neighbourhood law centres to the borough councils – as will be seen later in this chapter. Despite the promises offered by the Legal Aid and Advice Act 1949, the reality for settlement houses was harsh. Philanthropic funders were reluctant to fund work that was about to be taken over by the state, and making the case that the state – whether local, city or central – should fund it was not a straightforward matter.

Neighbourhood law centres

The first of the neighbourhood law centres opened in North Kensington in July 1970, in a former butcher's shop in Golborne Road. Peter Kandler, a solicitor, was the main instigator of the project, as he felt that lawyers were failing to act effectively in the interests of the working classes – for example, that they acted on behalf of landlords but not of tenants. A documentary in 1973 pointed out that the informality and shabby surroundings of the law centre belied a very efficient legal service. The law centre's funding came from legal aid and voluntary donations, which had allowed the centre to employ three solicitors, including Kandler, by 1973 – but they remained heavily reliant on volunteers. In the documentary, Kandler stated that the aim of the law centre was to bring law to the people and to prevent them from 'being crushed by the system they find themselves in'.[66]

Like their counterparts at Mary Ward and Cambridge House, the law centres had considerable problems with securing an income stream. The legal aid schemes were one source of income, and the shift to the green form scheme after 1973 helped with this. But the law centres required funding to keep their premises running and their staff in jobs, and they looked to various sources for this. The urban aid programme launched by the Labour Government in 1968 was an important source of funding for law centres, as well as a range of advice and support centres that could present law centres as a form of urban regeneration work.[67] Yet, as the 1970s progressed, the law centres experienced major difficulties with their finances. The Lord Chancellor, Elwyn-Jones, announced an additional £50,000 of funding to keep law centres afloat on 30 July 1974. The following July, Lord Gardiner, a previous Labour Lord Chancellor, asked for a statement on whether the Government would continue to fund the law centres. The Lord Chancellor stated that the £50,000 had been given with no future commitment to funding the centres. However, it had been possible to find £100,000 within the Lord Chancellor's budget that could be used for supporting the running of the law centres pending the approval of Parliament. Elwyn-Jones was clear that this, also, was not a commitment to future funding.[68] In April 1975, Thomas Williams, the Labour MP for Warrington and a working barrister, moved to introduce a Bill to formally establish neighbourhood law centres. Williams's logic in this was that inflation had rendered the statutory legal aid provision out of reach of most Britons, and that the law centres that had emerged in London, Cardiff and Manchester were a means by which the law could be made accessible to more people. The law centres were open in the evenings and weekends, when working people could get to them without having to take time off work. Home visits were also on offer to those who could not easily visit the law centres, such as disabled and elderly people and those caring for relatives. Williams pointed to the Lord Chancellor's £50,000 bailout that year of law centres in financial trouble and argued that his private member's Bill would allow the centres to be formally created with a sustainable funding stream.[69] A couple of weeks later, Elwyn-Jones said, in an answer to a parliamentary question, that he wanted to support them as fully as possible and thanked those local authorities who had funded them or supported them in other ways.[70] The Legal Aid Advisory Committee had called for a revision of the legal aid limits, which the Law Society and Supplementary Benefits Commission had undertaken. The limits were changed by the Legal Advice and Assistance (Financial Conditions) (No.2) Regulations 1975. During the discussion of this statutory instrument, Elwyn-Jones referred to the Advisory Committee's report, which drew his attention to the critical issue of the supply of legal advice. He was acutely aware of the shortage of solicitors and was impressed by how 'young people [had] taken it upon themselves to set up law centres' as well as how the Law Society was encouraging its solicitors to use the advice scheme.[71]

The key difference between the funding of the settlement centres and the law centres focused on the perceived political nature of the work in the latter. Robert Vigars, a Conservative member of the GLC and chair of its General Purposes Committee, wanted to know what funding the North Kensington law centre was getting, as it was 'publishing a monthly newssheet and sponsoring dramatic productions advocating a certain type of political action as a solution to local social problems?' The response was that that the law centre had been given £7,500, with no further commitment, and that it had been confirmed that the centre published a bulletin and offered 'short plays to demonstrate civil rights'. The GLC also received letters of concern about the behaviour or presence of the law centre, such as a letter of February 1975, which complained that the law centre was listed in the phone book as a solicitors' firm and that it was against the law for solicitors to make a profit using taxpayers' money; a letter of January 1975 wanted to know what parliamentary Act allowed the GLC to grant money to the law centres.[72] The replies to the last two letters mentioned were not kept in the archives, but the precarious finances of most law centres strongly suggested that profits were rare. The Local Government Act 1948 and the Local Government Grants (Social Need) Act 1969 were only two Acts of Parliament that facilitated this type of grant-making. The concerns of these letter-writers spoke to the abiding idea of lawyers as profiteers, taking public money for their own good; in the case of Vigars, they were also inflected with the idea that public money was being used to promote radical, left-wing politics. Unlike the CABx or the settlement houses, it was much harder for the law centres to present themselves as 'neutral' advice providers – and it went against their philosophical principles.

Law centres in action

The Brighton law centre opened in 1984. The law centre was a relatively small operation, with six staff, half of whom were part-time and half full-time; by 1990, the team had reduced to five staff members. They were funded by Brighton Borough Council with the rate negotiated each year. There were two solicitors, one development worker, one legal advice worker and one administrator. A typing assistant was provided by the Manpower employment training scheme, which the law centre topped up as necessary.[73] Whilst the staff had different, yet complementary, backgrounds and areas of expertise, all took part in the running of the centre. The 1987 Annual Report drew attention to the way in which the lawyers were 'self-servicing': essentially doing the majority of their own secretarial work. Like many other professionals, solicitors and barristers had passed their typing, copying and filing work to others. In the case of the legal profession, legal secretaries undertook this work. Although this meant that the lawyers could focus on their professional work, the fact that letters, contracts and other documents were passed from a solicitor to a legal secretary necessarily added to the cost of the service. For a law centre running on a tiny budget, a solicitor who typed his or her own letters and, in the case of Brighton, also helped out with answering the phones and greeting callers in person was a means of keeping staff costs down – but that solicitor then had more to do. The solicitors were also less distant from advice-seekers than they might otherwise have been. Advice-seekers came to the centre through a number of ways – the majority phoning for advice and being invited to a clinic in the early evening, or a Thursday lunchtime if this was appropriate in their case. Others visited in person, whilst others wrote in. The law centre staff were all involved in this work and in the triaging of the cases that came in.[74]

The aim of the law centre was to make the law as accessible as possible to people, partly through tackling the big, persistent issues of not knowing which problems might need legal remedy and the fear of taking a problem to a solicitor, and partly through proactive legal education. This took various shapes, from the publication of leaflets on common problems, which were translated into community languages, to collaborations with local activist groups. By 1990, development work had become an important area of their work. The law centres developed four distinct objectives to their work: legal education and encouraging people to use the law centre; making statutory organisations change their policies and procedures to better support citizens; supporting local voluntary and statutory organisations and community groups by providing advice on legal matters; and identifying areas in which legal needs were not being met.[75] As seen so far, three of these objectives were common to most types of free legal advice provision in terms of trying to make the public aware of their rights and the services that could help them to enforce them, finding out where problems were occurring, and working with other organisations. What was new was the objective to influence statutory organisations in terms of their policy.

The cases that came to the Brighton law centre reflected the nature of the city. With 21 per cent of Brighton residents living in private rented accommodation, a considerable amount of their work focused on supporting these tenants.[76] As the Housing Act 1988 proceeded through Parliament, the law centre worked with the Brighton Private Tenants' Action Group on a survey of private tenants' experiences. They found that 90 per cent of tenants had not been given any advice or direction on what to do if a fire broke out, a quarter were harassed by their landlords, 17 per cent had experienced an attempt at an unlawful eviction and half lived in damp conditions. This certainly painted a picture of tenants who were at best, ignored by landlords disinterested in dealing with suitable repairs and at worst, actively threatened. A further threat of the Housing Bill was the potential for rents to rise. The Housing Act 1988 essentially created a market in the private rental sector by removing protections around rent restrictions. In places like the south-east of England, where land and property prices have tended to be higher than in many other parts of the United Kingdom, this was an incentive to potential landlords to consider renting to private tenants. But it also meant that tenants faced the prospect of rents increasing further at the same time as landlords also gained enhanced powers of eviction for rent arrears. The law centre also acknowledged that, whilst council tenants also had problems, private tenants did not have one common landlord but rather, had to contend with a multiplicity of degrees of helpfulness, availability, avarice and awareness of the law. Living in a tourist destination, private tenants also had to navigate a market of so-called 'holiday lettings' and 'out of season lettings', which often ignored or compromised a tenant's rights in law.[77]

Immigration law was a further area that evolved in the late 1980s, as the centre believed that what would become the Immigration Act 1988 would make it progressively harder for black people to visit the country.[78] It also represented a further deterioration in the rights of Commonwealth citizens. The Immigration Act 1971 had clarified the status of Commonwealth citizens ahead of Britain's entry to the European Economic Community, allowing Commonwealth citizens the right to bring their families to join them in the United Kingdom. The Immigration Act 1988 introduced a requirement for Commonwealth citizens to prove that they could support their families without recourse to public funds before their families could join them.[79] During the run-up to the passing of the Act, one of the centre solicitors wrote to the MP for Brighton Kemptown, Andrew Bowden, to ask him to oppose the Bill on its first reading in Parliament in November 1987. He drew Bowden's attention to the discriminatory nature of the Bill: it intended to slow down or stop the movement of around 3,000 people per year from the Indian subcontinent but did nothing about the status of the millions of people with British-born parents or grandparents who could simply enter the United Kingdom and claim benefits without opposition. He also noted some further issues, such as the loss of the right to appeal against a deportation order unless there had been an error of law, which meant that appeals on compassionate grounds were no longer permissible. Another example highlighted how the proposed new requirement, predominantly for men from India and Bangladesh, to be able to support their families ignored the years of tax and National Insurance contributions they had made. As many were now elderly, not being able to bring their families to join them had an impact on their ability to look after themselves. The letter provided Bowden with points he could make in the debate some three days later.[80] Bowden did not speak in the debate in the House of Commons on 16 November 1987, and he voted in favour of the Bill proceeding.[81] The law centre also sought to directly help people who were affected by this law, such as 'Mr Green', who had spent sixteen years trying to persuade the Home Office that his family in Bangladesh were indeed related to him.[82] The advent of DNA testing in the 1980s – and its permissibility in legal cases – meant that the law centre had an additional tool for supporting people in making cases like Mr Green's, and they also worked on a number of cases where people had already been wrongly refused entry, using the DNA findings.[83] British citizens could also be caught up in immigration cases involving their spouses. One highlighted case involved a British woman whose Sudanese husband had been deported. The woman accompanied her husband to Sudan for a time, but she felt that she could not move there permanently and that it was an unsuitable environment in which to raise their child. The woman's mother, who had been looking after their child, became ill, and the woman returned to Britain, where she was split between caring for her child and her mother. The law centre was able to employ an independent social worker to investigate the case and to launch an eventually successful appeal, which reunited the family in Britain on compassionate grounds.[84]

Another emerging area of work was mental health, in the light of the Mental Health Act 1983, and particularly the detention of psychiatric patients against their will under Sections 2 and 3 of the Act. Section 2 allowed for detention up to 28 days, whilst extendable detention periods of six months were allowed under Section 3. As the law centre pointed out, individuals suffered a serious curtailment of their rights when 'sectioned'. In addition to issues around the treatment of individuals who were sectioned – such as being required to take medication – being sectioned had serious consequences for anyone trying to manage their personal affairs effectively. Some of the work of the law centre involved supporting patients to have their views on their treatment taken seriously, particularly when legal aid was not available for going before certain parts of the complaints and appeals process. A case highlighted in the 1990 annual report presented a woman who had gone into hospital for treatment voluntarily and who was consequently feeling better after a three-month stay but who had been sectioned so that the doctors could continue to assess her. As legal aid was not available for representation at the Hospital Managers' Board, the law centre had to take her case on without charge – and the woman was successful in making her case to go home. Restricted patients, or 'mentally disordered offenders', could also need legal assistance. Another case referred to a man who had been charged but not convicted of an offence and was released from hospital as his condition improved. However, the man was subject to highly restrictive conditions, which made settling back into his life difficult – such as needing Home Office approval for any job he was offered. On taking his case to the Mental Health Review Tribunal, the man came up against opposition from his consultant psychiatrist and the Home Office, which was only overturned by the law centre being able to provide the tribunal with an independent psychiatric report.[85] Although the law centre noted that improvements were starting to be made in enabling patients to make complaints, it was still a gargantuan task. The role of the law centre in this area was in ensuring that patients were not overwhelmed by trying to deal with an overly complex system as they were undergoing treatment and that they were not overruled by senior psychiatrists with considerable power and influence on Hospital Managers' Boards. Through this work, the law centre was concerned with ensuring that the system did not lose sight of the needs of already vulnerable individuals, who were likely to suffer enhanced risk and damage without independent support. It was also linked in with the growing user participation movement through a Brighton-based support group, Insight, who visited hospital wards on a weekly basis to promote awareness of patient rights. The anti-psychiatry movement peaked in the early 1970s but was closely connected with the civil rights movement of the 1960s and 1970s. The language of upholding rights and challenging the assumptions of the dominant power common to both social movements fed into what was first described as the 'patients' movement' and later as the 'users' or survivors' movement'.[86]

The law centre also responded to concerns about the introduction of the Poll Tax or Community Charge in April 1990. This was an attempt to radically overhaul the funding of local government. Local government was previously funded through the rates system, with 'rates' set according to the potential rental value of a house. Despite its imperfections, the rates system attempted to link the charge to the relative wealth of the household. The Poll Tax proposed a flat rate of contribution for all, with reductions for students and the unemployed, although the Poll Tax was set by councils and therefore varied from authority to authority. The Poll Tax was roundly rejected and disputed, with riots on the streets of London in 1990.[87] For the law centre, some of this work took the form of acting as a conduit for advice on the practicalities of the Poll Tax in terms of answering questions on who was required to pay. Other elements of it focused on supporting other organisations with regard to the situation of private tenants, whose rents had previously included rates. The law centre also provided training on the new tax, with the Brighton Housing Trust, for council officers and advised Brighton Borough Council on the leaflet they sent to tenants.[88]

The turmoil caused by the Poll Tax, its abolition and the creation of the Council Tax impacted on the law centres. Like all other law centres, it had benefited from urban aid funding, but it was mostly reliant on funding from Brighton Borough Council.[89] In the course of 1990, the council proposed cuts to the funding of the law centre and the Brighton Rights Advice Centre. The law centre staff felt that the council's proposed cut to their funding revealed its intention to force them to merge with the Brighton Rights Advice Centre.[90] The law centre worked with the Rights Advice Centre as a matter of course, but the purposes and aims of the two organisations were different. The law centre was concerned because it wanted to function as a law centre following the guidelines set by the Law Centres Federation.[91] These principles revolved around being community lawyers with management committees drawn from their local community and working with the community in different ways.[92]

The law centre management committee decided to shut in March 1992, as they could not find a way to work with the funding proposed by the council. In an interview with the *Guardian* later that year, Dr Neil Stammers argued that accepting the agreement would have resulted in having to drop advice work in favour of chasing legal aid work.[93] Advice work was funded by local authorities, originally empowered by the Local Government Act 1948; but legal aid came through a different route, which had no connection with local authority budgets. Brighton Borough Council's plan to merge advice and legal aid work was trying to cross-subsidise the two different types of work without necessarily thinking about the implications this would have on the nature of service offered. Taking on more and more legal aid work would have constrained the wider work the law centre undertook, particularly work in education and development. The Brighton Rights Advice Centre folded the following year, having found its grant unworkable.

The threat was to advice generally. The Housing Advice Centre, run by the Brighton Housing Trust housing association, with whom the law centre worked closely, was also under threat. The funding for the advice centre was to suffer a cut of 30–50 per cent, leaving the trust with a shortfall of £30,000. The Brighton Housing Trust was a citizen-led project developed in the early 1970s.[94] In a letter to the chair of the Council's Grants Sub-Committee, Stammers argued that the Housing Advice Centre was 'pivotal' in helping people with problems with mortgage payments and homelessness, and that reducing a grant to the centre would displace the advice-seekers to other agencies that did not have the capacity or the expertise to help them.[95] Whilst the CAB in the city was due to remain open, by January 1992, the law centre was due to shut, and the Rights Advice Centre would not survive much longer.

Although the Brighton law centre was the smallest of the sixty law centres running by 1990, its problems were by no means unique. The Brent Community law centre, one of the first to be founded and one of the most influential, also had its funding threatened in 1992. The London Borough of Brent was keen to reorganise its advice provision into three 'centres of excellence' rather than allowing fifteen different advice centres spread across the borough. The plan in Brent was to pass the work to the CAB to manage, and the CAB would then subcontract the work to the law centre and other bodies. In Brent, as in Brighton, the council wanted to be able to cross-subsidise advice and legal aid work through essentially topping up the advice work with legal aid.[96] As Kate Markus of the Brent law centre wrote in 1985, the tension arose from the fact that law centres were established to deal with some of the problems of the legal aid system rather than being created as a salaried version of it. They also supported local residents against the council, such as when the law centre helped residents force Brent Council to deal with asbestos in council homes.[97] Brent Community law centre survived this crisis in the early 1990s largely by working out a way of becoming independent of Brent Council. Hillingdon Legal Resource Centre (HLRC, later known as the Hillingdon law centre) became vulnerable when the control of Hillingdon Council changed after the local government elections of 1990. The budget that had been drawn up by the Labour members of the council was overturned by the newly dominant Conservatives, and the £150,000 grant to the centre was to be withdrawn.[98] The centre was given a temporary reprieve by a grant from the London Boroughs Grants Committee and a £10,000 holding grant from the council, despite some of the Conservative councillors viewing the centre as a 'fringe group'.[99] A widow in her eighties wrote to the *Uxbridge and West Drayton Gazette* to say that she had benefited from the Legal Resource Centre for several years and valued a service that was not trying to exploit her. Another resident, who had used the centre to help with an unfair dismissal case, wanted to know where local people would go for help with problems that ordinary solicitors would not want to be involved with. He felt that positioning funding the HLRC or social services as a choice was a false binary that insulted the intelligence of residents, and the council could look instead at selling unoccupied property.[100] These voices did not prevail. The HLRC was able to scrape by through reducing its opening hours, its staffing and the volume of cases it could take on.[101] It continued to receive funding from the London Borough Grants Committee, even though Hillingdon had the biggest Poll Tax rise in London.[102] The HLRC received funding in 1994 from the then Labour-controlled council, but it was still dwarfed by that given to the CABx in the borough and the area. Hillingdon CAB got £250,000, in comparison to the £10,000 for the Legal Resource Centre, and the council was also due to pay £66,550 to keep the Uxbridge CAB in its premises as well as £16,710 for the other CABx in the area.[103]

The Poll Tax was extremely disruptive to law centres, even if the majority were able to survive. Although local government had been empowered to fund advice and information by the Local Government Act 1948, legal advice was an easy target for councils that needed to save money. The Benson Commission had recommended the use of CABx as the preferred providers of advice and the gateway to legal advice, largely because of the facilities they offered as a national provider. With urban aid ending in the 1980s in England, the law centres lost another important source of funding, which had enabled them to undertake development and education work rather than relying on legal aid billing to keep afloat. The law centres were politically vulnerable, being cast as members of the 'loony left' by Conservative councillors, particularly after media coverage of GLC grants in the 1980s to law centres as such. With different and changing pressures on local government finance, being able to merge advice and law centres or to cut law centres off was tempting. Although law centres supported residents in ensuring that councils discharged their legal duties, they were nonetheless a potentially antagonistic force paid for by the council budget. The voices of local people who used those services were absent from decisions about what to keep and what to lose, with little or no evidence that moving to 'centres of excellence' would make a difference to people.

Making cases

Research into legal services had been undertaken from the 1920s, as seen earlier, with mapping work undertaken by the NCSS and LCSS for the Finlay Committee as well as Mervyn Jones and Egerton in the 1930s and 1940s. As before, mapping legal services formed part of the case-making for governmental support for legal and advice initiatives, and it also reveals much about the advisory world during this period.

The CPAG prepared a memorandum, which they sent to the Lord Chancellor's Advisory Council in 1972. This drew upon their earlier work, *A Policy to Establish the Legal Rights of Low Income Families*, which they had presented to the Lord Chancellor in 1969. In 1970, CPAG had resorted to setting up their own legal advisory service, named the Citizens' Rights Office (CRO), to support families on low incomes. To their minds, having access to 'basic legal services' was as important as having access to a basic income.[104] The CRO emerged from people writing to Tony Lynes at CPAG with questions about their benefits and for help with appeals. CPAG were successful in applying for funding from the Rowntree Charitable Trust for a part-time legal officer in 1969, and the trust then provided initial funding for the CRO.[105] In 1971, the CRO dealt with over 6,000 enquiries, which came from all over the country. Twenty per cent of cases dealt with by the CRO involved housing issues, whilst 10 per cent also needed help in dealing with National Insurance and constant attendance allowances. The CRO also offered representation at tribunals. As CPAG laid out in their memorandum to the Lord Chancellor, there was a pressing need for a National Civil Rights Council to raise awareness of rights as well as to support people to assert their welfare rights.[106] CPAG were well networked not just within voluntary action and social policy circles but also within the legal profession, not least through their solicitor. Henry Hodge worked as CPAG's solicitor, and he was the part-time director of the CRO and later deputy director of CPAG.[107] Hodge joined CPAG in 1970, shortly after being admitted as a solicitor. Hodge was also involved with the NCCL, serving as its chair in 1974–5, bringing himself and CPAG into contact with the NCCL's long interest in legal aid and connections with the left. Hodge would go on to set up a legal firm that specialised in legal aid cases and was also, later, chair of the Law Society's legal services council.[108]

Having left CPAG, Tony Lynes was secretary of the Review Committee on the CABx in London, which surveyed information and advisory services in London in 1974. This survey asked an array of different advice providers about their funding, their staffing, their opening hours and the types of advice that users wanted. The purpose was to find out why so many non-CAB advice centres were being established, particularly as this meant missing out on the central information services that CABx could offer.[109] As Charles Woodd, warden of Bede House Association in Bermondsey, south London, pointed out, the reasons could be complex and driven by local issues. Bede House was one of the partners running the advice centre in the Blue marketplace, which was open on Saturdays and run by volunteers.[110] The advice centre was set up in June 1973 as a project of Bede House, the Manor Methodist Church, two tenants' associations and the area Social Services Office as a means of dealing with the advice and legal needs of people in Bermondsey and Rotherhithe.[111] The settlement set up a welfare rights stall, which was proving much more popular than the centre in terms of people bringing enquiries to it – and therefore, Bede was considering putting in an application to the urban aid programme for a full-time worker.[112] Woodd stated that there was already one CAB in the London Borough of Southwark (where Bede was located), and there had long been pressure on the council from Bede and other settlement houses to fund a second CAB. Southwark refused to do this, and therefore, Bede and other charities set up advisory services to try to meet the local need for advice. Although Woodd acknowledged the benefits that came with being a branch of the CAB, Bede and other settlements were keen to provide advice as part of what he described as a 'broader based neighbourhood centre'. In time, the Bede centre and the BIAS (Blackfriars – Information

– Action – Support) at nearby Blackfriars Settlement would provide not just advice but also community support and advocacy. Southwark Council had warmed somewhat to the idea of advice provision, and the deputy town clerk had set up a 'forward planning group', with voluntary and statutory groups as members, which was looking at the development of advice and information provision and at the various urban aid applications that were being developed for advice work.[113]

Responses to the survey brought out a similar pattern of ad hoc arrangements in other parts of London. The Community House Information Centre in Marylebone was set up after the Feathers Clubs Association recruited a community worker who found herself inundated with requests for advice. The association provided funding for the information centre, whilst Westminster City Council offered the premises at a peppercorn rent.[114] The Manor Road Counselling Centre in north London offered a range of advisory services, including legal, on Wednesday evenings and was run by the Stoke Newington Council of Churches and Hackney Community Relations Council.[115] Harlesden Advice Centre had an urban aid grant via the Home Office and Brent Council. It also came out of grass-roots activism, being part of the Harlesden/Kensal Rise Project set up by the Willesden Christian Council with funding from the British Council of Churches and the Institute of Race Relations, the latter channelled through the City Parochial Foundation. This advice centre provided help to people mostly with housing and welfare issues. Two voluntary workers were supported by the British Council of Churches and Community Service Volunteers, but the project was able to expand to run a service with five full-time paid staff over five years through the urban aid programme.[116] The Brixton Advice Centre was a registered charity in its own right, providing legal advice five evenings a week, with funding from the Directorate of Social Services in Lambeth and the City Parochial Foundation.[117] The Family Advice Centre on Packington Square in Islington offered legal advice as just one part of a wider community and youth project.[118] Hackney Citizens Rights offered advice by volunteers on one evening a week and was part of the Centerprise bookshop and community centre. Robin Simpson, when completing the form, noted that the Rights Centre took many referrals from the local CAB.[119]

CABx were part of this landscape of advice in 1970s London, but it is clear that settlement houses, community organisations, tenants' associations, church groups and social work teams needed much more advice and information than the CABx could provide – or for it to be accessible in a different way. Advice centres were created at the points at which people connected with their community, whether that was through a community worker, a church or tenants' association or at a welfare rights stall on a market. Welfare rights stalls were found in places where people habitually went without involving a separate trip into a potentially forbidding office. Keith Elder, who ran an advice centre in Bilston in the West Midlands in the early 1970s, also found that people simply did not come into the centre and that he had to rethink how best to engage with people. Following an assessment of needs by the University of Birmingham, the centre team branched out into a jobs action project, engaging with tenants' associations and offering courses on consumer law. Whilst the white community in Bilston was somewhat readier to use the centre, the growing Asian community had a great need for advice and support around welfare services and entitlements, and this required Elder and colleagues to explore different methods of encouraging the Asians to use their services.[120] Similarly, in a 1978 documentary, Ranjit Sondhu of the Asian Resource Centre in Handsworth spoke of how the centre could, on the one hand, serve as a means by which social workers from white backgrounds could learn how to engage respectfully and helpfully with the Asian communities in the city. On the other, it was also a means of acting as a buffer between the individual and what Sondhu described as the 'insensitivity and bull-headedness' of the state.[121] The premise of all of this work, whoever provided it, was that for advice work to be owned and valued by the community, it had to be readily accessible to them, with as few impediments to engagement as possible. This did not sit easily with a desire to centralise and standardise services.

The Benson Commission found that there were 120 legal advice centres open in the late 1970s, which were mostly run by lawyers working for free; in 1976 alone, 3,300 solicitors were offering their services for free to the CABx, working on a rota basis to support local branches. Law centres employed seventy-five lawyers on salaries that did not compare favourably with private practice or being a solicitor on salary. Law centre lawyers made up a tiny percentage of the legal profession, but, through their expertise and campaigning around welfare law and rights, the Commission felt that they had exerted massive influence.[122] The Benson Commission was not in favour of a national legal service, favouring instead a system of citizens' law centres overseen by a small body.[123] Although there were limits on how far the Benson Commission could explore the work of CABx, they looked at general advice agencies. Their finding was that there needed to be a 'competent and accessible national network' of advice agencies, whose job it would be to provide advice and refer advice-seekers on to a legal service if this was appropriate. The Commission concurred with the National Consumer Council that the CABx should be the main local provider of general advice to the public.[124] Local CABx were funded by local authorities, whilst the NACAB was funded by central government and had used a £2.75 million grant from central government to improve central services, to create new CABx and to enhance existing ones.[125] Of the 130 or so free legal advice centres, the Commission noted that over half were in London, with most established in the preceding ten years. Although the Commission welcomed the voluntary efforts of solicitors and barristers in undertaking this work, they were firmly of the view that these should be stopgaps until a first-tier CAB advisory service could be established – or developed to be able to meet the needs of the community.[126] Law centres, on the other hand, with their different model of salaried legal staff, occupied a different position in the imagination of the Benson Commission. The Legal Aid and Assistance Act 1972 had empowered the Law Society and its local branches to directly employ solicitors to do work on behalf of the community.

BARS compiled evidence for the Benson Commission, revealing the diversity of types of advice provision in the country. Some of the examples given demonstrated how rights work had become an important part of advice provision, and it did not necessarily need a lawyer to do it. Check Rights Centre provided extensive notes on their service, outlining their foundation in April 1972 at the Liverpool University Settlement. They were due to close in 1977, as their five-year funding from the urban aid scheme and the Voluntary Services Unit was about to expire. They also had additional funds from Liverpool District Council and some revenue from offering training and consultancy. Their emphasis was on supporting welfare rights, and they did not employ any trained lawyers.[127]

The National Federation of Neighbourhood Advice Centres (NFNAC) was set up in 1979 to represent around 200 neighbourhood advice centres and also submitted evidence to the Benson Commission. NFNAC was keen that the Benson Commission should not see NACAB as the only national network for advice. NFNAC members were independent of both the CABx and the law centres and shared the same philosophy of promoting rights, being advocates for local people and the neighbourhood, rights advocacy and a willingness to campaign.[128] NFNAC were clear that whilst the term 'legal advice' assumed that the advice was given by a lawyer, advice about the law or on legal points did not have to be given by lawyers – and the individual neighbourhood advice centres were able to put people in touch with lawyers if needed.[129] NFNAC saw the difference between their advice centres and the CABx as coming down to engagement with a local community. The CABx were, in their analysis, well-meaning people who were not engaged with the problems of the community, whilst the neighbourhood advice centre, with its roots in community work and activism, was. The neighbourhood advice centre was happy to work with groups and to undertake community legal education in ways that the CABx would not or could not.[130]

The Benson Commission effectively recommended a shift away from community-focused advice provision in favour of the kinds of provision that CABx offered in conjunction with local authorities. There were distinct advantages to the CABx services, mainly in the form of access to a national framework of support and guidance, and a familiar brand name. But the CABx were, generally, not working to the same principles of community access as their counterparts in the neighbourhood advice or law centre worlds. As the incoming Conservative Government failed to respond to the Benson Commission until 1983, this meant that the potential threat of local authorities being encouraged – even required – to stop funding a plurality of advice providers went unrealised. This did not mean that the issues around funding were automatically resolved. Rather, advice providers felt that they remained in a period of crisis. One of the solutions to this was to establish the Advice Services Alliance (ASA) in May 1980, out of the Advice Services in Crisis Working Party. The ASA brought together the main interest groups: the Association of Housing Aid; BASSAC (previously BARS); the Federation of Independent Advice Centres; the Institute of Consumer Advisors; the NACAB; the National Association of Disablement Information and Advice Services; the National Association of Young People's Counselling and Advisory Services; the National Consumer Council; and the Welsh Consumer Council. A number of other organisations were happy to be involved but did not want to be named in publicity: the Community Information Project; the Consumers' Association; the Institute of Trading Administration; the Law Centres Federation; the Northern Ireland Consumer Council; the Scottish Association of Citizens Advice Bureaux; the Scottish Consumer Council; the Scottish Federation of Independent Advice Centres; and the Welfare Rights Officers' Group. The ASA planned to establish an annual conference in the autumn of 1980, which would allow the National Consumer Council's plan for a national policy for advice to be laid out. The ASA's members encompassed a diverse range of specialisms, from supporting teenagers to consumer advice, housing and welfare rights teams to legal aid lawyers, and also represented the four nations. As an umbrella group, the ASA's role was to provide a voice for what had become a wide field of advice provision. Its members were able to point to the need that they found, but how the funding to sustain their services could be found was unclear.

Conclusion

The failure to fully implement the Legal Aid and Advice Act 1949 caused numerous problems for those who provided advice, legal or otherwise. For the free legal advice centres, it caused major, ongoing uncertainty in their funding, with reluctance on the part of philanthropic funders to enter into what they saw as the province of government. The enabling of local government to fund advice and information work did not lead to an increase in the funding for voluntary-run organisations, though the projects run by some councils were innovative, useful and accessible to members of the public. The main tension in the period was about ensuring that the law was accessible. Accessibility was not just in terms of having a building that was near a major bus route or in the town centre; it was also about an environment that was welcoming, and where an advice-seeker could be sure of a sympathetic hearing with appropriately tailored advice. Accessibility was important in allowing people to challenge welfare decisions, tackle problems with landlords or deal with family matters; to negotiate bureaucracy and legislation at a pace that suited them and took their needs into account. The welfare state was not always benevolent or able to easily correct mistakes; the costs to an individual could be high without guidance or advocacy from a third party.

The neighbourhood law centres attempted to break the idea that lawyers were not for ordinary people and their problems through offering a different model for arranging legal work. The Benson Commission, with its aim to create a nationwide service, looked to the CABx as a national organisation of local branches with shared standards of delivery and practice as the place to which public funds could go. Yet the CABx and local authorities did not necessarily have the ability to reach out to needy individuals and excluded communities, or the ability to gain their trust, in the same way as community groups might. Legal advice was also reflected through the prism of political activity, which – correctly – saw the neighbourhood law centres as having their origins in Labour Party activism. Although demands for greater state funding of legal advice and aid had been made since the 1920s, what the Benson Commission promised was a standardised system that would crowd out the more diverse and innovative groups, which were often more responsive to the needs of hard-to-reach groups. Voluntarism and independence were both the curse and the strength of legal aid and advice providers in the period between 1949 and 1990.

Notes

1 M.P. Hall, *The Social Services of Modern England*, 4th edn (London: Routledge and Kegan Paul, 1959), pp. 142–5.

2 W.H. Snape, *How to Find out about Local Government* (London: Pergamon, 1969), pp. 8–12.

3 J. L'Etang, *Public Relations in Britain: A History of Professional Practice in the 20th Century* (London: Routledge, 2004), pp. 26–8.

4 National Citizens' Advice Bureaux Council (NCABC), *Report of National Citizens' Advice Bureaux Council to National Standing Conference of CABx, 1966–68* (London: National Citizens' Advice Bureaux Council, 1968), preliminary page and p. 3.

5 Ibid., pp. 1, 29.

6 Ibid., preliminary page.

7 L. Black, '*Which?* craft in post-war Britain: The Consumers' Association and the politics of affluence', *Albion*, 36:1 (2004); L. Black and N. Robertson, *Consumerism and the Co-operative Movement in Modern British History: Taking Stock* (Manchester: Manchester University Press, 2009); M. Hilton, *Consumerism in Twentieth-century Britain: The Search for a Historical Movement* (Cambridge: Cambridge University Press, 2003).

8 *Final Report of the Committee on Consumer Protection*, Cmnd. 1781 (London: HMSO, 1962), p. iii.
9 Ibid., pp. 157–64.
10 *Report of National Citizens' Advice Bureaux Council to National Standing Conference of CABx, 1966–68*, p. 29.
11 NCABC, *Report of National Citizens' Advice Bureaux Council to National Standing Conference of CABx, 1962–4* (London: NCABC, 1964), p. 20.
12 J. Citron, *Citizens Advice Bureaux: For the Community, by the Community* (London: Pluto, 1990).
13 LSE Archives (hereafter LSE), CAB/3/5 Hounslow Housing Aid Centre leaflet, n.d.
14 LSE, CAB/3/5 Consumer Advice Centre leaflets, n.d.
15 London Metropolitan Archives (hereafter LMA), 4016/IS/A/04/033 'Report on Free Legal Advice Centres', ca. 1945; 'Legal Advice Centres', *The Times*, 12 March 1951, p. 12.
16 LMA, A/TOY/021/020, Toynbee Hall, Warden's Letter, No. 1 October 1955, p. 2. There is a known caesura in the records of Toynbee Hall for the 1940s and 1950s.
17 Modern Records Centre, University of Warwick (hereafter MRC) MSS.292/850/3 Letter from Sir Luke Fawcett to Vincent Towson, General Secretary, 18 December 1953, attached: 'Notes on the Voluntary Legal Advice Service, Prepared by the National Council of Social Services', 7 December 1953.
18 See J. Lewis, *The Voluntary Sector, the State and Social Work in Britain: The Charity Organisation Society/Family Welfare Association since 1869* (London: Edward Elgar, 1995).
19 LMA, 4546/J/008/006, Family Welfare Association Annual Report April 1953–March 1954, p. 4.
20 A. Sackville, 'The Association of Family Case Workers 1940–1970', *Professional Associations and Social Work*, Working Paper 11 (1988).
21 S.J. Jenkins, 'The Intellectual Framework of Voluntary Social Service, c.1940–1960' (PhD dissertation, University College London, 2001), pp. 38, 100.
22 'Mr Benjamin Astbury', *The Times*, 26 May 1969, p. 8.
23 'Legal Aid', *The Times*, 8 August 1947, p. 5.
24 LMA, 4524/J/08/006, Letter Astbury to C. Walkinshaw, 23 August 1948.
25 LMA, 4524/J/08/006, Letter Astbury to Walkinshaw, 16 December 1949.
26 LMA, 4524/J/08/006, Letter J.V. Alexander to Astbury, 22 December 1949. Walkinshaw was warden of the Mary Ward Centre from 1935 to 1951, with Alexander taking over the role between 1951 and 1971. See Mary Ward Centre, 'Samples from the Mary Ward Settlement Archive', www.marywardcentre.ac.uk/wp-content/uploads/2012/07/Archive.pdf, correct at 26 May 2018.
27 LMA, 4524/J/08/006, Letter Astbury to Walkinshaw, 23 March 1950.
28 R. Davenport-Hines, 'Brooke, Henry, Baron Brooke of Cumnor (1903–1984)', *ODNB*.
29 LMA, 4524/J/08/006, 'London County Council: Free Legal Advice Centres – Grant', 1 August 1951.
30 See LMA, 4524/J8/08/001, Income and Expenditure Account for the Year Ended 31 March 1951 and Letter Howard Roberts to (LCC) to FWA, 5 November 1951.

31 LMA, 4524/J/08/001, Administration to 1960, letter from Noel Hans Hamilton, Secretary of the Society for the Discharge and Relief of Persons Imprisoned for Small Debts, 23 February 1948; letter from W.W. Badger, Senior Probation Officer, London Probation Service, 2 January 1951.
32 A. Alexander, 'Burton, Sir Montague Maurice (1885–1952)', *ODNB*.
33 LMA, 4524/J8/08/001, Letter from Montague Burton, 11 January 1951.
34 LMA, 4524/J8/08/001, Letter from Dorothy Howell-Thomas, Assistant Controller, Selfridges, 7 July 1951.
35 LMA, 4524/J8/08/001, Letter from JV Alexander to Harold Samuel, Martins Bank, 14 January 1953; cover note for donation on behalf of Gestetner Limited, 7 March 1960.
36 LMA, 4524/J8/08/001, Letter from JV Alexander to Nuffield Foundation, 13 March 1953; letter from Leslie Farrer-Brown, 19 March 1953.
37 'Legal Advice Centres', *The Times*, 12 March 1951, p. 12.
38 LMA, 4524/J8/08/001, Letters to L. Spero, H. Hewitt and B.R. Yorke, 30 May 1951.
39 LMA, 4524/J/08/001, Cambridge House (Trinity Hall) Legal Advice Centre, notice of change in hours 11 October 1951.
40 LMA, 4524/J/08/001, Report on Mary Ward Settlement Free Legal Advice Centre to July 1951.
41 LMA, 4524/J/08/001, Letter of 13 March 1953 to the Nuffield Foundation.
42 LMA, 4524/J/08/001, Report on Mary Ward Settlement Free Legal Advice Centre to July 1951.
43 LMA, 4524/J/08/001, Letter to supporters, 27 March 1953.
44 LMA, 4524/J/08/001, Letter from JV Alexander to PA Leach, Law Society, 13 March 1953.
45 LMA, 4524/J/08/001, Letter from Howard Roberts, LCC, 6 August 1953; letter from Roberts, 30 December 1953.
46 'Miss Kathleen Oswald', *Guardian*, 12 March 1964, p. 3.
47 'Liberty and the Law', *United for Peace and Progress: The Conservative and Unionist Party's Policy*, London: Conservative Party (1955), www.conservativemanifesto.com/1955/1955-conservative-manifesto.shtml, correct at 12 July 2018.
48 LMA, 4016/IS/A/04/032, Informal meeting to discuss arrangements for Legal Aid and Advice, 15 October 1956.
49 A.P. Baker, 'Haynes, Sir George Ernest (1902–1983)', *ODNB*.
50 LMA, 4016/IS/A.04/032, Letter K.M. Oswald to Sir G.E. Haynes, 20 November 1956.
51 LMA, LCC/CL/GP/1/250, Free Legal Advice Centres, 1958–1961.
52 LMA, LCC/CL/GP/1/250, Letter K.M. Oswald to Permanent Secretary of the Lord Chancellor's Department, 5 November 1948.
53 LCC/CL/GP/1/250, Letter Sir G.P. Coldstream to K.M. Oswald, 15 December 1958.
54 Derek Oulton, 'Coldstream, Sir George Phillips (1907–2004)', *ODNB*.
55 LCC/CL/GP/1/250, Letter Coldstream to Oswald, 15 December 1958.
56 LMA, 4524/J/08/010, Legal Advice Centre: Meetings and memoranda, 1963–1970, letter from W.O. Hart of LCC to J.S. Burt of FWA, 28 January 1963.

57 See 'Obituary: Hume Boggis Rolfe', *Daily Telegraph*, 6 September 2002, www.telegraph.co.uk/news/obituaries/1406391/Hume-Boggis-Rolfe.html, correct at 26 May 2017.
58 LMA, 4524/J/08/010, Legal Advice Centre: Meetings and memoranda, 1963–1970, notes on meeting at Lord Chancellor's Department, by Peter Archer for Mary Ward Settlement, June 1963.
59 LMA, 4524/J/08/008, Notes on meeting of Sir W.O. Hart, Mary Ward Settlement, Cambridge House and the Family Welfare Association, 15 November 1967.
60 LMA, 4524/J/08/010, Letter from Kenneth Nunn to J.V. Alexander, 20 May 1963.
61 LMA, 4524/J/08/008, Letter from E.A.L. Watts of London Marriage Guidance Council to Pamela Liverman, Mary Ward Settlement, 27 October 1967.
62 LMA, 4524/J/08/011, Cambridge House Branch, report by R.L.L. Guthrie, 'Memorandum concerning the present situation of the Legal Advice Centre', Cambridge House, January 1965.
63 LMA, LCC/CL/GP/1/251, Letter from Lord Chancellor's Office to Sir William Hart, 4 February 1965.
64 LMA, LCC/CL/GP/1/251, Joint Report by Clerk of the Council and Treasurer to the Council to the General Purposes Committee, 'Grants to Voluntary Bodies: Free Legal Advice Centres', 22 February 1965.
65 LMA, CL/GP/1/251, Joint Report by the Clerk of the Council and Treasurer to the Council to the General Purposes Committee, 'Grants to Voluntary Bodies: Free Legal Advice Centres', 28 July 1965.
66 E. Halliday, director, *North Kensington Law Centre*, 1973, available for free on BFI Player, https://player.bfi.org.uk/free/film/watch-north-kensington-law-centre-1973-online, correct at 22 August 2018.
67 See S.Y. Ho, *Evaluating British Urban Policy: Ideology, Conflict and Compromise* (London: Routledge, 2003).
68 *Hansard*, HL Written Answers, 8 July 1975, vol. 362, cols 771–2.
69 *Hansard*, HC Debate, 16 April 1975, vol. 980, cols 446–8.
70 LMA, GLC/DG/PR/R/6/115, Law Centres including North Kensington Legal Advice Centres. Letter from R.H.H. White, Lord Chancellor's Office, 12 May 1975, with insert *Hansard* 30 April 1975, p. 164, written answer.
71 *Hansard*, HL Debate, 12 May 1975, vol. 360, cols 540–1.
72 LMA, GLC/DG/PR/R/6/115, Letter GA Pilborough, 13 February 1975; letter EM Haynes, 16 January 1975.
73 The Keep, Brighton (hereafter, Keep) AMS7049/2/3 Profile of Law Centres. For Manpower, see D. Finn, 'The Manpower Services Commission and the Youth Training Scheme: A permanent bridge to work?' *Compare: A Journal of Comparative and International Education*, 14:2 (1984), pp. 145–56; R. O'Brien, 'The rise and fall of the Manpower Services Commission', *Policy Studies*, 9:2 (1988), pp. 3–8.
74 Keep, AMS7049/2/3 *Brighton Law Centre Review and Annual Report 1987*, pp. 1–2.
75 Keep, AMS7049/2/3 *Annual Report 1990*, p. 15.
76 Keep, AMS7049/2/3 *Annual Report 1987*.
77 Keep, AMS7049/2/3 *Annual Report 1988*.

78 Keep, AMS7049/2/3 *Annual Report 1987*, p. 7.
79 Keep, *1988*, p. 5.
80 Letter Fazilet Hadi on behalf of Brighton Law Centre to Andrew Bowden, 13 November 1987.
81 *Hansard*, HC Debate, 16 November 1987, vol. 122, col. 854.
82 Keep, AMS7049/2/3 *Annual Report 1988*, p. 5.
83 Keep, AMS7049/2/3 *Annual Report 1989*, p. 4.
84 Ibid., p. 5.
85 Keep, AMS7049/2/3 *Annual Report 1990*.
86 N. Crossley, *Contesting Psychiatry: Social Movements in Mental Health* (London: Routledge, 2006), p. 4.
87 D. Butler, *Failure in British Government: The Politics of the Poll Tax* (Oxford: Oxford University Press, 1994).
88 Keep, AMS7049/2/3 *Annual Report 1990*, p. 3.
89 Keep, AMS7049/2/3 *Annual Report 1989*, p. 14.
90 AMS7049/5/1 Brighton Law Centre: Staff Memos and Notes, Staff Memo 29 November 1990.
91 Ibid., AR 1988.
92 See J. Fitzpatrick, 'Standing up for Community Lawyers', *Law Centres Federation Annual Report 2007–8*, p. 4.
93 K. Barker, 'At the Centre of Controversy', *Guardian*, 6 May 1992, p. 25.
94 J. Symington, 'The Bishop Who Made a Difference', *The Times*, 7 February 2001, p. 19.
95 AMS7049/3/3 Brighton Law Centre: General Correspondence. Letter Neil Stammers to Jackie Lythell, Chair of Grants Sub-Committee, Brighton Borough Council, 17 January 1992.
96 Barker, 'At the Centre of Controversy', p. 25.
97 K. Markus, 'Legal, Decent, Honest – and Shut', *Guardian*, 4 June 1985, p. 22.
98 'Law Centre Set to Close', *Uxbridge and West Drayton Gazette (UWDG)*, Wednesday, 16 May 1990) p. 6.
99 'Still "No" to Law Centre', *UWDG*, Wednesday, 20 February 1991, p. 9.
100 'Legal Centre' and 'No Closure', *UWDG*, Wednesday, 6 June 1990, p. 18.
101 'Legal Centre Has to Cut Its Hours', *UWDG*, Wednesday, 17 April 1991, p. 9.
102 'Freeze on Helpers', *UWDG*, Wednesday, 11 March 1992, p. 5.
103 'Labour's Hand Out', *UWDG*, Wednesday, 23 February 1994, p. 6.
104 Child Poverty Action Group, *Establishing a Free Legal Service for Poor People: A Memorandum to the Lord Chancellor's Advisory Committee on Legal Aid and Advice* (London: CPAG, 1972), pp. 1–2.
105 P. Thane and R. Davidson, *The Child Poverty Action Group 1965 to 2015* (London: Child Poverty Action Group, 2016), pp. 12–13.
106 Child Poverty Action Group, *Establishing a Free Legal Service*, pp. 6–10.
107 Thane and Davidson, *The Child Poverty Action Group*, p. 13.
108 'Sir Henry Hodge', *Daily Telegraph*, 22 June 2009.
109 LSE, CAB/3/5, Letter from Tony Lynes to Charles B. Woodd, Bede House Association, 24 August 1974.
110 LSE, CAB/3/5, Bede House return.

111 LSE, CAB/3/5, 'Position statement' attached to letter from Charles B. Woodd to Tony Lynes, 10 June 1974.
112 LSE, CAB/3/5, Letter Charles B. Woodd to Tony Lynes, 10 June 1974.
113 LSE, CAB/3/5, Letter from Charles B. Woodd to Tony Lynes, 30 September 1974.
114 LSE, CAB/3/5, 'Short History of Community House Information Centre'.
115 LSE, CAB/3/5, Manor Road Counselling Centre return, 20 December 1973.
116 LSE, CAB/3/5, Harlesden/Kensal Rise Project First Annual Report August 1971–April 1973.
117 LSE, CAB/3/5, Brixton Advice Centre return.
118 LSE, CAB/3/5, Family Advice Centre return.
119 LSE, CAB/3/5, Hackney Citizens Rights Centre; K. Walpole, *Local Publishing and Local Culture: An Account of the Work of the Centerprise Publishing Project, 1972–77* (London: Centerprise, 1977).
120 British Library, Sounds collection: Keith Elder interviewed by Louise Brodie, National life stories: Pioneers in charity and social welfare. Recorded 4 April 2013, shelf mark C1155/18. 41:53–1:07, https://sounds.bl.uk/Oral-history/Charity-and-social-welfare/021M-C1155X0018XX-0003V0, correct at 2 August 2018.
121 Associated Television, *Here to stay* (1978), via Birmingham Black oral history project, http://bbohp.org.uk/node/29, correct at 2 August 2018, 3.30m, 16m.
122 Ibid., p. 16.
123 Ibid., p. 65.
124 Ibid., p. 70; National Consumer Council, *The Fourth Right of Citizenship: A Review of Local Advice Services* (London: National Consumer Council, 1977).
125 *The Royal Commission on Legal Services - Final Report*, Vol. 1, Cmnd. 7468, p. 74.
126 Ibid., pp. 76–7.
127 Cadbury Research Library, University of Birmingham (hereafter CRL) BAS5/20 Check! Rights Centre, Evidence to Royal Commission on Legal Services, March 1977, p. 1.
128 CRL, BAS5/20 National Federation of Neighbourhood Advice Centres, Evidence to the Royal Commission on Legal Services, p. 1.
129 Ibid., p. 2.
130 Ibid., p. 5.

Conclusion

Whilst there were various methods of obtaining legal advice before the 1890s, the last decade of the nineteenth century witnessed the growth of the idea that lawyers should volunteer to offer regular, structured 'Poor Man's Lawyer' sessions. These Poor Man's Lawyers found a ready home at settlement houses, which attracted socially aware graduates, many of whom were at the start of their careers in the law and happy to give over an evening a week to offering advice; retired lawyers and judges were often involved, and the settlements also provided a launch pad for the first women lawyers. This work was part of a wider reimagining and reconstruction of welfare, with the aim of trying to deal effectively with structural social problems through coordinating types of voluntary and state-paid work. It broadly coincided with the shift away from the more discretionary, localised application of the Poor Law to increasingly rules-based welfare, formally ushered in by the Liberal Governments of 1906–14. By the interwar period, those attached to the settlement movement and other reformist networks saw the potential for legal advice and new legislation to make a critical difference in working people's lives, from allowing people to be clearer about their rights and responsibilities to holding landlords and businesses to account, providing a mechanism for negotiating increasing legislation and welfare provision. Trade union members also had access to legal aid schemes as part of their union's mutual aid offer, which offered the possibility to obtain compensation for workplace injuries and individual help with workplace disputes that needed greater intervention. Newspapers and radio programmes were also a source of help and advice, whether personally or as part of wider educational projects. By the late 1930s, the establishment of the Haldane Society also provided a space for radically minded lawyers to meet, discuss reform, formulate legislation and campaign. However, the Lord Chancellor's Department and the senior members of the legal profession who were invited to sit on the Lawrence and Finlay Committees were not minded to make any radical changes to how legal aid and assistance were organised, preferring instead to leave this as a voluntary role undertaken by the legal profession. The legal profession was concerned about rationalising access to divorce for 'poor persons'; the other agencies were interested in empowering citizens to deal with the problems they faced, with legal advice and aid as part of that armoury.

The tipping point was the Second World War, when advising the citizen became of paramount importance. A network of CABx was set up nationally, building on the advice work undertaken by the NCSS and its associates in the interwar period. Whilst there was provision for divorce support for those in the armed forces, there was also an acknowledgement that legal advice on civil matters could be a critical part of trying to keep a household running in the most difficult of times – though legal advice was still to be given by lawyers on a pro bono basis. Whilst the Haldane Society called for a national legal service, the Rushcliffe Committee instead recommended a scheme in which lawyers would be reimbursed for their work on 'legal aid' cases, maintaining the split between the judiciary and the state. The ensuing Legal Aid and Advice Act 1949 introduced a system by which applicants were means-tested for their eligibility, and the lawyers who took on their cases would be refunded for this work. This Act did not try to reimagine or reform the legal profession, but it tried to make legal-aided work part of the everyday work of the legal profession. The legal profession, however, was not necessarily part of the everyday world of the working-class advice-seeker.

The Legal Aid and Advice Act 1949 was at best partially successful in this, and the next main piece of legislation, the Legal Advice and Assistance Act 1972, had a similar impact. Neither was implemented in full, with legal advice suffering in both cases. Whilst there was the political will to make legal advice more accessible, there was a critical failure to find the money to implement it. Until the late 1950s, there was no provision for legal aid in the county courts, which was where most cases involving working-class people were dealt with; or, indeed, within the growing number of tribunals that had been created by the welfare state. Whilst legal advice was eventually implemented, the plans to set up advice centres in particularly needy areas did not materialise. Instead, charities were required to try to fill the gap. As seen in the discussion of the Mary Ward and Cambridge House free legal advice centres, their funding was extremely precarious, with philanthropic foundations unwilling to fund work that they thought would shortly be taken over by a state scheme and disputations between layers of government as to who was responsible for funding them. The controversy caused by the work of Abel-Smith and others, and the party publications *Justice for All* and *Rough Justice*, were enough to force a review of the system. This was driven and accompanied by an interest in experiments in the United States. Whilst there was again consensus on the need to address the issue of making the law more accessible, there was a serious divide between the Conservatives, who were against any move towards nationalising the legal profession, and Labour, who were interested in the more radical idea of a national system of neighbourhood law centres. The proposals of the Law Society marked something of a middle ground between the two, and they led to the Legal Advice and Assistance Act 1972. This set up the £25 or green form scheme, which simplified and speeded up legal advice and aid, but the failure to fully implement the Act meant that a scheme to better embed legal advice within the CABx and create law centres in areas with shortages of solicitors was never realised.

Innovative work continued to be done in the voluntary sector, though its funding was vulnerable. New technologies better enabled groups to offer advice to people without the need to travel for an in-person conversation, as well as greater privacy and the option for advice to be accessed at any time of the day or night in an emergency. In addition to the continuation of free legal advice work at settlements and the growth of the neighbourhood law centres, there was a proliferation of legal advice work that drew upon new ideas about how better to reach out to people. Rather than following a uniform pattern, this work tried to meet the needs of people in neighbourhoods or those who had specific needs or interests but who were spread across the country. Much of this work was reliant upon the work of volunteers, or legal aid funding, or grants from local government and the urban aid scheme. The Benson Commission's 1979 report encouraged the development of a state-funded network of advice centres through the CABx. This was not implemented, but it reflected the position in the 1980s of trying to centralise legal advice work within the CABx, usually as part of cost-saving exercises in local government. Whilst the CABx could have much to offer, they were often stretched in the first place, and their model did not generally allow for the kinds of community-based work that were proving effective elsewhere. Although this was a form of 'nationalisation', it was devolved through local government and avoided creating a 'national legal service'.

From 1890 until the 1940s, the advice-seeker was portrayed as a 'poor person', as a recipient of welfare, as an imposition on the profession. In both cultural and legal terms, this had roots in the *in forma pauperis* and the Poor Laws through the person in need accepting poor relief and the status of a pauper. As historians of the eighteenth- and nineteenth-century Poor Laws have shown, the Old and New Poor Laws allowed for discretionary decision-making by officials at the local level and also for an epistolary culture in which paupers and their (non-lawyer) advocates could make a case for differential treatment. The emergence of demands for rigorous, planned and 'scientific' approaches to organising welfare from the 1870s led first to calls for stricter administration of the Poor Law, then to an increase in protective and preventative legislation, and then to the introduction of rules-based welfare under the Liberal Governments of 1906–14. This also coincided with the political shifts to greater enfranchisement of working men and the growth of the Labour Party by the start of the twentieth century. Whilst the social reformers of the late nineteenth century were attempting to understand society and social problems in new ways – to acknowledge the impact of structural issues on people's lives rather than explaining poverty as the sole result of fecklessness – these shifts did not readily provide a space for working-class people to assert their agency or to find advocates who could act on their behalf. Rules-based welfare systems could offer a fairer distribution of resources, but they could also steamroller people whose needs were complex or were unable to make their case in the language of bureaucrats. Legislation around standards of employment, housing and consumption needed to be intelligible to the people it sought to protect as a first step in asserting themselves against employers, landlords and businesses.

The need for discretion and advocacy did not diminish but emerged in the growing recognition of the need for all citizens to be able to understand the laws to which they were subject and to be able to assert their rights. This need became ever greater with the creation of the welfare state, in which people's welfare rights were derived from contributions to universal schemes, the permissive legislation of the 1960s and the greater regulation of immigration. Advice-seekers and their lawyers or advice workers could become 'impositions' in other ways, through effectively challenging decisions and holding local authorities and other bodies to account, rather than passively accepting or futilely protesting them. Work to make the law accessible had begun within the civil society arena, and it remained there, with the state only partially taking over the funding. Those involved in providing state-funded services were concerned either with the consistency of service that would be afforded through the CABx or with making savings, rather than engaging with a diverse range of needs and expectations. Although this reflected the long-held view that it was important to keep the state and the judiciary separate, and that it was equally important to have independent civil society bodies, it failed to adequately prioritise the citizen.

Money complicated this harnessing of the law to support citizens. Before 1949, the willingness of some solicitors and barristers to spend their evenings offering legal advice for free or for a very small fee to the advice-seeker was recognised – rightly – as a valuable public service. As a profession that was, largely, based on firms and chambers bringing in work and billing clients for the time spent and expenses incurred, and drew upon knowledge rather than needing specialist equipment, directly offering work for 'free' was a means of making lawyers available to the public. There was, however, nothing 'free' about this work, which was time spent in addition to a lawyer's daily, paid work. Although many of the lawyers were deeply committed to doing this type of work over many years, 'free' work in the evening needed to be justified against other calls on the lawyer's time, from family obligations to the demands of court cases. Poor Persons' divorce cases – which the

Lawrence and Finlay Committees had wanted to be done on a largely voluntary basis – also came with demands on the individual solicitor's willingness to work on matters to which they were opposed. The work also required a settlement house, church or other community space to make space available on a regular basis and to do a lot of the daily administration and accounting for the service – none of which was 'free'; rather, it was not charged for. This assumed, of course, that advice was all that was needed in order to deal with a situation. In many cases, this was true. However, writing a letter or taking a case to court incurred costs, with no obvious way of raising them, unless there were local arrangements for fundraising of one type or another. Unless a lawyer was able to give over a considerable amount of time through having an independent income or support from a spouse, or there was a particularly effective rota of committed volunteers, Poor Man's Lawyer services could only be available in the spaces between and after work, not during the working day. Evenings suited those in work during the day but narrowed the window in which a wider range of people – such as older people or those with small children – could easily get to their services.

The Finlay Committee in particular saw this 'freeness' as a valuable service offered by the legal profession as well as maintaining standards by not exploiting working-class divorce applicants. The giving of professional time for free was a means of avoiding interference from the state, which had the potential to both take away professional autonomy and threaten the democratic separation of judiciary and state. Volunteering in the Poor Man's Lawyer model used a model of personal advocacy, which was important and useful to the individuals who needed it, but the demand for a lawyer to commit to non-paying work did not offer a mechanism for sustainability. The objection to paying lawyers for this work diminished through the Second World War as the role of the state greatly expanded. Information, advice and the need for effective advocacy were highlighted in the war, with the interwar calls for supporting citizens gaining traction. The involvement of the media in offering advice columns and bureaux very publicly highlighted the problems individuals faced; these could hold government departments, landlords and business to account whilst also offering direct help and advocacy to people in those situations. This also demonstrated that legal advice and advocacy did not have to come from the 'traditional' legal profession. Trade unions could offer legal services to their members through their mutual aid offer; newspaper advice bureaux drew on revenue from readers buying papers and advertising. Newspapers were by no means the mutually driven, associational cultures that trade unions were, but through their idea of a readership, they offered a service to that community. Mutualism and mass media audiences offered a different mechanism for access to legal advice and aid that was brokered through community contributions – albeit with gatekeeping to minimise free-riding on the schemes. Powerful as these could be, they were not universal schemes, and the trade unions by definition excluded non-members.

The solution offered by the initially partially enacted Legal Aid and Advice Act 1949 involved refunding solicitors and barristers for their work on court cases that qualified for legal aid; over the next twenty years, legal aid was extended to the county courts and to tribunals, and the legal advice scheme was introduced. The idea of refunding lawyers for legal aid work essentially substituted the state in place of a private individual or business paying for the work; more radical ideas involving the development of state-funded legal services for the public did not find favour. The rejection of this avenue centred upon questions of professional independence from the state and the avoidance of public money being used to sue the state. Yet it was clear throughout the 1950s and beyond that citizens were struggling to find accessible sources of advice and help on consumer law or on the tribunals that were supposed to make navigating the welfare state easier. Although councils were empowered to fund advisory services from the 1950s, the potential of greater state funding and intervention made it harder for free legal advice providers to offer a more accessible service, open for longer hours and using paid lawyers – albeit on very low salaries. The emergence of social scientific research into access to justice and the interventions of philanthropic research funders threw questions about public funding and the structure of the legal profession into relief, energising prior conversations about how to use public money to enable vulnerable people to access their rights. Creative use of grants that were supposed to be used for other types of social action – such as urban regeneration funding – offered new opportunities for innovative legal services, though neighbourhood law centres and others remained highly vulnerable to constraints on local government funding. Legal advice was harder to prioritise than other welfare services, particularly if the legal advisory service adopted a critical approach to local councils and their policies.

Harnessing access to the law as a means of developing citizenship had significant potential, as activists and reformers acknowledged from the 1890s. It offered a means for working-class people to assert themselves against unfair decisions and treatment by welfare agencies, rogue landlords, negligent employers, unreliable businesses or powerful pillars of the community. The advent of rules-based, universalist welfare and increasing legislation removed much local discretion from the system at the same time as it aimed to offer greater protection and fairness in resource distribution. Mutual aid forms of accessing legal services could be highly beneficial to those who were members of those associations, but they were not an inclusive or universal solution; increasing the amount and type of state funding was one way of expanding citizens' access, but this came with concerns about how public money would be used and its impact on professional and judicial independence. Whilst there was the political will to offer support to citizens through a system of legal advice and aid, there was not enough to ensure that there could be funding to offer a full system and to radically rethink how a profession of private practitioners could operate in a welfare state. These concerns about using public money to pay for lawyers – including those working on salaries for government or non-governmental organisations – remain unresolved.

Select bibliography

Unpublished primary sources

Bodleian Library, University of Oxford, Special Collections

MS.Eng.hist.d.315 Viscount Haldane Papers

Cadbury Research Library

BAS5/20 BASSAC, Royal Commission on Legal Services
UB/COU/18 University of Birmingham Council minutes

The Keep, Brighton

AMS 7049 Papers of the Brighton Law Centre

London Metropolitan Archives

4016/IS/A/04 Citizens' Advice Bureaux papers
4546/J/008 Mary Ward Settlement papers
ACC/1888/250 London Council of Social Services, Legal Advice Centres including Neighbourhood Law Centres
ACC/2486 Toynbee Hall
A/TOY/021/020 Toynbee Hall papers
GLC/DG/PR/6/115 Law Centres including North Kensington
LCC/CL/GP/01/250 and 251 Free Legal Advice Centres

London School of Economics

FABIAN SOCIETY/H Fabian Women's Group
HALDANE SOCIETY Haldane Society Papers
SLL/6 and SLL/7 Society of Labour Lawyers
CAB/3/5 Review Committee of Greater London Citizens' Advice Bureau Service

Modern Records Centre, University of Warwick

547/FLA/L/1/1 National Union of the Footwear, Leather and Allied Trades
MSS126/TG/507/1/4–6 Transport and General Workers' Union
MSS.229/NU/1/2/1 National Union of County Officers
MSS.292/850/3 Trades Union Congress, Legal Advice
MSS.56/BIFU/box 20/2 Banking Insurance and Finance Union
MSS.880/36/7 National Union of Teachers
MSS.229/NU/1/2/1 National Union of County Officers

National Archives

LCO/2/981–87 Lord Chancellor's Office

Published primary sources

Blackburn, R. *The Soldier's Guide to His Rights and Duties*. London: Frederick Muller, 1943.

Child Poverty Action Group. *Establishing a Free Legal Service for Poor People: A Memorandum to the Lord Chancellor's Advisory Committee on Legal Aid and Advice*. London: CPAG, 1972.

Egerton, R. *Legal Aid*. London: Kegan Paul, Trench, Trubner, 1945.

Gurney-Champion, F.C.G. *Justice and the Poor in England*. London: George Routledge and Sons, 1926.

Haldane Society. *Annual Report for the Year 1937–8*. London: Haldane Society, 1938.

Haldane Society. *The Law and Reconstruction*. London: Haldane Society, 1942.

Haldane Society. *Annual Report 1942–3*. London: Haldane Society, 1943.

Haldane Society. *Annual Report 1943–4*. London: Haldane Society, 1944.

Hall, M.P. *The Social Services of Modern England*. 4th edn. London: Routledge and Kegan Paul, 1959.

Jones, J.M. *Free Legal Advice in England and Wales*. Oxford: Slatter and Rose, 1940.

National Consumer Council. *The Fourth Right of Citizenship: A Review of Local Advice Services*. London: National Consumer Council, 1977.

National Council for Civil Liberties. *The Record of a Decade of Work for Democracy and Civil Liberty, 1934–1945*. London: National Council for Civil Liberties, 1945.

Nixon, E. *John Hilton: The Story of His Life*. London: George Allen and Unwin, 1946.

Page Arnot, R. *History of the Labour Research Department*. London: Labour Research Department, 1926.

Platts-Mills, J. *Muck, Silk and Socialism: Recollections of a Left-Wing Queen's Counsel*. Wedmore: Paper Publishing, 2001.

Pritt, D.N. *From Right to Left: The Autobiography of D.N. Pritt*. London: Lawrence and Wishart, 1965.

Roberts, B.C. *Trade Union Government and Administration in Great Britain*. London: G. Bell and Sons, 1956.

Samuels, H. *The Industrial Worker's Guide to His Rights and Duties*. London: Haldane Society and Pitman & Sons, 1943.

Society of Conservative Lawyers. *Rough Justice*. London: Conservative Political Centre, 1968.
Society of Labour Lawyers. *Justice for All*. London: Fabian Society, 1968.
Williams, G.L. (ed.) *The Reform of the Law*. London: Victor Gollancz, 1951.
Williams, J.L. *The Airman's Guide to His Rights and Duties*. London: Frederick Muller, 1942.

Secondary works

All references to the *Oxford Dictionary of National Biography* are to the online version, H.C.G. Matthew, B. Harrison, L. Goldman and D. Cannadine (eds), Oxford: Oxford University Press, up to 2018; and *Who's Who* and *Who Was Who*, published by AC Black and hosted online, Oxford: Oxford University Press, up to 2018.

Abel, R.L. *The Legal Profession in England and Wales*. Oxford: Blackwell, 1988.
Abel-Smith, B. and R. Stevens. *Lawyers and the Courts: A Sociological Study of the English Legal System 1750–1965*. London: Heinemann, 1967.
Abel-Smith, B. and R. Stevens. *In Search of Justice: Society and the Legal System*. London: Allen Lane, 1968.
Abel-Smith, B., M. Zander, and R. Brooke. *Legal Problems and the Citizen: A Study in Three London Boroughs*. London: Heinemann, 1973.
Batlan, F. *Women and Justice for the Poor: A History of Legal Aid, 1863–1945*. Cambridge: Cambridge University Press, 2015.
Beers, L. *Your Britain: Media and the Making of the Labour Party*. Cambridge, MA: Harvard University Press, 2010.
Bingham, A. *Family Newspapers? Sex, Private Life and the British Popular Press, 1918–1978*. Oxford: Oxford University Press, 2009.
Black, L. 'Which? craft in post-war Britain: The Consumers' Association and the politics of affluence'. *Albion* 36, no. 1 (2004): 52–82.
Black, L. and N. Robertson. *Consumerism and the Co-Operative Movement in Modern British History: Taking Stock*. Manchester: Manchester University Press, 2009.
Blake, N. and H. Rajak. *Wigs and Workers: The Haldane Society of Socialist Lawyers 1930–1980*. London: Haldane Society of Socialist Lawyers, 1980.
Box, M. *Rebel Advocate: A Biography of Gerald Gardiner*. London: Victor Gollancz, 1983.
Bradley, K. *Poverty, Philanthropy and the State: Charities and the Working Classes in London, 1918–1979*. Manchester: Manchester University Press, 2009.
Bradley, K. '"All human life is there": The John Hilton Bureau of the *News of the World* and access to free legal advice, c.1938–1973'. *English Historical Review* 129, no. 539 (2014): 888–911.
Brasnett, M. *Voluntary Social Action: A History of the National Council of Social Service, 1919–1969*. London: National Council of Social Service, 1969.
Byles, A. *Unmet Need: The Case of the Neighbourhood Law Centre*. London: Routledge & Kegan Paul, 1977.
Calder, L. 'Saving and spending'. In *Oxford Handbook of the History of Consumption*, edited by Frank Trentmann. Oxford: Oxford University Press, 2012.

Cohen, D. *Family Secrets: The Things We Tried to Hide*. London: Penguin, 2014.

Conboy, M. *Tabloid Britain: Constructing a Community through Language*. London: Routledge, 2006.

Citron, J. *Citizens Advice Bureaux: For the Community, by the Community*. London: Pluto, 1990.

Crang, J.A. *The British Army and the People's War, 1939–1945*. Manchester: Manchester University Press, 2000.

Cullen, L. 'The first Lady Almoner: The appointment, position, and findings of Miss Mary Stewart at the Royal Free Hospital, 1895–99'. *Journal of the History of Medicine and Allied Sciences* 68, no. 4 (2013): 551–82.

Davis, J. 'A poor man's system of justice: The London police courts in the second half of the nineteenth century'. *Historical Journal* 27 (1984): 309–35.

Fielding, S., P. Thompson, and N. Tiratsoo. *'England Arise!' The Labour Party and Popular Politics in 1940s Britain*. Manchester: Manchester University Press, 1995.

Finlayson, G. 'A moving frontier: Voluntarism and the state in British social welfare, 1911–1949'. *Twentieth Century British History* 1 (1990): 183–206.

Finlayson, G. *Citizen, State and Social Welfare in Britain 1830–1990*. Oxford: Clarendon, 1994.

Garrard, J. *Democratisation in Britain: Elites, Civil Society and Reform since 1800*. Basingstoke: Palgrave, 2002.

Goriely, T. 'Law for the poor: The relationship between advice agencies and solicitors in the development of poverty law'. *International Journal of the Legal Profession* 3, no. 1–2 (1996): 215–48.

Goriely, T. 'Gratuitous assistance to the "ill-dressed": Debating civil legal aid in England and Wales from 1914–1939'. *International Journal of the Legal Profession* 13, no. 1 (2006): 41–67.

Gosling, G.C. 'Gender, money and professional identity: Medical social work and the coming of the British National Health Service'. *Women's History Review* 27, no. 2 (2017): 310–28.

Gosling, G.C. *Payment and Philanthropy in British Healthcare, 1918–1948*. Social Histories of Medicine. Manchester: Manchester University Press, 2017.

Graves, P. *Labour Women: Women in British Working Class Politics 1918–1939*. Cambridge: Cambridge University Press, 1994.

Harris, J. 'Political thought and the welfare state 1870–1940: An intellectual framework for British social policy'. *Past and Present*, no. 135 (1992): 116–41.

Harris, J. 'Between Civic Virtue and Social Darwinism: The Concept of the Residuum'. In *Retrieved Riches: Social Investigation in Britain, 1840–1914*, edited by D. Englander and R. O'Day, 67–88. Aldershot: Ashgate, 1998.

Harris, J. *Civil Society in British History: Ideas, Identities, Institutions*. Oxford: Oxford University Press, 2005.

Hennock, E.P. 'Poverty and social theory in England: The experience of the eighteen-eighties'. *Social History* 1, no. 1 (1976): 67–91.

Heuston, R.F.V. *Lives of the Lord Chancellors, 1940–1970*. Oxford: Clarendon, 1987.

Hilton, M. *Consumerism in Twentieth-century Britain: The Search for a Historical Movement*. Cambridge: Cambridge University Press, 2003.

Holton, S.S. *Feminism and Democracy: Women's Suffrage and Reform Politics in Britain, 1900–1918*. Cambridge: Cambridge University Press, 2003.

Jones, B. 'The uses of nostalgia: Autobiography, community publishing and working-class neighbourhoods in post-war England'. *Cultural and Social History* 7, no. 3 (2010): 355–74.

Jones, B. *The Working Class in Mid-Twentieth Century England: Community, Identity and Social Memory*. Manchester: Manchester University Press, 2012.

Keating, J. *A Child for Keeps: The History of Adoption in England, 1918–1945*. Basingstoke: Palgrave Macmillan, 2008.

Latta, G. and R. Lewis. 'Trade union legal services'. *British Journal of Industrial Relations* 12, no. 1 (1974): 56–70.

Lewis, J. *The Voluntary Sector, the State and Social Work in Britain: The Charity Organisation Society/Family Welfare Association since 1869*. London: Edward Elgar, 1995.

Lobban, M. and J. Moses. 'Introduction'. In *The Impact of Ideas on Legal Development*, edited by J. Moses and M. Lobban. Comparative Studies in the Development of the Law of Torts in Europe, 1–33. Cambridge: Cambridge University Press, 2012.

McKibbin, R. *The Ideologies of Class: Social Relations in Britain 1880–1950*. Oxford: Clarendon, 1990.

Meacham, S. *Toynbee Hall and Social Reform 1880–1914: The Search for Community*. New Haven: Yale, 1981.

Morgan, R.I. 'The introduction of civil legal aid in England and Wales, 1914–1949'. *Twentieth Century British History* 5, no. 1 (1994): 38–76.

Norton, P. 'The growth of the constituency role of the M.P'. *Parliamentary Affairs*, no. 47 (1994): 4.

Norton, P. 'Roles and behaviour of British M.Ps'. *Journal of Legislative Studies* 3, no. 1 (1997): 17–31.

Paterson, A. *Legal Aid as a Social Service*. London: Cobden Trust, 1971.

Regan, F., A. Paterson, T. Goriely and D. Fleming. *The Transformation of Legal Aid*. Oxford: Oxford University Press, 1999.

Richards, J. *Inform, Advise and Support: 50 Years of the Citizens Advice Bureau*. Cambridge: Lutterworth, 1989.

Searing, D.D. *Westminster's World: Understanding Political Roles*. Cambridge, MA: Harvard University Press, 1994.

Spencer, M. 'Public subsidies without strings: Labour and the lawyers at the birth of legal aid'. *International Journal of the Legal Profession* 9, no. 3 (2002): 251–82.

Steedman, C. 'At every bloody level: A magistrate, a framework-knitter, and the law'. *Law and History Review* 30, no. 2 (2012): 387–422.

Steedman, C. 'A lawyer's letter: Everyday uses of the law in early nineteenth-century England'. *History Workshop Journal* 81, no. Spring (2016): 62–83.

Taylor, R. *The T.U.C.: From the General Strike to New Unionism*. Basingstoke: Palgrave, 2000.

Thane, P. and R. Davidson. *The Child Poverty Action Group 1965 to 2015*. London: Child Poverty Action Group, 2016.

Thorpe, A. 'Conservative party agents in Second World War Britain'. *Twentieth Century British History* 18, no. 3 (2007): 334–64.

Thorpe, A. *Parties at War: Political Organization in Second World War Britain*. Oxford: Oxford University Press, 2009.

Trentmann, F. *The Making of the Consumer: Knowledge, Power and Identity in the Modern World*. Cultures of Consumption, edited by F. Trentmann. Oxford: Berg, 2006.

Unpublished theses

Blaiklock, O. 'Advising the Citizen: Citizens Advice Bureaux, Voluntarism and the Welfare State in England, 1938–1964'. PhD dissertation, Kings College London, 2012.

Jenkins, S.J. 'The Intellectual Framework of Voluntary Social Service, c.1940–1960'. PhD dissertation, University College London, 2001.

Logan, A. 'Making Women Magistrates: Feminism, Citizenship and Justice in England and Wales, 1918–1950'. PhD dissertation, University of Greenwich, 2002.

Moores, C. 'From Civil Liberties to Human Rights?: British Civil Liberties Activism'. PhD dissertation, University of Birmingham, 2010.

Steel, A.M. 'Explaining Changes in Political Party Fortunes in Greater London, 1918–1931'. PhD dissertation, Queen Mary, University of London, 2005.

Index

EU authorised representative for GPSR:
Easy Access System Europe, Mustamäe tee 50,
10621 Tallinn, Estonia
gpsr.requests@easproject.com

www.ingramcontent.com/pod-product-compliance
Ingram Content Group UK Ltd.
Pitfield, Milton Keynes, MK11 3LW, UK
UKHW021839100926
8556IPUK00004B/447
* 9 7 8 1 5 2 6 1 3 6 0 5 3 *